Interreligious Curriculum for Peace Education in Nigeria

Interreligious Curriculum for Peace Education in Nigeria

A Praxeological Intervention
for the Advanced Training of Religious Leaders

ISAIAH EKUNDAYO DADA

Foreword by Jacob K. Olupona

◥PICKWICK *Publications* · Eugene, Oregon

INTERRELIGIOUS CURRICULUM FOR PEACE EDUCATION IN NIGERIA
A Praxeological Intervention for the Advanced Training of Religious Leaders

Copyright © 2019 Isaiah Ekundayo Dada. All rights reserved. Except for brief quotations in critical publications or reviews, no part of this book may be reproduced in any manner without prior written permission from the publisher. Write: Permissions, Wipf and Stock Publishers, 199 W. 8th Ave., Suite 3, Eugene, OR 97401.

Pickwick Publications
An Imprint of Wipf and Stock Publishers
199 W. 8th Ave., Suite 3
Eugene, OR 97401

www.wipfandstock.com

PAPERBACK ISBN: 978-1-5326-4861-8
HARDCOVER ISBN: 978-1-5326-4862-5
EBOOK ISBN: 978-1-5326-4863-2

Cataloguing-in-Publication data:

Names: Dada, Isaiah Ekundayo, author. | Olupona, Jacob K., foreword.

Title: Interreligious curriculum for peace education in Nigeria : a praxeological intervention for the advanced training of religious leaders / Isaiah Ekundayo Dada.

Description: Eugene, OR : Pickwick Publications, 2019 | Includes bibliographical references.

Identifiers: ISBN 978-1-5326-4861-8 (paperback) | ISBN 978-1-5326-4862-5 (hardcover) | ISBN 978-1-5326-4863-2 (ebook)

Subjects: LCSH: Christian Education—Nigeria. | Religious Education—Nigeria. | Christianity And Other Religions—Islam. | Islam—Relations—Christianity. | Peace—Religious aspects. | Peace-Building—Religious Aspects

Classification: BL65.P4 D33 2019 (print) | BL65.P4 D33 (ebook)

Manufactured in the U.S.A.　　　　　　　　　　　　　　　APRIL 8, 2019

This book is dedicated to my grand children,
Ifedayo, Ayomikun & Ifeoluwa

"So it goes. Returning violence for violence multiplies violence, adding deeper darkness to a night already devoid of stars. Darkness cannot drive out darkness, only light can do that. Hate cannot drive out hate, only love can do that."

~Martin Luther King Jr.

Table of Contents

List of Tables | x
Foreword | xi
Preface | xiii
Acknowledgments | xv
List of Acronyms | xvi

1. INTRODUCTION | 1
1.1 Description of Nigeria | 1
1.2 Role of Religion in Nigeria | 3
1.3 Peace Education Curriculum | 5
1.4 Aim of the Book | 9
1.5 Praxeological Theory and Methodology | 9
1.6 Content of the Book | 11

2. INTERRELIGIOUS RELATIONS IN NIGERIA | 13
2.1 Religious Violence in Nigeria from 1999 to 2015 | 13
2.2 Analysis of this Religious Violence | 21
2.3 Interreligious Initiatives in Nigeria | 23
2.4 Synthesis of the Observation | 33
2.5 The Challenges of Interreligious Dialogue in Nigeria | 36
    2.5.1 Choosing a Specific Model of Interreligious Dialogue | 36
    2.5.2 The Missing Link of Grassroots Community Participation in Dialogue | 38
2.6 Problématique | 39

3. THE EFFECTS OF RELIGIOUS VIOLENCE ON INTERRELIGIOUS RELATIONS IN NIGERIA | 40
3.1 Theological Interpretations | 40
    3.1.1 Jihad | 41
    3.1.2 "Jesus the Only Way to Salvation" | 53
3.2 Political Interpretations | 56
3.3 Socio-economic Interpretations | 60
3.4 Interreligious Dialogue and Inter-Ethical Dialogue Problems | 62
3.5 Disparity between Those Taking Part in Dialogue | 63
3.6 Unequal Theological Development | 64
3.7 Conclusion | 64

4. PRECONDITIONS OF PEACE EDUCATION IN NIGERIA | 66
4.1 Peace Education | 66
    4.1.1 Definitions and Concepts of Peace Education | 66
    4.1.2 Goal and Objectives of Peace Education | 69
    4.1.3 Philosophy of Peace Education | 70
    4.1.4 Theories of Peace Education | 71
4.2 Transformative Peace Education | 73
4.3 Pedagogy of Peace | 75
4.4 A New Pedagogy of Interreligious Peace Education | 76
4.5 Peace Education in the Yoruba Religion | 81
4.6 Peace Education in Islam | 85
4.7 Peace Education in Christianity | 87
4.8 Conclusion | 92

5. PEACEBUILDING INTERVENTION AND INTERRELIGIOUS CURRICULUM FOR PEACE EDUCATION | 94
5.1 Definitions of Curriculum | 94
5.2 Interreligious Curriculum for Peace Education | 96
    5.2.1 Unit I: Overview of the Interreligious Curriculum for Peace Education | 97
    5.2.2 Unit II: Violence | 109
    5.2.3 Unit III: Peace Education | 149
    5.2.4 Unit IV: Human Security | 187
    5.2.5 Unit V: Practices | 213
5.3 Conclusion | 264

6. GENERAL CONCLUSION | 267
6.1 Conclusion of the Book | 267
6.2 Prospective | 274

Bibliography | 283

List of Tables

Table I. Religious Violence in Nigeria from 1999 to 2015 | 13
Table II. Vocabulary for Feelings | 255
Table III. Student Attitude Survey | 262

Foreword

The interreligious peace education for religious leaders in Nigeria developed by the author is premised on the ongoing history of violence and incessant religious conflicts in Nigeria. The author has rightfully identified Yorùbá communities of Southwestern Nigeria for his primary focus because of the nature of religious affiliation in the region. There, among the Yoruba people, the practice of Indigenous religion, Islam, and Christianity lend themselves to peaceful co-existence that make it amenable to a robust and workable curriculum that could be put in place for developing an interfaith curriculum for lasting dialogue. For centuries, the Yoruba have imbibed the principle of live and let live in matters of religious life. He has therefore produced a curriculum that reflects this world view and lived experience. Dada's cardinal objective of testing the adequacy and appropriateness of this curriculum in the Department of Religious Studies at the University of Ibadan, Nigeria is brilliant.

I am aware that the Department of Religious Studies at Ibadan, Nigeria is the best place to test this work. It is one of the earliest Departments of Religious Studies in Africa, and its Journal, *ORITA*—which literally means where the three roads of Indigenous religion, Islam, and Christianity meet—is a testimony to the success of the department in interfaith dialogue. Nigeria, a nation of 170 million people with diverse religious practices, is an ideal place for developing interreligious peace education for religious leaders. I share the author's optimism that if properly run, the education curriculum will serve as an excellent model for reducing the growing religious violence in Nigeria and provide a viable solution to the recurrent Christian-Muslim conflicts in the region.

The content of the work is very rich, and its theoretical and practical dimensions are in-depth. The work provides important social, theological, and historical interpretations, and the intervention proposed will go a long way to achieve the objectives of the project. A curriculum on peace education such as this can be transformative, particularly if it has an important ingredient: ensuring that educators, who are key players in the peace-building process, are empowered to carry out what is required to ensure peace.

This book points in many ways to how best to achieve the objective of communal and national peace in Nigeria, especially given the fact that the issue of religious violence in Nigeria places a strong responsibility on the roles of religious leaders themselves. The pastoral and educational interventions Dada prescribes for ensuring adequate peace education are very important to Nigeria and indeed other countries going through similar experiences as well. What is also significant about this work is that even though it is very strong in building a theoretical framework for peace building, the work has also mapped out practical responses to the problems that the author has adequately identified.

This work also provides a fascinating anthropological and theological ethnography of interfaith relations in Yorùbáland. It is a holistic approach, which enables him to draw on social, ecological, and literary dimensions of the theory and practice of peace education. The work provides a deep historical trajectory of religious violence in Nigeria. Because of the current situation in Nigeria, the importance of this historical overview cannot be overemphasized. The Boko Haram menace today cannot be grasped adequately if one does not also have this deep historical knowledge. His discussion of the Qur'an and the Hadith, particularly as those texts relate to his work, is important, as are his references to Christian scriptures in similar context. He rightly observes that what we often regard as religious conflict may indeed be more political than religious. This is an explanation that is commonly vocalized by scholars in Nigeria as well.

The references Dada provides are more than adequate for others wishing to carry out similar projects in their own national and regional contexts. They point to the relevance of this work in the global understanding of religious conflict and the possibility of a peaceful resolution to these conflicts.

This is a brilliant work that reflects Dada's deep training in interdisciplinary work. The book will have important impact on the resolution of religious violence in contemporary Nigeria.

Professor Jacob K. Olupona
Harvard University

Preface

Since the end of the Cold War, we have witnessed the increasing role religion plays in shaping worldviews as well as global fragmentation, part of which is through its being directly involved in violent conflicts. This situation is no better reflected than in the ethno-religious politics of Nigeria. Since the transition from a military to a civilian regime in 1999, violent conflicts between Christians and Muslims continue to erupt, constituting one of the gravest dangers facing Nigeria today. In the last few years, interreligious riots in Nigeria have even become routine events.

What have Nigerians done about this situation, especially in educational circles? Although the field of Peace Education developed a new educational reform movement in the early 1980s aimed at addressing such problems of violence directly, this reform has hardly reached Nigerian higher education (both religious and non-religious institutions of higher learning). It has left the educated elites with little formal educational training to understand the causes of this violence and especially how to provide alternatives for more peaceful relations within Nigeria.

Using a praxeological theory and method, this book addresses this doubly bleak situation by presenting the context for and the details of an interreligious curriculum for peace education for religious leaders in Nigeria. Understanding the role religious discourse plays in fostering much of the current violence, this book focuses in particular on the need to educate better religious leaders through the eventual dissemination of an interreligious curriculum for peace education adapted to the Nigerian multi-religious reality and long history of interreligious conflicts. This one-year curriculum builds upon religious Yoruba, Islamic, and Christian conceptions of peace with the goal of creating a safe, caring, spiritual, peaceful, and successful interfaith relationship between all Nigerian religious communities. It is contextualized for use as an example in the Department of Religious Studies at the University of Ibadan.

This book argues that the development of an interreligious curriculum for peace education for religious leaders in Nigeria will, in the long term, reduce the growing religious violence in Nigeria by addressing the tensions between Traditional, Christian, and Muslim populations and by enabling religious peacemakers to create interreligious islands of peace as well as to actively participate in finding ways to reduce the ongoing violence.

Acknowledgments

This book would not have been possible without the support, help, and challenges of many parties. I wish to express my utmost gratitude to Patrice Brodeur, who assisted in steering me in the right direction and helping me to shape my interreligious peace education and multicultural sensitivity. I appreciate the efforts of all my professors, especially Jean-Marc Charron, who stayed the course on this project and who jointly challenged me to articulate my passion. They shared their own resources as it developed and instructed me step by step. Their focus and feedback has enabled my passion to see the invaluable insights to this book.

Furthermore, I acknowledge the support and help of God, who sent people to facilitate and make my journey easy and smooth: Pr. Jacob K. Olupona, Rev. Dr. Merle Bailey, Bishop Mary-Ann Swenson, Rev. & Mrs. Karl Gudberlet, Denise Couture, Lucie Duval, David Robert, Jean-Marc Breton, Jean-François Roussel, and Solange Lefebvre. I cannot image having completed this project in the same way without the input, support, and friendship of Jason Sparkes and Loletta Barrett, who read this book in draft form, offering their criticism, suggestions, and their own experiences.

I am deeply grateful to my family members: my wonderful wife Victoria Dada and my precious children, Muyiwa, Olubanke, and Oluwayinka. Their constant assistance and steadfast sympathy have greatly encouraged me in all my efforts. Finally, my deepest appreciation goes to my sister-in-law Comfort Ogeleka, my brother Philip Dada, and my sister Iyabo Dada, who were able to support me.

List of Acronyms

AIDS	Acquired Immune Deficiency Syndrome
BBC	British Broadcasting Corporation
CAN	Christian Association of Nigeria
CIA	Central Intelligence Agency
CSN	Catholic Secretariat of Nigeria
HIV	Human Immunodeficiency Virus
IDP	Interreligious Dialogue for Peacebuilding
ICPE	Interreligious Curriculum for Peace Education
ITP	Integrative Theory of Peace
JNI	Jamalat-ul-Nasril Islam
NIREC	Nigeria Inter-Religious Council
NGO	Non-Governmental Organizations
NPA	National Peace Academy
NSCIA	Nigerian Supreme Council for Islamic Affairs
NRSV	New Revised Standard Version
OIC	Organization of Islamic Cooperation
TB	Tuberculosis
UNESCO	United Nations Educational, Scientific and Cultural Organization
WLACM	World Leadership Alliance Club de Madrid

CHAPTER I

Introduction

In the face of the scaling problems of violence in Nigeria, this book intends, through praxeological theory and method, to analyze the educational needs and formulate an interreligious curriculum for peace education for religious leaders in Nigeria. This study addresses the absence of any interreligious peace education curriculum that forms an integral part of a peace education core program, which is identified as one of the main problems encountered when analyzing the effectiveness of peaceful living in a multicultural society. The curriculum developed in this book is built upon Yoruba Religion, Islamic, and Christian conceptions of peace with the goal of creating a safe, caring, spiritual, peaceful, and successful interreligious relationship of communities. This book aims to respond to the need for peace education in general and for an interreligious curriculum for peace education adapted to Nigeria in particular.

The introduction briefly describes Nigeria, explains the role of religion, discusses the importance of the peace education curriculum, enumerates the aim and methodology of the book, and details the content of the book.

DESCRIPTION OF NIGERIA

The Federal Republic of Nigeria, as an economically developing nation, is facing different challenges ranging from political tensions to religious and tribal violent conflicts. These events constitute factors that have been stifling the economic and social development of the country. Left unattended due to the difficulty of resolving these issues, these situations of conflict keep occurring and are gradually becoming part of the national culture. The Federal Republic of Nigeria (Nigeria) is a West African country that shares borders with the Republic of Benin in the West, Chad and Cameroon in the East, and Niger in the North. Its coast lies on the Gulf of Guinea in the South.

On October 1st, 1960, Nigeria gained its independence from the United Kingdom. It now consists of thirty-six states and the federal capital territory.[1] Nigeria occupies 923,768 sq km/336,667 sq mi.[2] According to a 2006 census, its population is estimated to be one hundred and sixty million, with a life expectancy of around fifty-two years. It is the only country in the world with an equally high number of adherents to both Christianity and Islam (64 million for each religion).

Nigeria is the most populous country in Africa, the seventh most populous country in the world, and the most populous country in the world in which the majority of the population is black. Nigeria's diverse ethnic, linguistic, and religious characteristics contribute to cultural and artistic riches as well as to its fractious political conditions. It is an ethnically and religiously complex country with over two hundred and fifty ethnic groups. "The major ethnic groups include the Hausa (21 percent), Yoruba (21 percent), Ibo (18 percent), and Fulani (9 percent). The Hausa have traditionally dominated the Northern region of the country while the Yoruba have a pronounced influence in Nigeria's Western region, and the Ibo reside largely in the country's Eastern region."[3]

The official language of Nigeria is English, but over two hundred and fifty other languages are spoken as well. It is a country that not only includes a large Christian and Muslim population of a roughly equal size but also is home to ancient religions often under the nomenclature of traditional African religions. In much smaller numbers, there are also adherents to other religious belief systems like the Baha'i faith, Sat Guru Maharaji, and Hare Krishna. Approximately 40 percent of Nigerians are Muslim, 40 percent are Christian, and approximately 20 percent practice either a form of traditional African religions or another religion as mentioned above.

---

1. The 36 states are Abia, Adamawa, Akwa Ibom, Anambra, Bayelsa, Benue, Borno, Cross River, Delta, Ebonyi, Edo, Ekiti, Enugu, Gombe, Imo, Jigawa, Kaduna, Kano, Katsina, Kebbi, Kogi, Kwara, Lagos, Nassarawa, Niger, Ogun, Ondo, Osun, Oyo, Plateau, Rivers, Sokoto, Taraba, Yobe, and Zamfara.

2. Ulaval, *Nigeria 2010*.

3. Encyclopaedia of the Nations, "World Leaders: Nigeria," 1.

ROLE OF RELIGION IN NIGERIA

Religion plays a central, often divisive role in the ethno-regional politics of Nigeria. The problem is far more complex than simply the presence of religious "fanatics" enacting violence on other Nigerian citizens. There has often been as much violence amongst Muslims and disagreements between Christian groups as there was between adherents of these two faiths. The Bible and the Qur'an have become part of the staple religious discourse in Nigeria, with a too often divide-and-conquer strategy in the geopolitics of this demographically very large country.

Nigeria has not yet experienced a peaceful period from the colonial period to the present. There is an increasingly frightening picture of the destructive consequences of human violence taking many different forms: between children on the streets, at school, in family life, and between ethnic, religious, and political groups in the community. There are also different forms of violence: physical, psychological, socioeconomic, environmental, and, of course, political. Since the transition from military to civilian regime in 1999, religious violence constitutes one of the gravest dangers facing Nigeria. According to Roger A. Johnson in *Peacemaking and Religious Violence*: "Religious violence is . . . the type of violence organized, motivated and/or justified by the leadership, scriptures, and rhetoric of religious communities."[4] David Hicks defines violence as "acts of aggression with the deliberate intention of causing pain or discomfort to others, directly or indirectly."[5] "Violence, in the broadest sense, includes physical, psychological, and structural violence and can be caused by thoughts, words, and deeds—any dehumanizing behavior that intentionally harms another."[6] Gerald A. Arbuckle asserts that "violence is not about damaging or destroying things. It is about abusing people. The tragedy is that it lowers their self-confidence; they experience it as sense of powerlessness and subjugation. Violence crushes the spirit of people and makes them submissive to violators for their purpose."[7] Religious riots have become routine events in Nigeria, no longer even making many news items. In *The Political History of Religious Violence in Nigeria*, S. P. I. Agi affirms that: "Burning houses, destroying property, and maiming and killing innocent people have become a

---

4. Johnson, *Peacemaking and Religious Violence*, 8.
5. Hicks, *Education for Peace*, 6.
6. Harris, "Types of Peace Education," 16.
7. Arbuckle, "Violence, Society, and the Church," xii.

normal way of religious life, and religious violence is often seen as one of God's unwritten commandments that must be obeyed."[8] Nigeria has joined the league of the religiously restless nations with both intra- and interreligious conflicts. Religion has remained a majorly divisive element in the ethno-regional politics of Nigeria. Some critics claim that because of "religion-fuelled conflict, complicated politics, retarded social development, and impaired human relations across the world . . . one is often tempted to propose that Religion is innately an enemy of Humanity, if not indeed of itself a crime against Humanity."[9]

Religion, however, can also be a source of stability—and even harmony—in Nigerian peace. To distinguish between when it is a source of violence and when it is a source of peace requires an adequate understanding of religion and conflict, including an understanding of the internal dynamics and ongoing development of doctrines, norms, and religious practices within diverse religious traditions, as well as a willingness to make informed judgments about which doctrines, norms, and practices contribute to peacebuilding—and which do not.[10]

Among the most critical challenges facing Nigeria today is the need to distinguish between when religious discourse is used to promote peace and when it is used to promote violence. It is not enough only to focus attention on the increasingly serious and devastating terrorist activities of the *Boko Haram* group in the North or the equally expanding militancy in the South. The situations of tension and conflict only continue to increase in numbers, and the new generation is not aware of the issues behind these terrorist group's actions. Of course, they are also mostly unaware of how to resolve them, in part because most Nigerians are raised according to the beliefs and customs of their respective ethnic groups with insufficient inter-group knowledge and contacts. Consequently, in times of crises and situations of violence, few Nigerians know how to practice prevention, peacemaking, and post-conflict peacebuilding in order to reduce violence and increase sustainable peace amongst themselves. A brief overview of the university and high school curricula seem to indicate the paucity of courses or even elements thereof that teach those knowledge and skills necessary to resolve conflict peacefully. Such

---

8. Agi, *Political History of Religious Violence in Nigeria*, 2.
9. Soyinka, "Religion Against Humanity," 1.
10. Appleby, *Ambivalence of the Sacred*, 322.

peace education courses and programs have become urgent in the face of the scaling problems of violence.

PEACE EDUCATION CURRICULUM

In this book, I define a "peace education curriculum" as a pedagogical tool to encourage and support students in discovering personal and existing material and non-material human resources—including their own personal resources—that can empower them to become better peacebuilders and global citizens. A student that goes through this curriculum will indeed be transformed to develop his or her own set of preferred resources, which will lead them to make more self-conscious and better informed choices as peacebuilders. In "Peace Education and School Curriculum," Adesina and Odejobi explain that in Nigeria, the current education system has failed to serve as a means of transmitting the main ingredients of a culture of peace to the younger generation. They recommended that peace education be included in the school curriculum in Nigeria to promote peace in a country with a long, ongoing history of violence.[11]

My research as well as my previous personal experience confirms this assertion. I was trained at Immanuel College of Theology, Ibadan, as well as the University of Ibadan, both being among the oldest seminaries and universities in Nigeria, training generations of Methodist and Anglican pastors. While to this day, there is no peace education course in their curriculum, they offer a course on interfaith dialogue with the aim of reducing violence. Having had access to its syllabus—and by the very nature of its focus on interfaith dialogue (only one small component fostering peace education)—I know that it does not provide the breadth and depth of knowledge necessary for more serious training in peace education.

Since the aim of peace education is to help individuals become better global citizens, which includes respect for diversity of identities of all kinds, any peace education curriculum must be non-sectarian and non-religious in nature.[12] Peace education constitutes one of the key means to reach positive peace. Peace is a virtue,[13] a state of mind, and a

---

11. See Adesina and Odejobi, "Peace Education and School Curriculum."
12. See Brodeur, "Identity and Power Dynamics," 1.
13. See Galtung, "Peace by Peaceful Means," 25.

disposition for benevolence, non-violence, justice, and confidence.[14] This aim of peace education is also found in the three religions surveyed in this book, which I will introduce in the following order: Yoruba Religion, Islam, and Christianity.

In Yoruba Religion, peace is "the totality of well-being: fullness of life here and hereafter, what the Yoruba call *alafia*, that is the sum total of all that man may desire: an undisturbed harmonious life."[15] Therefore, if one is lacking any of the basic things—such as good health, a wife or husband, children, means of sustenance of one's family—or if a person, though possessing these things, does not enjoy a good relationship with the other members of their community (living or dead), one cannot be said to have peace.[16]

In Islam, peace is understood as a state of physical, mental, spiritual, and social harmony, living at peace with God—through submission—and with one's fellow human beings by avoiding wrongdoing.[17] Peace encompasses harmony and tranquility within individuals in their relation to their creator, their relation to others, and their relation to their environment.[18]

In Christianity, "Jesus, he is our peace, in his flesh, he made both groups into one and has broken down the dividing wall, that is the hostility between us. He has abolished the law with its commands and ordinances, that might reconcile both groups to God in one body through the cross, thus putting to death that hostility through it" (Eph 2:14–16). With the coming of Jesus Christ, the way was opened for the restoration of the lost *shalom* to humankind. True peace includes personal wholeness, corporate righteousness, political justice, and prosperity for all creation. Perhaps no term better describes God's perfect paradise than "peaceful," the world full of wholeness, righteousness, justice, and prosperity.

The peace education curriculum proposed as part of this book aims specifically to empower students with knowledge, attitudes, values, and behaviors to live in harmony with themselves, others, and their environment. Moreover, the program will enhance the development of the necessary skills to resolve situations of injustice and conflict and will encourage

---

14. See Harris and Morrison, *Peace Education*, 5.
15. Rweyemamu, "Religion and Peace," 381.
16. Rweyemamu, "Religion and Peace," 382.
17. Abu-Nimer, *Nonviolence and Peace-building in Islam*, 60.
18. Abdalla, *Peace Education: Islamic Perspectives*, 5.

a culture of peace based on the specific identity components that make up the unique identity of each student. By developing a curriculum that does this for all students in the same classroom, it becomes obvious that the pedagogical approach is one that fosters pluralism, building on not only the respect for a diversity of identities and perspectives but also for cultivating this respect on the basis of arguments that are respectful, rooted in what each student considered to be their own respective cultural or religious worldviews. When doing this in presence of one another, an even greater mutual respect is fostered.

In particular, because of the multi-religious context of the Nigerian population and the increasingly interreligious tensions and conflicts that growing radicalization has fostered, this peace education curriculum includes interreligious dialogue training at its very core. This assertion is based on my conviction that an understanding and acceptance of religious differences—as well as collaboration between adherents of various religious and non-religious worldviews—has essential value. The interreligious Peace education includes the interreligious education goal that reveals that the creeds and holy books of the world's religion teach about spiritual systems that reject violence and the individualistic pursuit of economic and political gain, instead calling their followers to compassion for every human being. It also seeks to lead students to an awareness that the followers of religions across the world need to be and to grow in dialogical relationships of respect, understanding, and engagement with people of different religions. It has great potential to contribute to the common good of the global community.

In the International Handbook of Interreligious Education, Engebretson affirms that:

> Interreligious education is cognitive, affective, and experiential. The cognitive dimension refers to learning about the world of religion its many dimensions, and its focus may encompass breadth or depth of studies in religion or both. Interwoven with the cognitive aspect is the affective process of appropriating the cognitive at a personal level. In all of education, the student learns not only at an intellectual level but inevitably seeks to extract meaning from content. This affective process consists of reflecting on the implications of the content, integrating the content with life experience, being challenged by the content to

deeper awareness or sensibility, responding in a personal and creative way to the content.[19]

Today, the potential ways in which religious people can contribute to peace is made more and more explicit. Hans Küng affirms that there is "no world peace without peace between the religions."[20] In addition, religious leaders are increasingly sought out for training/educating in institutions that offer peace studies, such as the universities of Ibadan, Ilorin, and Calabar. There is a growing recognition that, depending on the issue, multireligious efforts can often be more powerful than those of a sole religious community. This new understanding implies the need for a paradigm shift: from the dominant, present approach of separate religions addressing and solving problems themselves to a collaborative and inclusive interreligious approach. In order to help religious adherents shift in this direction, they require an experience of interreligious dialogue that is transformative to them personally. This is where interreligious dialogue within an interreligious curriculum for peace education becomes vital.

Like many other Nation-states, Nigeria is experiencing serious crises that need urgent responses, including planting seeds—as long term investments—toward longer term results. While the current radicalization obviously needs to be addressed by a variety of immediate political and social responses, it is equally important to understand that this currently growing religious violence can be reduced in the short (minimally), medium (more), and long (root out radicalization discourses) term by the development of an interreligious curriculum for peace education for religious leaders in Nigeria. Prominent peace educators—such as David Hicks, Ian Harris, and Betty Reardon—all endorse the power of education as a means of transforming society. I believe that religious leaders have stronger and longer impacts in promoting peace because of their relationship and authority within their communities. The curriculum proposed is based on an Integrative Theory of Peace which posits that peace has its roots at once in the satisfaction of human need for survival, safety, and security; the human quest for freedom, justice, and interconnectedness; and in the human search for meaning, purpose, and righteousness. Therefore, my present research not only focuses on the development of an Interreligious Curriculum for Peace Education

19. Engebretson, *International Handbook*, vi.
20. Küng, *Global Ethics and Education in Tolerance*, vi.

(ICPE) specifically tailored for the pressing needs of Nigeria in particular but also as my humble contribution to the field of peace education and the world in general.

The year-long curriculum presented in this book intends to be usable by any institution of higher learning in Nigeria, knowing that adaptation to local contexts is always necessary. Yet, it is important to choose a particular case as a point of contextual anchoring in the development of any curriculum. In our case, I have chosen the Department of Religious Studies at the University of Ibadan. This university has been selected because it includes in its Religious Studies department a set of courses directly related to all three main religions in Nigeria (Traditional African Religions, Islam, and Christianity), as well as courses related to theory in the study of religions and interreligious relations, both in Nigeria and beyond. It is posited that the development of an interreligious curriculum for peace education for religious leaders will eventually reduce the growing religious violence in Nigeria by addressing the root-causes of tensions between Christian and Muslim populations and by enabling Nigerian peacemakers to consolidate and/or create interreligious islands of peace amidst this violence.

AIM OF THE BOOK

Using a praxeological process,[21] the general aim of this book is to enable religious leaders to assume positions of interreligious leadership in their local communities by assuming the social and political responsibility to (1) guide and challenge people, (2) to encourage them to explore their own contributions and possible alternatives to resolving and transforming problems, and (3) to enable them to achieve better living conditions, both individually and collectively.

PRAXEOLOGICAL THEORY AND METHODOLOGY

This book is interdisciplinary in nature, rooted in the three overlapping disciplinary fields of religious studies, interreligious dialogue, and peace education. The methodology used is theoretical, and tends toward a constructive and praxeological approach. It rejects the empirical methods of the natural sciences for the study of human action because the

---

21. Nadeau, *La Praxéologie Pastorale*, 93.

observation of how humans act in simple situations cannot also predict how they will act in complex ones. Etymologically defined as "the science of human action," praxeology is a theory influenced by both pastoral theology (with its later development of practical theology) and liberation theologies (also linked to practical theology). It argues for a science of religious action as essential to pastoral studies, which shifted from a model of the application of religious theories to the study of various practices.[22] Based in the practice of observation, praxeology uses multiple empirical tools and theoretical, hermeneutical approaches. After defining a central *problématique*, it explores referents in many disciplines to interpret the problem. Then, it evaluates the pastoral intervention and action itself to elaborate a prospective vision.[23]

The theoretical approach of this book will provide numerous ways of unfolding the difficulties of interpreting theories on peace, peace education, interreligious peace education, and the selected five religious practices, which are: community building, service, teaching, preaching, and worship. In order to have an effective Interreligious Curriculum for Peace Education, my theoretical research will be based on a rationale that can be evaluated rigorously. These theories will therefore be assessed and compared according to their strength and weaknesses.

In addition, the Integrative Theory of Peace (ITP) will be adapted to our design of an interreligious curriculum for peace education. The ITP is based on the concept that peace is, at once, a psychological, social, political, ethical, and spiritual state with its expressions in intrapersonal, interpersonal, intergroup, international, and global areas of human life. The theory holds that all human states of being, including peace, are shaped by our worldview; that is, our view of reality, human nature, the purpose of life, and human relationships. The theory also holds that all human states of being, including peace, are the outcome of the main human cognitive (knowing), emotive (loving), and conative (choosing) capacities.[24]

Finally, the theory of an Interreligious Dialogue for Peacebuilding (IDP) will be used as a methodological approach because it enhances the results of research. It will also be used to help increase understanding of our object of study through creating a higher level of trust and

---

22. Nadeau, *La Praxéologie Pastorale*, 94.
23. Charron and Gauthier, *Entre l'Arbre et l'Écorce*, 25.
24. Danesh, "Towards Integrative Theory of Peace Education," 55–78.

greater local impact on various areas in which Muslims and Christians dialogue. This will help in the formulation of how to evaluate the theory I am developing and undergird this interreligious curriculum for peace education.

The development of this curriculum will be based on several inputs. First, I shall make use of the following five principles of peacemaking: (1) comprehensive; (2) interdependent; (3) architectonic; (4) sustainable; and (5) integrative, since peacebuilding is not a task for religious actors only.[25] Second, I will integrate the seven principles of "inclusive education," developed by the Tanenbaum Center, into our proposed interreligious curriculum for peace education (ICPE) to acquire skills and behaviors such as: (1) acceptance of differences as normal; (2) viewing difference as something interesting, as that which promotes curiosity rather than fear; (3) skillfully asking questions about differences; (4) being an attentive listener; (5) identifying a stereotype and having the skills to debunk it; and (6) recognizing that there are many different religions, religious beliefs, and practices.[26]

CONTENT OF THE BOOK

The book is divided into an introduction, four chapters, and a conclusion. Its order and the content of each chapter are following my theoretical method, based on using a praxeological approach.

The introduction presents, in a cursory fashion, the Nigerian context that both propelled me to have embarked on this book as well as to have selected a particular praxeological approach for later application of the ICPE. In addition, the introduction presents the theoretical elements underpinning this book. It briefly describes Nigeria, explains the role of religion, discusses the importance of the peace education curriculum, enumerates the aim and methodology, and details the contents of the book.

Chapter 2, "Interreligious Relations in Nigeria," provides insight into the various kinds of interreligious relations in Nigeria. It includes an analysis of violence in Nigeria, a description of interreligious initiatives, as well as an enumeration of the obstacles and challenges facing interreligious dialogue in Nigeria.

25. Appleby, *Ambivalence of the Sacred*, 40.
26. Dubensky, *Look at Religion, Diversity, and Conflict*, 16.

Chapter 3, "The Effects of Religious Violence on Interreligious Relations in Nigeria," focuses on interpreting religious violence experienced in Nigeria and its effects on interreligious relations. It presents various theological, political, and socio-economic interpretations, concluding with an analysis of how these interpretations affect interreligious dialogue and its sub-set of inter-ethical dialogue.

Chapter 4, "Preconditions of Peace Education in Nigeria," discusses preconditions of peace education in Nigeria and analyzes the principles and theory of peace education as well as various perspectives on peace education: from a Yoruba religion, Islamic, and Christian approach respectively.

Chapter 5, "Peacebuilding Intervention and Interreligious Curriculum for Peace Education," focuses on peace education as the pastoral intervention required in a praxeological methodology and analyzes the principles and theory of peace education as well as various perspectives on peace education intervention: from a Yoruba Religion, an Islamic, and a Christian approach respectively. It presents the content of the interreligious curriculum for peace education (ICPE). The interreligious curriculum for peace education is divided into 5 units.

CONCLUSION

The interreligious curriculum for peace education (ICPE) is not a quick-fix solution or a pre-packaged tool to be imposed either locally or globally. It is a paradigm shift that shapes content and pedagogy by incorporating issues of human security with sensitivity to the inherited cultural, religious, and spiritual traditions of all those involved and/or affected by conflict. This section focuses on the conclusion of the book—my prospective for interreligious peace education—which includes my prophetic vision of using religious leaders to establish the kingdom of God on earth. Finally, this book ends with important elements and factors contributing to new knowledge in both theory and practice.

CHAPTER II

Interreligious Relations in Nigeria

This chapter provides insights into various kinds of interreligious relations in Nigeria. It includes an analysis of violence in Nigeria, a description of interreligious initiatives, as well as an enumeration of the obstacles and challenges facing interreligious dialogue in Nigeria.

RELIGIOUS VIOLENCE IN NIGERIA FROM 1999 TO 2015

The period highlighted is the beginning of the process of democratic rule after long years of military rule. The clashes selected are based on the number of victims and include the whole country.

Table I. Religious Violence in Nigeria from 1999 to 2015[27]

No	Date	State(s)	Nature	Remarks
1	1 Jul 1999	Ogun	Violent clashes between Yoruba traditional worshippers and Hausa groups in Sagamu.	The crisis originated from the killing of a Hausa woman by the Oro Masqueraders for violating traditional rites.

---

27. Adapted from Onuoha, "Islamist challenge," 54–67; Wikipedia, "Boko Haram."

2	22 Jul 1999	Kano	Reprisal to the Sagamu crisis above.	The casualty figure was not reported.
3	20 Dec 1999	Kwara	Muslim Fundamentalists attacked and destroyed over 14 churches in Ilorin.	Properties worth several millions of naira were destroyed and an unspecified casualty reported.
4	21–22 Feb 2000	Kaduna	Riots over the introduction of *shari'a* law.	An estimated 3,000 people died.
5	28 Feb 2000	Abia	Religious riots in Aba and minor disturbances in Umahia.	Over 450 persons killed in Aba, Abia state, in reprisal for Kaduna crisis.
6	8 Sept 2000	Gombe	The Kaltunga religious crisis.	The crisis erupted over the implementation of *shari'a* in the state.
7	12 Oct 2000	Kano	Religious riot in Kano.	In protest to USA Invasion of Afghanistan over Osama bin Laden. Over 150 persons were killed.
8	7–17 Sep 2001	Plateau	A religious riot between Muslims and Christians in Jos. Mosques, churches, and several properties were damaged or torched.	The riots broke out when the Islamic brigade attacked a Christian woman who attempted to cross a public highway barricaded by Muslim worshippers on Friday. Over 300 people were killed.

9	16 Nov 2002	Kaduna	The Miss World crisis in which Muslims attacked Christians and Churches.	The crisis was triggered by an article by Osioma Daniel in *This Day* newspapers alleging that Prophet Muhammad would have loved to have the girls. Over 250 people were killed and several churches destroyed.
10	8 Jun 2004	Adamawa	Religious conflict between Christian and Muslims in Numan town.	Caused by the location of the town's central Mosque close to Bachama paramount ruler's palace. Over 17 persons were killed.
11	18 Feb 2006	Borno	Religious conflict between Christians and Muslims in Maiduguri.	The riot was caused by the Danish Cartoon on Prophet Muhammad, the *Jyllands-Posten* newspaper. Over 50 persons killed and 30 churches destroyed; over 200 shops, 50 houses and 100 vehicles vandalized.

12	22 Mar 2007	Gombe	Muslim pupils killed their Christian teacher, Mrs. Oluwatoyin Olusesan.	The pupils claimed that their teacher desecrated the Qur'an while attempting to stop a student from cheating in an examination hall.
13	28 Nov 2008	Plateau	Religious violence between Muslims and Christians in the city of Jos.	The crisis, which was triggered by the controversial results of a local election, later turned religious. Over 700 people killed and thousands internally displaced.
14	21 Feb 2009	Bauchi	Ethno-religious conflict at Makama New extension.	Over 11 people were killed, more than 400 houses burnt, and over 1,600 families displaced.
15	26–30 Jul 2009	Bauchi, Borno, Kano, Yobe	Religious violence unleashed by the Boko Haram sect on Christians.	Over 700 persons killed, 3,500 persons internally displaced, 1,264 children orphaned, 392 women widowed, and several properties destroyed
16	29 Dec 2009	Bauchi	Religious violence unleashed by the kala-kato sect on Christians.	Over 38 persons killed, about 20 suspected members of the sect arrested, over 1,000 people internally displaced.

17	17–20 Jan 2009	Plateau	Resurgence of religious crisis in Jos.	Police announced at least 320 killed, but aid workers and local leaders place death toll at over 550. Over 40,000 persons displaced.
18	7 Mar 2010	Plateau	Attacks by Fulani Moslems on Christian-dominated villages of Dogo Nahawa, Shen, and Fan in Jos.	Over 500 people, mainly women and children, were killed.
19	17 Mar 2010	Plateau	Suspected Fulani militia men attacked residents of Biye and Batem in Jos.	13 persons killed
20	11 Apr. 2010	Plateau	Attack on a Christian village of Berom Stock, some 30 kilometers South of Jos, by suspected Fulani Herdsmen.	The attackers targeted the homes of some officials in Kura Jenta in reprisal to the killing of about 150 Fulani Muslims, who were allegedly killed and dumped in wells on 19 January 2010. No life was lost, but 3 houses and 6 vehicles were torched. This violence was ethno-religious.
21	22 may 2010	Plateau	Murder of three Muslim Fulani herdsmen at Tusung village in Barkin Ladi local government, Plateau state.	The attackers were alleged to be Berom Christian Youths. It was ethno-religious.

22	22 May 2010	Plateau	Attack on some Christians who were returning from their place of worship along Bauchi Road in Jos.	Reprisal attack by Muslims over the killing of 3 Fulani Muslims. At least 1 person died while many were injured.
23	17 Jul 2010	Plateau	Muslim Fulani herdsmen launched an overnight attack on a Christian village, Mazah, North of the city of Jos.	About eight people were reportedly killed, including the wife, two children, and a grandson of a pastor. Seven houses and a church were also burned during the attack.
24	29 Aug 2011	Plateau	Clashes between Muslims and Christians at Rukuba road and Farin Gada in Jos during the Ramadan prayers.	No less than 20 persons were killed, 50 injured, over 50 motor vehicles, and 100 motorcycles were torched.
25	16 Jun 2011	Abuja	Suicide bomb attack at the police headquarters, Abuja, by suspected Boko Haram islamists, whose ideology is framed around religion.	Authorities said 6 persons were killed and 73 vehicles destroyed.
26	26 Aug 2011	FCT	Suicide bombing at the UN house, Abuja, by suspected Boko Haram Islamists.	23 persons (11 UN personnel and 12 non-UN personnel were killed).

27	5 Nov 2011	Plateau and Borno	Coordinated attacks on churches and police stations by suspected Boko Haram Islamists.	More than 90 persons were reportedly killed; several churches and police stations torched.
28	25 Dec 2011	Niger and FCT	Bombs were alleged to have been planted at a church's parking lot.	At last count, 45 persons were killed. Some died instantly, others from injuries sustained from the explosion. Over 80 others were receiving treatment for various degrees of injuries.
29	5–6 Jan 2012	Gombe	Gunmen stormed a Deeper Life church in Gombe, shooting indiscriminately at worshippers. The Boko Haram sect claimed responsibility for the shooting.	6 persons were reportedly killed and many others were injured.
30	5–6 Jan 2012	Adamawa	Suspected Boko Haram militants stormed a gathering of Igbo Christians and shot sporadically, killing over a dozen and injuring others, in apparent execution of an ultimatum given by the Boko Haram Islamists sect to Southern Christians living in the North to leave.	22 persons were reportedly killed, a dozen others were injured.

31	10 Jan 2012	Yobe	Boko Haram attack on a beer parlor garden.	8 persons, including 5 police men and a teenage girl, were killed.
32	28 Jan 2012	Kaduna	Nigerian army attacked Boko Haram.	Nigerian army killed 11 Boko Haram.
33	8 Feb 2012	Kaduna	Boko Haram claims responsibility.	Suicide bombing at the army headquarters in Kaduna
34	8 Mar 2012	Sokoto	British hostage rescue attempt to free Italian engineer Franco Lamolinara and Briton Christopher McManus, abducted in 2011 by a splinter group of Boko Haram. The Nigerian army assists British attempt to free them.	Both hostages were killed.
35	3 Jun 2012	Bauchi	Boko Haram claimed responsibility for the bombing of churches in Bauchi state through spokesperson Abu Qaqa.	15 church-goers were killed and several injured.
36	17 Jun 2012	Kaduna	Suicide bombers strike three churches in Kaduna State.	At least 50 people were killed.
37	3 Oct 2012	Adamawa	Boko Haram claimed responsibility for the massacre in the town of Mubi in Nigeria during a night-time raid.	Around 25–45 people were massacred.

38	18 Mar 2013	Kano	Boko Haram claimed responsibility for the suicide car bomb that exploded in Kano bus station.	2013 Kano Bus bombing: At least 22 killed and 65 injured.
39	7 May 2013	Yobe	Boko Haram claimed responsibility for the coordinated attacks on army barracks, a prison, and police post in Bama town.	At least 55 killed and 105 inmates freed.
40	6 July 2013	Yobe	Boko Haram claimed responsibility for Yobe State school shooting.	42 people, mostly students, were killed.
41	29 Sep 2013	Yobe	Boko Haram claimed responsibility for attack at College of Agriculture in Gujba.	40 students killed.
42	14 Jan 2014	Borno	Boko Haram claimed responsibility for the suicide bombing in Maiduguri, Borno.	At least 31 people killed, over 50 people injured.
43	16 Feb 2014	Borno	Boko Haram claimed responsibility for the Izghe massacre.	106 villagers were killed.
44	25 Feb 2014	Yobe	Boko Haram claimed responsibility for the Federal Government College attack at Yobe	Fury at military over Yobe deaths. At least 29 teenage boys dead at Federal Government College BuniYadi.
45	14 Apr 2014	Borno	Boko Haram claimed responsibility.	At least 16 killed.

ANALYSIS OF THIS RELIGIOUS VIOLENCE

The amalgamation of Northern and Southern Nigeria in 1914 brought together the two religions—Christianity and Islam—that had started to be demarcated by ethnicity. These two religions subdued the Traditional Religion hitherto known by various ethnic groups that make up Nigeria. Hence, conflicts of ethnic chauvinism, border disputes, and Islam versus Christianity remain the main source of how profound inequalities and various forms of political and social instability are interpreted in Nigeria. Meanwhile, Islam versus Christianity crises have reached such a level that it could be referred to as localized and periodic civil wars, ranging from the Kano revolt (1980); Bulunkutu Bizarre (1982); Kaduna crisis (1982); Jimeta War (1984); Gombe revolt (1985); Kastina crises (1999); Kano riot (1995); *shari'a* law crises in Zamfara, Kaduna, Bauchi, Sokoto, etc. (1999); *shari'a* law reactions in Aba, Onitsha, and Owerri (1999); Jos crises (2008); and *Boko Haram* (2009–present). The more recent, on-going violence and the insurgence of *Boko Haram* is just the latest form of a pattern of religious violence that erupts, to different degrees, in different regions, at different times. These conflicts result in disintegration, dispersion, instability, loss of lives and properties, and discontinuing economic programs and projects—to mention but a few of the negative impacts of such on-going conflicts within Nigeria.

In summary, these religious crises have brought physical and emotional hardship and overall socio-economic retrogression on the Nigerian people. Various causes have been identified and will be discussed later to explain or interpret this religious violence. Whatever they are, the results are negative and can be summarized in the following list: injury and pain, death, mental agony, psychic terror, feelings of helplessness, destruction of property, damage to infrastructural facilities (such as electric installations, police posts, and schools), diversion of public funds from socio-economic development to security, abuse of human dignity and rights, losses of resources, and the desecration of property. These religious conflicts have had adverse consequences on the growth and building of the nation. They have brought psychological trauma and the destruction of properties. It has caused the breakdown of law and order, weakened the government's ability to govern, threatened the unity of the country, and discouraged foreign investors. It has destroyed the image of Nigeria in the world. Many initiatives have been taken to deal with the current state of violence—one type is interreligious in nature.

INTERRELIGIOUS INITIATIVES IN NIGERIA

Interreligious dialogue has been going on in Nigeria since the late 1970s. The tension built conflicts that have existed between the two communities and have challenged religious leaders to come together for dialogue. The Nigerian Supreme Council for Islamic Affairs (NSCIA) was created in 1973. The *Jamalat-ul-Nasril Islam* (JNI) and the council of *Ulema* and Christian Association of Nigeria (CAN) were formed in 1976.[28] The role of these organizations is to respond to the various religious, social, political, cultural, and missionary challenges within Nigeria. They meet to discuss, to issue joint statements, and offer advice on affairs of common concern and religion to enhance the process of dialogue. They also organize seminars, symposia, and conferences.

Some political events made the interreligious dialogue positive such as: (1) the strong Islamic character of the Shagari (1979–1983) and Babangida (1985–1993) regimes made the whole nation aware that Islam is a national concern, not confined to the far North. Christians throughout the country, whether reacting positively or negatively, realized that they could not ignore Islam and Muslims. (2) The 1983 return of the military and the later annulled election of Abiola, who had enjoyed the support of Christians and Muslims throughout the country, opened the eyes of Christians and Muslims, and during the bitter Babangida-Abacha (1993–1998) days, drew them together to face the common problem.

Rama Mani indicates that in Nigeria, the interreligious initiatives "have scored concrete successes in mediating"[29] religious violence. For example, at a grassroots level, "Pastor James Wuye and Imam Muhammad Ashafa in Kaduna were initially enemies in the Christian-Muslim violence. The pastor lost an arm and the imam lost his spiritual guide and relatives in the conflict. They reconciled and forged a partnership to establish the Muslim-Christian Interfaith Mediation Centre that resolves religious conflicts in Nigeria."[30] This religious grassroots organization has successfully mediated between Christians and Muslims throughout Nigeria. Their organization, now with over ten thousand members, reaches into the militias and trains the country's youth—as well as women, religious figures, and tribal leaders—to become civic peace activists. Under

---

28. Umaru, *Christian-Muslim Dialogue in Northern Nigeria*, 169.
29. Mani, "Cure or Curse?," 152.
30. Mani, "Cure or Curse?," 152.

their leadership, Muslim and Christian youth jointly rebuild the mosques and churches they once destroyed through war and violence.[31]

Their goal is to achieve peaceful coexistence through interfaith cooperation, and community education. Their organization, the Interfaith Mediation Center of the Muslim-Christian Dialogue Forum, deals with the psychology of religious violence and addresses its causes and effects. Their education and media outreach strategies have afforded them widespread support and legitimacy for their efforts to promote peaceful coexistence. They have designed a strategy to both prevent religious and political violence and resolve it when it happens. Their early-warning mechanism, developed in 1996, helps communities identify inflammatory situations and provides the means to reduce tensions. Another early-warning technique is the "deprogramming" of violent youth through Christian and Islamic instruction that emphasizes forgiveness and non-violence.

In 1998 Ashafa and Wuye developed a curriculum entitled "The Ethical Code for Religious Instructions in Schools," which is now used in schools and by other organizations interested in promoting peace. Coupled with Peace Clubs, the curriculum is reducing religious violence in schools. To date, over thirty schools in the majority Muslim Kaduna state and primary schools and universities in Plateau, Kano, and Bauchi states have Peace Clubs and peace curricula. They also created "deprogramming" Youth Camps, which bring together militant youths from different communities for five days of intensive interaction. Camp participants are involved in humanizing activities that replace the demonization of those of a different faith. These militant youth attend skill-building activities such as financial and computer literacy classes. In 2003, a five-day interfaith workshop for Christian and Muslim youth held in Kaduna focused on confronting and revising religious stereotypes, misconceptions, and prejudices among the youth. Led by Imam Ashafa and Pastor Wuye, they organized seminars with opinion leaders and elders that encouraged dialogue about differing views on politics, society, and law.

The pair also offers trauma counseling for those who have suffered losses at the hands of religious violence and trains religious and community leaders to assist those affected by violence. Ashafa and Wuye use scriptures from their two holy books to help people deal with suffering and tragedy. In 2004, when religious violence broke out in the village of

---

31. Bennett, "Interfaith Peace," 1.

Yelwa Shendem and 600 people were killed, the two men traveled to the village more than a dozen times to mediate and preach peace. Gradually, trust was restored. Eventually, the village came together in a Festival of Peace. They have been spreading the practice of tolerance and reconciliation for nearly two decades since forming the Interfaith Mediation Center in Kaduna, in Northern Nigeria, where they train staff in dialogue techniques that bridge divides of ethnicity and religion.

Another interreligious organization working to promote peace, instead formed out of a top-down approach, is the Nigeria Interreligious Council (NIREC), established by the government on September 29th, 1999, in response to the various religious crises. The NIREC is made up of fifty leaders, twenty-five Christian and twenty-five Muslim. The organization is co-chaired by two eminent Nigerians: the Sultan of Sokoto and President-General of the Nigeria Supreme Council for Islamic Affairs (NSCIA), Alhaji Muhammed Saad Abubakar, and the President of the Christian Association of Nigeria Ayo Oritsejafor. According to the NIREC constitution, the goals of the council are:

> To honestly and sincerely endeavor by themselves and through them, their followership, to understand the true teachings of the two religions—Christianity and Islam—including their peculiarities and personal mannerisms, through dialogue, discussions, workshops, seminars, conferences, pamphleteering, etc. To create a permanent and sustainable channel of communication and interaction, thereby promoting dialogue between Christians and Muslims in Nigeria so that the members of both faiths may have mutual understanding of each other's religious position, co-existence among all the people of Nigeria irrespective of their religious or ethnic affiliations. . . . To create forums and channels for the peaceful resolution of any friction or misunderstanding that may arise from time to time.[32]

According to World Leadership Alliance Club de Madrid (WLACM), the NIREC is to provide a formal channel for addressing interreligious strife, thus creating a mechanism for addressing sectarian problems before they escalate into violent strife, and to allow religious leaders in Nigeria to meet at a regular interval, thus helping build channels of trust and understanding between religious leaders on both sides.

The Nigeria Interreligious Council meets once a quarter to dialogue and discuss ways to improve relations. Its members then disseminate the

32. Nigeria Interreligious Council, *Constitution 2010*.

joint message of tolerance and cooperation to their respective communities. After a few years, there was a lull in cooperation, but things have improved over the last few years. So far, the leaders at the elite national level seem to be cultivating a good degree of understanding. At the national level, they tried to foster deeper understanding between Muslims and Christians. At lower levels, their efforts are less well-developed. A few states have created state NIRECs or NIREC like structures. Unfortunately, further cooperation is still limited due to the high level of suspicion that still exists at these lower levels. The majority do not yet understand each other. This misunderstanding is why conflicts are still erupting today. NIREC is trying to carry out damage control at the national level. NIREC will intervene with the government to quarantine the violence, preventing it from spreading elsewhere.

NIREC has also been working to support interreligious projects, which sometimes receive external funding. The Roll Back Malaria Project is perhaps the most prominent example of this cooperation. The United States provided the initial $2 million to start this program. Interreligious cooperation is a work in progress. It is always difficult building relationships of trust with the Muslim community. There is a battle to hold the various Christian denominations together at the same time and promote dialogue with the Muslim community.

NIREC has been known to be very active in addressing the challenges of violence not only in Nigeria but even in neighboring countries, like Cote d'Ivoire. Among many other issues on the agenda of NIREC are freedom of religion and credible elections in a peaceful atmosphere. On Tuesday, October 30, 2012, the *Nigeria Observer* reported that the Nigeria Interreligious Council (NIREC) has advised Nigerians to disregard threats by anyone in the country, meant to intimidate them out of their places of abode. However, the increase in terrorism in the country appears to prove NIREC wrong. The report by Waheed Bakare in *Punch* on October 8, 2012, indicates how much the people are expecting from NIREC. Sha'afi urged the leadership of the Nigeria Interreligious Council to curb religious violence and ensure that there is peaceful co-existence between Muslims and Christians in the country. He said that, "The leadership of NIREC should be blamed for the perennial religious violence in the country. It is a minus for them and it is an indication that we are not being well led."[33] He suggested that if NIREC is not able to assist in

---

33. Sha'afi quoted in Omonokhua, "Where is NIREC?," 1.

stopping terrorism in the country, then the government should look beyond it.

NIREC has been criticized as "Gala club" of prominent Nigerian religious leaders who meet occasionally at Nigeria's most costly hotels to enjoy themselves. NIREC is also accused of only pacifying the masses without being committed to any practical action towards ensuring that its message of interreligious cordial relationship and peaceful coexistence reaches the levels needed. Most state governors accuse the NIREC of inefficiency and instead advocate support of interreligious organizations at the state level.

Another group that has been a strong advocate for the dispossessed in Northern Nigeria is the interfaith forum of Muslim and Christian Women's Association, it is also known as Women's Interfaith Council (WIC). The organization was established in 2010 and is based primarily in Kaduna. The organization has a vision of expanding to other parts of Nigeria. WIC brings Christian and Muslim women from different denominations and groups in Kaduna for creative dialogue, to address women's common concerns, and to embark on peacekeeping initiatives. The group has worked together to give concrete meaning and testimony to interfaith solidarity in action. Whether it is by cleaning the streets or organizing seminars and workshops on topics such as justice and healing, women in security process, peacemaking and peacekeeping, and violence against women, the organization has provided a formidable forum for dismantling some of the barriers that separate women in Kaduna.

The department of Mission and Dialogue of the Catholic Secretariat of Nigeria (CSN) has created a forum for dialogue between Catholic and Muslim Women. The department has also initiated dialogue between Catholic and Muslim Youths. Some Non-Governmental Organizations (NGOs)—such as Society for Peace Studies and Practice and Movement for Peace in Nigeria—are now springing up and seeking recognition on a regular basis.

In spite of the present challenges, there are also areas where dialogue has worked in Nigeria. According to Cornelius Afebu Omonokhua:

> In the Dialogue of life, many Muslims, Christians, and traditional worshippers live in the same family, attend the same school, and work together in the same office and other places of work. In the Dialogue of Social Engagements, some people of different religions in Nigeria often meet in different life situations, like ceremonies, trade, and even join together to fight injustice and

diseases. In Nigeria, some Muslims and Christians have issued joint statements to condemn terrorism and other forms of social ills. In the Dialogue of Theological Exchange, scholars of different religions in Nigeria organize seminars and workshops to discuss theological issues. In the Dialogue of Religious Experience, people of different religions in Nigeria sometimes share their religious experiences and dreams.[34]

Local and international organizations sponsor various conferences in order to mobilize youth toward interreligious dialogue. For example, since 2009, the New Era Educational and Support Foundation has organized an annual conference on youth and interfaith. In 2013, 156 delegates from three continents gathered at the Treasures Inn & Suites, Jos, Nigeria to reflect on the topic: "The Role of Free and Responsible Media toward a Peaceful Society Imbued with Dignity and Mutual Respect."[35] These rounds table discussions brought an interfaith group of youth together from Europe, North America, and Africa to engage in a dialogue with political, social, and faith leaders on a variety of topics—from the media's role in creating and promoting a peaceful society to what role can young people take in promoting world peace and Christian/Islam peacebuilding efforts in Nigeria.[36] By the end of the two-day event, participants resolved to do the following: (1) Establish the Golden Rule Chapter in Nigeria to serve as a platform for the entrenchment of mutual respect, tolerance, and upholding of human dignity; (2) the citizenry and mass media should have an attitudinal and behavioral change on their content; (3) the mass media and people working in the area of peace should give voice to younger people and involve them in peacebuilding activities; (4) the mass media and people working in the area of peace should create an inclusive and divergent platform; (5) the media should promote responsible citizenship so as to cultivate the culture of nonviolence through reports that promote human dignity and patriotism; (6) we should all be committed to peacebuilding process and not leave it in the hands of few individuals or groups; and (7) all citizens must show practical commitments to peacebuilding in their respective communities.

The New Era Educational and Charitable Support Foundation is a Nigeria-based registered NGO. It is a diverse group of dedicated, young

34. Omonokhua, "Need for Interreligious Dialogue," 1.

35. New Era Educational and Support Foundation, "5th International Conference," 1.

36. United Religious Initiative, *Bound for Peace 2013*, 1.

men, women, and community leaders ushering in a new way of thinking that demands inclusiveness in the form of sustained human relationships and dignifies all individuals as equals. They are replacing the old, top-down order that separates and fuels the flames of unnecessary separation and exaggerated fear. They understand that "you cannot want misery for someone else without being in misery yourself."[37] Consequently, they believe forgiveness is imperative for transcending Nigeria's conflicts and establishing co-existence. For them, the entry point is listening-to-learn, one of the great acts of love. Since 2007, as part of their public peace process, they have invited and hosted religiously diverse groups of young women and men of excellence to begin long-term dialogue together. Through this, former adversaries are realizing that nothing replaces face-to-face relationships; we are each other's best advocates. These innovative Nigerians are beginning to seek a standard of excellence and culture of peace not only for themselves but also—and more importantly—for the perceived "other"; they are beginning to see the "other" as equally deserving.

Forward Action for Conservation of Indigenous Species (a Cooperative Circle, based in Bauchi State) is a non-profit organization working to promote quality health care, environmental education and management, leadership development, and youth interfaith communication and integration. On January 4th, 2014, they organized a one-day training on Listening and Negotiations in Bauchi State in the North, including different communities of the Yelwan Tudu area. The goal of the training was to strengthen the capacity of thirty-five Muslims and Christians youth leaders from fourteen communities in their listening and negotiation skills for sustainable interfaith relationships and peaceful coexistence. The thirty-five Muslim and Christian youth at the training were introduced to: (1) theories and concepts in listening and negotiation; (2) strategies and practical examples of successful listening and negotiation; and (3) skills for continuing dialogue for understanding, listening to learn to one another, experience sharing, and discovering that "an enemy is one whose story we have not heard."[38] The training provided the participants with an avenue where they learned and re-learned new skills for active listening and negotiation for peaceful coexistence.

---

37. New Era Educational and Support Foundation, "5th International Conference," 1.

38. United Religions Initiative, "More than 30," 1.

The International Communities are also becoming interested in assisting Nigeria in fighting terrorism through dialogue. November 18–19th, 2011, The UFUK Dialogue Foundation (a Turkish foundation) organized an international conference at the Transcorp Hilton, Abuja, with the theme "Establishing a Culture of Coexistence and Mutual Understanding." On March 3rd, 2012, the Canadian Embassy called a meeting of a few scholars to discuss what the Canadian Government can do to assist Nigeria in fighting terrorism. The theme of the discussion was religious freedom. On March 6th, 2012 United States Commission on International Religious Freedom had a meeting at the Transcorp Hilton, Abuja, with some religious leaders on what the American government can do to help Nigeria achieve peaceful coexistence and promote human dignity.

In addition, some scholars and peacemakers produce literature to reduce the current violence through interreligious dialogue. In his book *Defibrillation of Peace* (2008), Isaiah Dada, a Methodist pastor, explains that peace has been a major factor in economic, political, emotional, and social development, but when communal identities—particularly religious identities—are key causal factors in violent conflicts in an underdeveloped, illiterate, and poor Nigerian community, there is a need for each faith tradition to stop the unnecessary violence and not allow for religion to be the root cause of it. This book explores how to empower pastors to live in peace with others, proposing nine healthy practices and a year-long curriculum outline for in-depth understanding and assimilation of peace education designed for children in Sunday school, youth in Bible study, and adults in women's and men's fellowship groups. The book contains nine chapters and uses library research, including reviews of published studies, books, and articles written from the perspective of peace education, conflict resolution, and reconciliation.

In 2014, Akintude E. Akinade published a book entitled *Christian Responses to Islam in Nigeria: A Contextual Study of Ambivalent Encounters*. This book investigates the complex networks of competition, conflict, and cooperation in interreligious encounters in Nigeria. It studies how both contextual methods and holistic engagement can clarify and untangle some of the intricate conundrums that are discernible in the various ways Christians have responded to Islam in Nigeria.

Another scholar, Umaru Thaddeus Byimui, in his doctoral book, entitled *Toward Christian-Muslim Dialogue and Peace-building Activities in Northern Nigeria: Theological Reflection*, examines critically the incessant interreligious conflicts in Northern Nigeria, identifies the real causes of such conflicts, and suggests theological and practical ways to sustain peacebuilding endeavors. Conflicts as an inevitable part of human existence can be triggered and exacerbated by numerous factors. According to Umaru, religion is a powerful impulse in human existence and has been used to fuel conflict in Northern Nigeria. Radical religious strife, the quest for more converts, colonization, ethnicity, as well as perceived and real political domination have all strengthened stereotypical views of the self and of the other. Religion is closely intertwined with culture and thus central to the understanding and establishment of peace in society; it continues to play a paradoxical role in society. Obviously, religion can be both a cause of conflict as well as a source for conflict resolution and harmonious living.

Umaru's book considers the theological potential of the interreligious encounter (or dialogue) between Islamic and Christian traditions in general and the possibilities and difficulties of dialogue between Muslims and Christians in Northern Nigeria in particular. It explores the theology of interreligious dialogue as a means for a promising peacebuilding process in Northern Nigeria. Religion as a significant part of the problem is equally essential in providing solutions. Taken on their own terms, however, neither religion nor politics have comprehensive answers. Hence, any peacebuilding project in Northern Nigeria must be multi-faceted. In an attempt to consider and strengthen peace-building endeavors within the region, it could be modeled on a theological approach for encounter and dialogue that examines common grounds for collaboration within the two faith traditions.[39] Interreligous dialogue has been used in Nigeria to help people resolve long-standing conflicts and build a deeper understanding of contentious issues. Dialogue is not about judging, weighing, or making decisions, but rather, first and foremost, it is about understanding and learning. Dialogue dispels stereotypes, builds trust, and enables people to be open to perspectives that are very different from their own. Dialogue is one sure way to heal memories and wounded hearts.[40] In dialogue, education, formation, awareness, and understanding are key words. Nigerians have gone through many faces of violence, slavery, and colonialism to the extent that the value of trust has been replaced with prejudice, preconception, and mutual suspicion.

---

39. Umaru, *Christian-Muslim Dialogue in Northern Nigeria*, 12.
40. Omonokhua, "Where is NIREC?," 1.

Another significant contribution to the interreligious initiatives is that Christian leaders have identified the urgent need for education and training of religious preachers, leaders, and teachers. It is essential that religious authorities be responsible for training religious leaders to prevent incompetent men/women from preaching. Seminaries like Immanuel College of Theology, Vining College, and some universities offer courses on Interfaith-dialogue. In some Christian seminaries, Islam is a required course. This gives Christian ministers a more accurate understanding of what Islam actually teaches and aims at reducing misunderstandings between religions. In some academic institutions, such as the Religious Studies Department at the University of Ibadan, there are courses on interreligious dialogue as well as courses whose theme is interreligious in nature, such as "Common Themes in Islam and Christianity." The Islamic leaders trained in various universities are also craving to understand the teachings of Christianity and acquire interreligious skills in dialogue.

In teaching interreligious dialogue in institutions training future religious leaders (such as seminaries or universities), the curriculum focuses on certain historical roots which the two religions have in common. It helps in focusing on many aspects of religion that can assist in living in peace, but the curriculum does not teach peace directly as shown below in the goals or objectives of their curriculum:

a. In both religions, there is the prophetic tradition, the acceptance of self-critical analysis within the community of the faithful, and the questioning of authority where it exceeds the limits set by the will of God.
b. Both religions recognize that the sacred and so-called "secular" together, in their totality, belong to God and come under his sovereignty. Therefore, the social and political dimensions of faith are taken seriously.
c. At present, there is the increasing mobility of people and mixing of populations, particularly students, migrant workers, and refugees. This fact has increased the responsibility of Christians and Muslims to find ways of living together, of spiritual nurture, and of religious education.
d. Finally, at a time when belief in God is being corroded by the acids of modernity, both Christians and Muslims are called upon to restate their belief in a convincing manner.

The General objectives are:

a. To initiate a better relationship between Christians and Muslims on the basis of informed understanding, critical appreciation, and balanced presentation of the other's basic beliefs.
b. To see how the spiritual resources of the two living faiths can contribute to the solution of some of the common problems we face in society today, problems which are not just Muslim or Christian but also human problems, which we all face.
c. To suggest practical ways of co-operation between Christians and Muslims in particular situations and, of course, ways of extending it to neighbors of other living faiths.
d. To raise basic questions on human life and existence for long-range reflection and action together. This can lead each of the communities of faith to a deepening and a renewal of its own spirituality.

SYNTHESIS OF THE OBSERVATION

From the observations above, in Nigeria, religion has failed to establish the peace which it has claimed to promote because deep historical feuds have found religious expression. Religion is thus at the core of the strife experienced primarily in contemporary Northern Nigeria. The theology of the Second Vatican Council, in which the Roman Catholic Church reflects on its self-understanding as a community and its role in the world, provides a vivid model for the encounter between Christianity and other religions in mutual understanding.

There are a number of international and local faith-based organizations operating in Nigeria, and they are making impressive moves towards peace and reconciliation among the divergent religious groupings in the country. Some of the early efforts at reconciliation proved to be ineffective and, in some cases, counterproductive because most of these conferences are round table discussion with people who are not involved with the grassroots life. Such conferences are: The UFUK Dialogue Foundation (a Turkish foundation), which organized an international conference at the Transcorp Hilton, Abuja, with the theme "Establishing a Culture of Coexistence and Mutual Understanding"; the Canadian Embassy, which called a meeting of a few scholars to discuss what the Canadian Government can do to assist Nigeria in fighting terrorism with the theme of "Religious Freedom"; and the United States Commission on International Religious Freedom, which had a meeting at the Transcorp Hilton, Abuja, with some religious leaders on what the American government can do to help Nigeria achieve peaceful coexistence and promote human dignity.

In addition, the annual interfaith conferences organized by the New Era Educational and Support on "The Role of Free and Responsible Media toward a Peaceful Society Imbued with Dignity and Mutual Respect"[41] are round-table discussions among unknown selected youth to engage in a dialogue with political, social, and faith leaders on a variety of topics—from the media's role in creating and promoting a peaceful society to what role can young people take in promoting world peace and Christian/Islam peacebuilding efforts in Nigeria. There is no grassroots transfer of the knowledge acquired.

There are many impediments to interreligious dialogue that affect development of good descriptive models. For example, there is a lack of conviction about the value of interreligious dialogue. One can also encounter an attitude of self-sufficiency or a lack of real openness. Among practitioners of dialogue, one can also find different forms of intolerance based on: ethnic, social, economic, political, and/or racial factors. The best example is the NIREC, which was unable to reduce the interreligious violence in Nigeria, neither able to open any offices in various states nor trained or create a grassroots center.

For example, Sha'afi affirms: "The leadership of NIREC should be blamed for the perennial religious violence in the country. It is a minus for them and it is an indication that we are not being well led."[42] He suggested that if NIREC is not able to assist in stopping terrorism in the country, then government should look beyond it. Ezegbobelu described them as "Gala club" of prominent Nigerian religious leaders, who meet occasionally at Nigeria's most costly hotels to enjoy themselves.[43] Finally, NIREC is also accused of only pacifying the masses without being committed to any practical action towards ensuring that its message of interreligious, cordial relationships and peaceful coexistence reaches the levels needed. Most state governors accuse the NIREC of inefficiency and instead advocate supporting interreligious organizations at the state level.

41. United Religions Initiative, "5th International Conference," 1.
42. Omonokhua, "Where is NIREC?," 1.
43. Ezegbobelu, "Challenges of Interreligious Dialogue," 156.

The understanding that many religious leaders have about peace is very limited. They do not know about the variety of instruments and techniques that can promote peace, and thus, in the face of some more difficult challenges, they can too easily fall prey to calling for the use of violence in order to achieve a "solution" to their problems. Many grew up in environments that encouraged violence, supported by often selective interpretations of specific passages in their sacred texts. The best example is the goals and objectives of the curriculum of Seminaries like Immanuel College of Theology, Vining College, and some universities that offer courses on Interfaith-dialogue. The curriculum in which they have been educated can be qualified as dysfunctional since education should teach religious leaders to avoid resorting to violence.

The dialogue based upon extreme religious relativism is not very useful in diffusing mass conflict in Nigeria today because this type of dialogue suffers from insufficient grounding in their daily life. In addition, other things that can seriously affect the quality of interreligious dialogue can be found in all the following aspects: religious indifference, religious extremism, lack of self-criticism, and/or lack of respect. All of these potential and sometimes real challenges and impediments affect the quality of how to go about teaching interreligious dialogue, and most scholars involved are not physically present in Nigeria (e.g., Isaiah Dada, Akintude E. Akinade, and many others).

The analysis of various religious problems in the Nigerian society brought the understanding of how religion has been "instrumentalized" and maintained by the policy of both colonial and post-colonial powers. This describes the dramatic situations, misfortunes, poverty, conflicts, and wars caused by religious violence. These horrible tragedies will help to understand that there was no peace in Nigeria. The observation compels us to put faces, events, and history behind what we are talking about and will allow us to establish the problematization of religious violence, how to reduce violence in Nigeria, and what is the place of a curriculum for interreligious peace education in advanced religious training.

The following obstacles to peacebuilding have also been identified: (1) the two major tendencies that have contributed to the unfortunate transformation of Christianity and Islam into obstacles to peacebuilding: (a) the intolerance and, at times, violent treatment of differences, both internally and externally and (b) forced conversions;[44] (2) the limitations

---

44. Bartoli, "Christianity and Peacebuilding," 150–53.

that revolve around the secularist framing of religion as a belief and as a distinct variable, empirically manifest but thoroughly historical and transcultural;[45] (3) the lack of imagination and creative political leadership; and (4) the co-optation of religious leaders by political regimes, the patriarchal social structure, and authoritarian regimes.[46]

THE CHALLENGES OF INTERRELIGIOUS DIALOGUE IN NIGERIA

This section deals with various challenges facing interreligious dialogue in Nigeria.

Choosing a Specific Model of Interreligious Dialogue

The first challenge of interreligious dialogue from the Christian perspective is choosing a model. According to Alan Race in *Christians and Religious Pluralism*, there is a tripod model of interreligious dialogue.[47] The first leg of the tripod model is traditionally called exclusivism. Exclusivists are convinced that believers of other religions or non-believers can only be considered to be on the right path when they convert to the one true religion—namely, the religion they confess themselves. For Christian exclusivists, for example, this means that people can only be saved when they convert to Christianity and explicitly accept Jesus as Christ and Redeemer. This Christian exclusivism is mostly christological in nature but it may also be ecclesiological: "*extra ecclesiam nulla salus*" (no salvation outside the Church). Because religious truth is revealed only through Christ and the Church, exclusivist Christians believe that they are obliged to proclaim the Christian message to everyone—that this is a Christian mission. Christian missionary activities have been an important dimension in the history of Christianity.

According to Christians, their central tenet is that God has revealed Godself in an unique mediator or medium and that only through the explicit recognition of this mediator or medium can one find liberation or salvation. In the course of its history, however, this tenet came to be linked to an exclusivistic theology—accompanied by powerful

---

45. Omer, "Religious Peacebuilding," 9.
46. Abu-Nimer, *Nonviolence and Peace-building in Islam*, 119–25.
47. Race, *Christians and Religious Pluralism*, 11–60.

institutional structures—that were sometimes linked to political ideologies, such as colonialism.

The second leg of the tripod model is called "inclusivism." An inclusivist position does not deny the value of other religious traditions and theological claims in advance. The central idea of Christian inclusivism, for example, is that salvation outside Christianity is possible but only thanks to the salvific work of God through Jesus Christ. Christian inclusivism accepts the idea that God wanted salvation for all people, of all times and places, and that God's salvation can take many forms. For this reason, one cannot reject all other religions in advance. Explicit knowledge or recognition of Christ as one's Savior is not necessary in order for one to be saved. This approach was initially developed before and during the time of the Second Vatican Council (1962–1965) by the Catholic theologian Karl Rahner: "If it is true that a person who becomes the object of the church's missionary efforts is or may be already someone on the way towards salvation—and if it is at the same time true that this salvation is Christ's salvation, since there is no other salvation—then it must be possible to be . . . an anonymous Christian."[48] Rahner's particular form of inclusivism is necessarily linked to the notion of "anonymous Christians."

The third leg of the model is that of pluralism, in which there is a recognition that all religions are equal. All religions are partial expressions of the Ultimate Reality. All these religions are parallel ways to reach Ultimate Reality or, in a Christian language, salvation. Pluralism is the most amenable position for interreligious dialogue.

From the Islamic perspective, there is no interreligious model but rather three Muslim interfaith initiatives with varied interfaith theologies and religion-state relations: The Movement, Jordan's A Common Word and Saudi Arabia's interfaith efforts. These three prominent cases have attracted much publicity and are likely to influence future interfaith dialogue efforts in the Muslim world. The Gülen movement will be studied because of his engagement on a grassroots level.

The leader of the Fethullah group offers a very accommodating interfaith theology grounded in orthodox Sunni (Hanafi) thought and informed by his Sufi teachings. Gülen has written extensively on interfaith dialogue, for "the very nature of religion demands [it]."[49] This

---

48. Rahner, *Concise Theological Dictionary*, 24.
49. Gülen, *Advocate of Dialogue*, 242.

accommodationist approach is built around three principles: (1) the commonalities among faiths, (2) a history of revelation and prophecy, and (3) the Qur'an's explicit sanction of interfaith dialogue.[50] Like other traditional Sunni scholars, Gülen understands the Qur'an as calling for universal dialogue primarily—but not exclusively—with Christians and Jews. The Qur'an (such as Qur'an 3:64) provides scriptural support for a Muslim dialogue with the People of the Book (Jews and Christians) and is stressed by those verses in which Muslims are asked to believe "in what is sent to you [Muhammad] and what was sent before you" (Q 2:3–4) and to "not argue with the People of the Book unless in a fair way" (Q 29:46).

Gülen, however, also expands this accommodation to non-Abrahamic religions. He holds that Judaism, Christianity, Islam, as well as even Hinduism and other world religions all accept the same divine source for themselves. These religions—along with non-theistic religions, like Buddhism—are all in pursuit of the same goals: love, compassion, tolerance, and forgiveness.[51] This accommodating approach to other faiths is rooted in Gülen's understanding of the spiral history of religion. Embedded in an Islamic understanding of religion and history, assuming oneness and the basic unity of religions, this spiral view of history suggests that God sends prophets and revelations to establish and re-establish the universal principle of God's existence. This inclusive interfaith theology constructed from the elements of mainstream Sunni and Sufi tradition is further buttressed by the Ottoman-Turkish tradition. Gülen refers to the teachings of Rumi (1207–1273), the famous Sufi poet, on universal values. Gülen indicates how religious tolerance encouraged Muslims and non-Muslims to embrace these universal values.

The Missing Link of Grassroots Community Participation in Dialogue

Another challenge in interreligious dialogue is the missing link of grassroots community participation.[52] Too often, dialogue takes place exclusively among elite religious leaders and experts. Tariq Ramadan affirms: "To be involved in dialogue between two religions while being completely cut off from the believers of one's own religion is problematic and can

---

50. Kayaoglu, "Explaining Interfaith Dialogue," 236.
51. Gülen, *Advocate of Dialogue*, 253.
52. Umaru, *Christian-Muslim Dialogue in Northern Nigeria*, 172.

be counterproductive. Many specialists in interreligious dialogue move from conference to conference totally disconnected from their religious community as well as the grassroots realities."[53]

PROBLÉMATIQUE

The various violent religious conflicts in Nigeria have a devastating impact on the citizenry and disrupt any hope for peaceful coexistence. Any possible solution calls for a sound contextual analysis that is rooted in a careful understanding of the complexities of the Nigerian situation. In addition to finding connections between the religious traditions, it must also take the social, economic, political, and cultural dynamics into consideration. The institutionalization of religious violence and the aggressive competition for dominance by Christians and Muslims continue to have a particularly deleterious impact on the Nigerian nation. The current policy and strategy of interreligious mediation in terms of religious conflict management, prevention, and peacebuilding has neither reduced religious violence nor improved the grassroots engagement of religious leaders. Practical, alternative ways of enhancing the capacity of the interreligious mediation group to effectively resolve religious conflict in the country must be developed. Religious leaders must be empowered and charged with the responsibility for the process of peace at the grassroots level. Peace education and training is a viable alternative to violence, but it can only be effective if it brings together participants in an interreligious peace education experience. The absence and neglect of interreligious peace education as part of the peace education core program and the lack of interreligious curriculum for peace education in the training of religious leaders are identified as two of the main problems encountered when analyzing the effectiveness of Nigerian academic studies in creating a peaceful living experience.

---

53. Ramadan, *Western Muslims and the Future of Islam*, 209.

CHAPTER III

The Effects of Religious Violence on Interreligious Relations in Nigeria

This chapter focuses on interpreting religious violence experienced in Nigeria and its effects on interreligious relations. First, I present various theological interpretations. Second, I give an overview of different political interpretations. Third, I give a variety of socio-economic interpretations. After presenting those different kinds of interpretations, this chapter concludes with an analysis of how these interpretations affect interreligious dialogue and its subset of inter-ethical dialogue.

THEOLOGICAL INTERPRETATIONS

Today, while we know that there are three general religious traditions in Nigeria (Traditional African, Islamic, and Christian), the vast majority of cases where religious people are involved in promoting violence relate to Islam and Christianity. Within both of these two traditions, there is a wide spectrum of religious interpretations, only a small segment of which condone violence. For example, there are Muslims who promote an interpretation of *"jihad"* that legitimizes violence and there are Christians who promote an interpretation of "Jesus is the only way" to also legitimize violence.

Jihad

The word "*jihad*" is commonly used today by many Muslims worldwide, including in Nigeria, but with very different meanings. More recent events and increased media coverage of new technologies have often focused attention on sad events that have popularized, among both Muslim and non-Muslim communities worldwide, the part of the spectrum of interpretations that defines *jihad* in a more violent way. In the name of *jihad*, for example, many Nigerian Muslim militants have killed Christians as well as Muslims that they disagree with, especially in the Northern part of Nigeria. These movements, the most famous of which today is *Boko Haram*, are part of a transnational phenomenon that can best be described as a family of extremist Jihadist groups, with various degrees of militancy. One can give a few examples, such as the Egyptian Islamic *jihad* that killed Anwar Sadat in 1981 or the *Laskar jihad* that is responsible for the murder of more than ten thousand Christians in Indonesia. For two decades, the Jihadists in Sudan have physically attacked non-Muslims, looted their belongings, and killed their men. Al-Qaeda Jihadists killed nearly three thousand people on September 11th, 2001, in the United States of America. So-called "home grown" Jihadists caused terror attacks on July 7th, 2008, in London. And of course, *Boko Haram* Jihadists continue to attack Christians and Muslims in Northern Nigeria in particular. Such instances, especially in recent years (but also throughout Islamic history), have led many non-Muslims to view Islam as a violent, destructive, and even barbaric religion. Yet the concept of *jihad* is a rich, polysemic concept that includes a spectrum of interpretations, some of which promote violence, while others promote peaceful self-introspection and battle against the human propensity for unethical thoughts and actions. In the face of these wide differences in interpreting the concept of *jihad* today, it is distortive to reduce all use of the terminology to only its violent usages.

The concept of *jihad* is an ancient one, with a complex subsequent history. According to Rudolph Peters, there are six main varieties of *jihad*: the classical doctrine, *jihad* as propaganda, modern "defensive *jihad*," anti-colonial *jihad*, pacifist *jihad*, and Islamist *jihad*.[1] The first variety, the classical doctrine of *jihad*, was first formalized around the tenth century as part of the general process whereby Islamic doctrine and law were codified from the source texts of Islam: the Qur'an and the

---

1. See Peters, *Islam and Colonialism*.

Hadith compendia. The result of this general process was the emergence of *sharia*, a fully worked-out system of rules and principles that govern all aspects of the lives of devout Muslims.[2] One reason for this process of codification was that the text of the Qur'an, taken on its own, often permitted contradictory conclusions on significant matters—including, importantly, *jihad*.

The second variety, *jihad* as propaganda, is exemplified by when *jihad* played a small part in the First World War as propaganda rather than as religious or legal doctrine. At the start of the war, the *Shaykh al-Islam*—the senior Ottoman religious dignitary—publicly proclaimed a *jihad* against England, France, and Russia. The hope was that this proclamation would help to motivate the Ottoman war effort and might also create disaffection among the Muslim populations of the three empires in question.[3]

The third variety of *jihad*, according to Mark Sedgwick, is what might be called "defensive *jihad*," an understanding of *jihad* that was advanced by most Muslims during 2006 in response to Pope Benedict XVI's ill-advised quotation from Theodore Khoury's quotation from Emperor Manuel II. These understandings of "defensive *jihad*" differ significantly from the understandings at the time of Manuel II's captor Bayezid I, but they represent the consensus of most Muslims today. Few of today's Muslims realize that they have little or no basis in the classic doctrine.[4] Their origin, as Peters shows, lies in the nineteenth century.[5]

The fourth variety of *jihad* is called "anti-colonial *jihad*." Although the classical doctrine of *jihad* had become irrelevant to states by the nineteenth century, it remained relevant for irregular and rebel forces. Once European armies had defeated Muslim states in various parts of

2. *Sharia* is often translated as "holy law," but it is rather more than that. It is very similar to the Jewish *halakha*. The *sharia* not only covers most branches of law (from family law through criminal law to commercial law) but also regulates ritual, ethics, and even clothing and table manners. It derives principally from the Qur'an and Hadith but also makes use of analogy and certain forms of reason, and it takes account of consensus and precedent. In Shi'i Islam, the words *(akhbar)* of the infallible Imams are also a source of the *sharia*. The *sharia* is recorded in the writings of religious scholars, who disagree among themselves on (usually minor) points, but it exists independently of these writings rather as historical truth exists independently of the writings of historians. See Sedgwick, "Jihad, Modernity, and Sectarianism."

3. Sedgwick, "Jihad, Modernity, and Sectarianism," 1.

4. Buchan, *Greenmantle*, 16.

5. Sedgwick, "Jihad, Modernity, and Sectarianism," 10.

the Muslim world, a number of sub-state resistance movements came into being. Such *jihads* were, of course, also defensive *jihads*, even if the defense was sometimes pre-emptive. The most famous of these anti-colonial *jihads* were those against the French in Algeria, against the Russians in Daghestan, against the Italians in Libya, and against the British in Somalia—all of which established short-lived political structures that might be called states.[6]

The fifth variety of *jihad* is "pacifist *jihad*." This is a development of "defensive *jihad*" that takes the logic of self and community improvement as a religious duty to its pacifist end.

The sixth and final variety of *jihad*, Islamist *jihad*, is that which is nowadays most familiar in the West, and is exemplified by al-Qaeda. Of the six main varieties of *jihad*, all of them but two—the classical doctrine and the pacifist variety—are modern in nature. *Jihad* as propaganda retains the basic idea of religious duty and religious rewards, but it is fundamentally just a form of propaganda. "Defensive *jihad*," the current mainstream interpretation, is of relatively recent origin and is essentially compatible with contemporary mainstream Western "just war" theories.[7]

Jihad, according to Firestone is divided into the medieval and the modern.[8] In medieval legal sources, *jihad* generally referred to a divinely sanctioned struggle to establish Muslim hegemony over non-Muslims as a prelude to the propagation of the Islamic faith. The medieval theory included elaborate rules on the right conduct of *jihad*. No war was a *jihad* unless authorized and led by the *imam*, the leader of the Islamic state. Enemies were to be given fair warning, and, should they choose not to accept Islam or to fight, they were offered protected *(dhimmi)* status, which allowed them to retain communal autonomy within the Islamic state in return for collective tax payments.

Three broad approaches to the modern reinterpretation of *jihad* may be discerned. The first approach is apologetic and arose in the late nineteenth century in response to Western criticism that *jihad* meant "holy war" and Islam was spread by force. Muslim apologists argued that the Qur'an and Prophetic traditions only allow war for self-defense against persecution and aggression. The second approach is modernist and also diminishes *jihad*'s military aspects, emphasizing its broader

---

6. Esposito, *Unholy War*, 5.
7. Sedgwick, "Jihad, Modernity, and Sectarianism," 10.
8. Firestone, "Jihad," 2.

ethical dimensions within Islamic faith and practice. Like the apologists, the modernists dismiss the medieval theory as a distortion of Qur'anic ethics, pointing out, for example, that the division of the world into *Dar al-Islam* and *Dar al-Harb* is found nowhere in the Qur'an or Prophetic traditions. A war is a *jihad*, therefore, only if it is fought in defense of Muslim lives, property, and honor. Unlike the apologists, however, the modernists are motivated less by Western criticisms of *jihad* than by the desire to interpret this concept in a way compatible with modern international norms. *Jihad* in the modernist view is the Islamic equivalent of the Western idea of just war, a war fought to repel aggression with limited goals and by restricted means. The third approach, the revivalist, arose in response to the apologist and modernist writings. By limiting *jihad* to self-defense, the revivalists claim, the apologists and modernists have debased the dynamic qualities of *jihad*. The goal of *jihad* today ought not to be to coerce people to accept Islam because the Qur'an clearly encourages freedom of worship (especially Q 2:256); rather, it ought to be to overthrow un-Islamic regimes that corrupt their societies and divert people from service to God.[9]

Islamic scholar Majid Khadduri asserts that: "God enjoins all believers to slay the polytheists wherever they may be found until they believe."[10] The verses of the Qur'an cited by the protagonists of this view in support of their stand include: "Fight in the cause of God those who fight you; but do not transgress limits. . . . There is no more tumult for oppression" (Q 2:190–193).[11] Commenting on the verse, which enjoins Muslims to slay the idolaters not on account of their religion but rather on account of their (the idolaters') unruly behavior, M. M. Ali opines that in view of the clear exception given in verse 4 of chapter 9, the idolaters identified are the idolatrous tribes of Arabia, assembled at the pilgrimage, who made treaties with the Muslims but later violated them—and not all idolaters of the world.[12]

According to Kaltner in *Islam: What Non-Muslims Should Know*, the term *jihad* occurs only four times in the Qur'an, but "words etymologically associated with it are found about forty times in the text."[13] The

---

9. Firestone, *Jihad*, 2.
10. Khadduri, *War and Peace in the Land of Islam*, 37.
11. See also Q 2:217, 246; 9:5, 13–14, 29, 123.
12. Ali, *Holy Qur'an*, 385.
13. Kaltner, *Islam*, 1.

concept awakens fear and misunderstanding of Islam by non-Muslims. Therefore, there is a great need to provide a detailed explanation of what *jihad* means. According to B. A. Robinson: "Muslims generally classify *jihad* into two forms, *jihad al-akbar*, the greater *jihad*, [which] is said to be the struggle against one's soul (*nafs*), while *jihad al-asgar*, the lesser *jihad*, is external and is in reference to physical effort, i.e., fighting."[14]

According to John Esposito in "Jihad: Holy or Unholy War," the importance of *jihad* is rooted in the Qur'an's command to struggle (the literal meaning of the word *jihad*) in the path of God and in the example of the Prophet Muhammad and his early Companions. In its most general meaning, *jihad* refers to the obligation—incumbent on all Muslims, individuals, and the community—to follow and realize God's will: to lead a virtuous life and to extend the Islamic community through preaching, education, example, writing, etc.[15] *Jihad* also includes the right—indeed, the obligation—to defend Islam and the community from aggression. Throughout history, the call to *jihad* has rallied Muslims to the defense of Islam. Another important dimension of *jihad*, according to Esposito, is rooted in the Qur'an's command to "struggle or exert" (the literal meaning of the word *jihad*) oneself in the path of God.[16] The Qur'anic teachings have been of essential significance to Muslim self-understanding, piety, mobilization, expansion, and defense. *Jihad* as struggle pertains to the difficulty and complexity of living a good life: struggling against the evil in oneself, making a serious effort to be virtuous and moral, to do good works, and to help reform and transform society. Depending on the circumstances in which one lives, it also can mean fighting injustice and oppression, spreading and defending Islam, and creating a just society through preaching, teaching and, if necessary, armed struggle or holy war.[17]

Esposito shows the two broad meanings of *jihad*—non-violent and violent—are contrasted in a well-known Prophetic tradition. Muslim tradition reports that when Muhammad returned from battle, he told his followers: "We return from the lesser *jihad* to the greater *jihad*. The

---

14. Robinson, "Concept of Jihad in Islam," 1.
15. Esposito, "Jihad," 2.
16. Esposito, "Jihad," 2
17. Esposito, *What Everyone Needs to Know about Islam*, 133.

greater *jihad* is the more difficult and more important struggle against one's ego, selfishness, greed, and evil."[18]

The Qur'anic verses dealing with the right to engage in a "defensive" *jihad*, or struggle, were revealed shortly after the *hijra* (emigration) of Muhammad and his followers to Medina in flight from their persecution in Mecca. At a time when they were forced to fight for their lives, Muhammad is told: "Leave is given to those who fight because they were wronged—surely God is able to help them—who were expelled from their homes wrongfully for saying, 'Our LORD is God'" (Q 22:39–40). The defensive nature of *jihad* is clearly emphasized in the Qur'an as well: "And fight in the way of God with those who fight you, but aggress not: God loves not the aggressors" (Q 2:190). At critical points throughout the years, Muhammad received revelations from God that provided guidelines for *jihad*.[19]

According to David Cook in *Understanding Jihad*, *jihad* plays a major role in Muslim apocalyptic literature as well. Since the early Muslims' existence was largely dominated by fighting and conquest, it is hardly surprising to find that their vision of the future just before the end of the world, as well as their vision of the messianic future, was characterized by a state of continuous war.[20]

Both *jihad* literature and apocalyptic literature are very frank in their assessment of the economic reasons that drew the early Muslims to conquest. Fantastic amounts of booty and slaves are described in the sources. In describing the eventual conquest of Constantinople, the apocalyptic sources speak of gold, jewels, and virgins, saying fighters "will ravish 70,000 as long as they wish in the Royal Palace."[21] These baser motives are acknowledged in the *jihad* literature, but at the same time, they are dismissed as ancillary to the spiritual goals of *jihad*: "A man came to the Prophet and said: 'Some men fight for spoils, some for fame, some to show off; who is fighting in the way of Allah?' He said: 'The one who fights to lift the Word of Allah to the highest, he is fighting in the path of Allah.'"[22]

---

18. Esposito, *Unholy War*, 117.
19. Esposito, *Unholy War*, 120.
20. Cook, *Understanding Jihad*, 24.
21. Cook, *Understanding Jihad*, 25.
22. Cook, *Understanding Jihad*, 25.

In understanding the concept of *jihad* in the Qur'an, there is a need to distinguish between what the Qur'an says and how it has been interpreted. According to Clinton Bennett in *The Concept of Violence: War and Jihad in Islam*: "There are several *Qur'anic* verses, however, where the word *Jihad* has been interpreted as being synonymous with the words war and fighting, as in Q 2:215; 8:41; 49:15; 61:11; 66:9."[23] The most commonly cited verse used to justify the equation of *jihad* with violence reads, "Strive (*Jihad*) your utmost in the cause of Allah with your property and your persons" (Q 61:11).[24] But in reality, those verses mentioned are not *jihad* but something different from the meaning of *jihad*. The four times *jihad* is mentioned, it has been used in the sense of effort and strength and not in the sense of war and fighting.[25] The first verse in the Qur'an in this connection is 9:24. In this verse, Muslims are enjoined to extend their full support to the mission of the prophet, to the extent of making sacrifices. Here the phrase "*jihad fisabilillah*" appears for helping the prophet in his mission of dissemination of the message of Islam and not for waging war. The second verse of the Qur'an that mentions *jihad* says: "Do not listen to the unbelievers, but strive with them strenuously with it [the Qur'an]" (Q 22:52). Clearly, here the word *jihad* is again used for the mission of the Prophet. No other sense can be implied by the word *jihad* in this context of doing *jihad*. The word *jihad* appears in the Qur'an for the third time in chapter 60: "If you have come out to strive in My Way and seek My Good pleasure" (Q 60:1). This verse was revealed shortly before the conquest of Mecca. The Prophet was preparing for the journey from Medina to Mecca. It was indeed a peaceful journey, made for achieving peaceful results in the form of a *hudaiybiya* peace treaty. One incident makes it clear that it was a march of peace, for during this march, one Muslim uttered these words aloud: "Today is the day of fighting." The Prophet responded immediately, saying, "No, today is the day of mercy." The fourth time the Qur'an uses *Jihad* comes in chapter 22: "And strives in his cause as you ought to strive" (Q 22:78). Here, too, *jihad* is used as struggle for the cause of God's religion.

According to Farida Khanam in "Understanding Jihad": "Fighting and war came from another word, *qital*."[26] *Qital* is to engage in war at the time of aggression on the part of the enemies. The *qital* or war is

23. Bennett, "Interfaith Peace," 1.
24. Khadduri, *War and Peace in the Law of Islam*, 1.
25. Kaltner, *Islam*, 120.
26. Khanam, "Understanding Jihad," 1.

purely in self-defense in accordance with God's commandment, which also involves a struggle that came to be called *jihad* as well.

The following is what Muhammad had to say about *jihad* as recorded in the Hadith:

> Allah's Prophet was asked, "What is the best deed?" He replied, "To believe in Allah and His Prophet Muhammad." The questioner then asked, "What is the next in goodness?" He replied, "To participate in *jihad* [religious fighting] in Allah's Cause." The questioner again asked, "What is the next [in goodness]?" He replied, "To perform Hajj [Pilgrimage to] *mubrur*, [which is accepted by Allah and is performed with the intention of seeking Allah's pleasure only and not to show off and without committing a sin and in accordance with the traditions of the Prophet]."[27]

> Allah's Prophet said a pious slave gets a double reward. Abu Huraira added: "By Him in Whose Hands my soul is but for *jihad* (holy battles), Hajj, and my duty to serve my mother, I would have loved to die as a slave."[28]

> Allah's Prophet said: "Allah guarantees [the person who carries out *jihad* in His Cause and nothing compelled him to go out but *jihad* in His Cause and the belief in His Word] that He will either admit him into Paradise or return him with reward or booty he has earned to his residence from where he went out."

The close connection of *jihad* with the struggle for justice is reinforced in Hadith literature. One of the best-known ways that a Muslim must strive to avert injustice is first by actions, and if that is not possible, by words, and if that is not possible, at least by intentions.

In the Hadith, the second most authoritative source of the *shari'a* (Islamic law), *jihad* is used to mean armed action, and most Islamic theologians and jurists in the classical period (the first three centuries) of Muslim history understand this obligation to be in a military sense. Although the language of the Qur'an and Hadith is quite militant in many places, this is a reflection of the Muslims' world in the seventh century, which consisted initially of resistance to a variety of more powerful non-Islamic tribes and then successful military campaigns to spread the faith. Besides

---

27. Bukhari, *Sahih al-Bukhari*, 25.
28. Bukhari, *Sahih al-Bukhari*, 724.

containing exhortations to fight, however, Islamic sacred texts have also laid out the rules for the engagement of war, which include prohibitions against the killing of non-combatants such as women, children, the aged, and the disabled. These texts also require notice to the adversary before an attack, requiring that a Muslim army must seek peace if its opponent does, and forbids committing aggression against others as well as suicide.

According to Sohail H. Hashmi in his article "*Jihad*," during the period of Qur'anic revelation, while Muhammad was in Mecca (610–622), *jihad* meant essentially a nonviolent struggle to spread Islam.[29] Following his move from Mecca to Medina in 622, and the establishment of an Islamic state, fighting in self-defense was sanctioned by the Qur'an (Q 22:39). At each place *jihad* was used, the focus was on the sense of effort and strength and not the sense of war and fighting. The life of the Prophet Muhammad was full of striving to gain the freedom to inform others and convey the message of Islam. During his stay in Mecca, he used non-violent methods, and after the establishment of his government in Medina, by the permission of Allah, he used armed struggle against his enemies whenever he found it inevitable. Allah admonishes Muslims in the Qur'an: "And why should you not fight in the cause of Allah and of those who, being weak, are ill-treated (and oppressed)? Men, women, and children, whose cries are Our Lord! Rescue us from this town, whose people are oppressors; and raise for us from You, one who will protect; and raise for us from You, one who will help" (Q 4:75). The mission of the Prophet Muhammad was to free people from tyranny and exploitation by oppressive systems. Once free, individuals in the society were then free to choose Islam or not.

In its literal sense, *jihad* in Arabic simply means struggle, striving to one's utmost to further a worthy cause. There is a difference, however, between the word struggle and *jihad*. The word struggle does not connote the sense of reward or worship in the religious sense of the word. But when the word *jihad* became a part of Islamic terminology, the sense of reward or worship came to be associated with it; that is to say, if struggle is struggle in the simple sense of the word, *jihad* means a struggle which is an act of worship, the engagement of which earns reward for the person concerned. Inasmuch as *jihad* is a struggle, it is a struggle against all that is perceived as evil in the cause of that which is perceived as good. It is a struggle across time and all dimensions of human thought and

---

29. Hashmi, "Jihad," 425.

action. Although *jihad* is improperly used by some fanatics and fundamentalist Muslims, coupled with press propaganda, *jihad* is relevant in our world and deserves to be emulated for the following reasons: it is rooted in the basic tenets of Islamic pillars, in the Qur'an and Hadith, not only for spiritual growth and political and economical freedom but also for peace, solidarity, and love in the community. Living in a worried world gives each religion the impetus to demonstrate the tenets of their faith that make each religion distinct, attractive, and accommodating for peace, love, and spirituality.

Jon Brockopp describes *jihad* as a religious doctrine that has little place in modern statecraft. Wars in the Middle East and elsewhere are termed "*harb*" not *jihad*. *Jihad* means "struggle" and the Prophet stated that the lesser *jihad* is the struggle to spread Islam, whereas the greater *jihad* is the struggle with one's own evil inclinations. In the medieval period, like the Crusades, *jihad* was waged to spread Islam, and just as the word crusade is still used in a metaphorical sense, so one also hears *jihad*. It is a perversion of medieval doctrines of warfare to use *jihad* to justify individual terrorist acts, and these acts have always been condemned by Muslim authorities in the strongest terms.[30]

According to Jawad Khaki, other forms of practices in human struggle that have been mentioned in the Hadith literature are as follows: (1) *jihad-un-nafs*, spiritual struggle for self-purification; (2) *jihad-ul-lisan*, struggle to engage in a civil dialogue by way of the tongue; (3) *jihad-ul-qalam*, intellectual struggle by the use of the pen; (4) *jihad-ut-tarbiyya*, educational *jihad*; (5) *jihad-ud-da'wa*, spreading the message of monotheism and servitude to God with wisdom and goodly admonition; (6) *jihad bi-l-maal*, struggle to part with one's wealth to help in a humanitarian cause; and (7) *jihad bi-s-sayf*, military engagement for self-defense and self-preservation when all peaceful methods fail to achieve a resolution to the dispute.[31] *Jihad* is a central and broad Islamic concept whose primary significance is in reference to spiritual purification, including the struggle against evil inclinations within oneself, the struggle to improve the quality of life in society, and the struggle in the battlefield for self-defense or fighting against tyranny or oppression. It is recognized, however, that there will be times in society where evil and mischief may arise. In such cases, Muslims are urged to defend themselves. Again,

---

30. Brockopp, *Islamic Ethics of Life*, 93.
31. Khaki, "What are the Basic Teachings," 1.

referring to the Qur'an: "Fight in the way of God against those who fight against you, but begin not hostilities. Lo! God loveth not aggressors" (Q 2:190). *Jihad* is an "effort against evil in the self and every manifestation of evil in society."[32] In fact, many would argue that anyone willing to carry out suicide missions cannot be considered a Muslim, or at least must be considered a grave sinner who will suffer in hell. Muslims are deeply opposed to suicide, even in cases of war. Further, war is understood to be run by the state, and a majority of Muslims support non-violent means to end their conflicts.

For Omid Safi, *jihad* is a term that means many different things to many different people. There are many Sufis who would talk about the need to be perpetually vigilant of one's own being and self to fight egoism and to transform the self towards a higher reflection of divine qualities. Safi points out that there have also been many Muslim rulers who have called for waging *jihad* against the infidels. He believes there has to be a theory and a method of *jihad* in which the closest analogy is the just war theory in medieval Christian thought. He notes that you just can't go around massacring civilians. Muslims jurists have identified a very specific set of criteria whereby one may undertake *jihad*. For example, they have said that perhaps only an authentic Muslim ruler can initiate offensive *jihad*. A defensive *jihad* is a different situation if the Muslims are under attack, but even in those situations, jurists have said you cannot kill civilians, you cannot kill women, you cannot kill children, you cannot kill the elderly, you cannot kill somebody that has his back to you and is running away, you cannot poison water wells, you cannot cut down trees, and you can't kill animals. Once you begin to get a broader sense of the legalistic framework that has been in place precisely to prevent a kind of war of all against all, you begin to see just how abnormal something like September 11th is, even from a Muslim perspective.[33]

Giles Kepel explains that over time, *jihad* became a resource essential to finance the Ottoman Empire. The failure of the Muslim army at Vienna in 1683, followed by the "roll-back" inflicted by gradual European states, dried up this flow of goods and money and precipitated the decline in the Ottoman system of taxation to support military and political resources, leading to an inevitable collapse. Since then, the Islamic expansion has been in decline.

32. Pipes, "What is Jihad," 1.
33. Safi, *Progressive Muslims*, 8.

What are the ethical considerations of striving in the path of God in the contemporary period, when that path traverses communities and economies of rapid technological development and political change, bringing profound social and cultural dislocations for Muslims in virtually every corner of the globe? The single most important point about *jihad* is that participation is a religious duty that brings religious rewards. Religious duties in Islam may be either individual duties *(fardayn),* such as prayer, which every Muslim must perform, or communal duties *(fardkifaya),* such as the study of Arabic grammar (necessary for Qur'anic exegesis), which must be performed by a sufficient number of Muslims but not by every Muslim. Participation in *jihad* is normally a communal duty, but under certain circumstances, it can become an individual duty.

The terms "strive" and "struggle" may be used by Muslims as well as non-Muslims in a community because in our daily life, we strive to achieve what is important to us. In this sense, a student struggles and strives to obtain an education and pass course work; a worker strives to discharge his/her job and maintain good relations with his/her employer; and a politician strives to maintain or increase his/her reputation with constituents. *Jihad* is still relevant in modernity because it is indeed a struggle for Muslims to put Allah ahead of their loved ones, their wealth, and their worldly ambitions. *Jihad* is worthy to be practiced when we read from the Qur'an: "So obey not the rejecters of faith, but strive *(jahidhum)* against them by it (the Qur'an) with a great endeavor" (Q 25:52). When *jihad* is understood as having courage and steadfastness to convey the message of Islam, it helps to convey the message of the Divine. In the Qur'an, Allah specifically praises those who strive to convey His message: "Who is better in speech than one who calls (other people) to Allah, works righteousness, and declares that he is from the Muslims" (Q 41:33). In defending Islam and the community, *jihad* encourages the defense of the self, the community, and the religion.

The Qur'an permits fighting to defend the religion of Islam and the Muslims. This permission includes fighting in self-defense and for the protection of family and property. The early Muslims fought many battles against their enemies under the leadership of the Prophet Muhammad and his representatives. For example, when the pagans of *quraysh* brought armies against the Prophet Muhammad, the Muslims fought to defend their faith and community. Allah declares *jihad* is gaining freedom to inform, educate, and convey the message of Islam in an open and free environment (Q 22:39–40).

In conclusion, after reviewing the views of sixteen scholars, one cannot help but notice how many different interpretations of this concept there are among Muslims and non-Muslims alike. While some put the emphasis on interpretations that emphasize *jihad* as a form of violence, others lean towards the opposite. What emerges is not only the sheer variety of interpretations but the need to contextualize different interpretations as well, both past and present.

The Qur'an and the Hadith show how the notion of *jihad* differs distinctly from the notion of holy war against unbelievers, as it is commonly understood today by some militant Islamists, as well as their foes. *Jihad*, in its original sense, simply meant striving in the path of God. Such striving could take various forms. Helping the poor and the distressed could equally be a form of *jihad* as could defense of the community from hostile attacks. Indeed, *jihad* as war was originally intended as defense of the faith and the community in the face of aggression. In normal times, relations between Muslims and people of other faiths were intended to be peaceful and violence the exception, rather than the norm.

"Jesus the Only Way to Salvation"

Christian exclusivism interprets Christianity from the perspective that allegiance to Christianity presents itself as a worldview that entails renouncing all other religious options. Christians who hold strongly to this worldview are concerned that engaging other religions might be disloyal, might lead to falling away from righteous behavior or belief, or might even lead to conversion to other faiths. The exclusive statement on the nature of salvation has not only contributed to daily conflict but also to crusade and war, fighting against other religions for the supremacy of Christianity and forcing the conversion of people of other faiths.

Exclusivism in Christianity is based on multiple biblical passages; the Gospel according to John is particularly relevant, interpreted to show "Jesus is the only way to salvation": "For God so loved the world that he gave his one and only Son, so that everyone who believes in him may not perish but we may live eternal life. Those who believe in him are not condemned; but those who do not believe in him are condemned already, because they have not believed in the name of the only son of God" (John 3:16-18). Thomas said to him, "Lord, we do not know where you are going. How can we know the way?" (John 14:5). Jesus answered him, "I am the way, and the truth and the life. No one comes to the Father except through me" (John 14:5–6). Exclusivist Christians believe that Jesus is the one for whom the scripture says: "The stone that was rejected by you, the builders, it has become the cornerstone. There is salvation in no one else, for there is no other name under heaven given among mortals by which we must be saved." (Acts 4:11–12). In pursuit of this concept, it is difficult for exclusivist Christians to live in peace with their neighbors. It allows them to provoke circumstances that may end up leading to killing instead of following the prince of peace in his call to love one's neighbors as oneself. "Jesus is the only way to salvation" is problematic because it means imposing Jesus on others. Therefore, the concept of "Jesus is the only way to salvation" creates an epistemological framework rooted in a form of reductionist positivism that makes dialogue almost impossible.

Christian inclusivism includes a concept of universal salvation as the grace of Christ operates in and through other faith traditions—whether the adherents of these faiths know and acknowledge Christ or not. This approach believes God sent Jesus Christ to die for all people (2 Cor 5:14), hence God's spirit brings salvation to all people, regardless of their religious affiliation. Persons holding this belief argue that the followers of other religions do not necessarily have to become Christians and evangelization is not necessary. Jesus is the one mediator of all humanity, says Paul: "This is right and is acceptable in the sight of God our Savior, who desires everyone to be saved and to come to the knowledge of the truth. For there is one God; there is also one mediator between God and humankind, Christ Jesus, himself human, who gave himself as a ransom for all" (1 Tim 2:3–6). In this inclusivist approach to interpreting Christianity, it is believed that the spirit of Christ infuses all religions and therefore all of humanity is saved. Other alternatives exist, including understanding that each religion identifies and promotes its own view of reality, some with concepts of "salvation" and some with other concepts and ideals.

Both exclusivist and inclusivist Christian perspectives bring their own respective challenges to dialogue. In both cases, it may not be so much their respective perspectives that are in need of change as the exclusivist perspective carries the danger of being more easily manipulated or instrumentalized for political purposes that may lead to exclusivist and even violent behaviors.

In a pluralist Christian interpretation, other biblical passages and theological implications are emphasized. For example, in order to foster communal harmony, pluralist Christians will stress the importance of following the life and example of Jesus, the Prince of Peace. Today, when all the people in the world are in a frantic search for peace, this pluralist Christian perspective proclaims that Jesus Christ is "the Prince of Peace" and that that prophecy to ancient Israel was realized with the coming of Jesus Christ, the Lord. In this interpretation, the meaning of peace from a biblical perspective is emphasized.

The most common word in the Bible translated into "peace" is the Hebrew word "*shalom.*" Its verbal form, *shalem*, means "to make whole" and derivatively "to bring to completion," "to complete," "to restore" and "to compensate," as in the following passage: "Thus all the work that King Solomon did on the house of the Lord (Jerusalem Temple) was finished (*shalem*)" (1 Kgs 7:51). Second, the adjectival form of the word, *shalem*, means "whole" or "full": "A full (*shalem*) and just weight you shall have a full (*shalem*) and just measure you shall have" (Deut 25:15). Third, the noun form of the word, *shalom*, means, basically, "wholeness," "fullness," "totality," or "completeness."

When *shalom* is referred to in a communal context, it means the harmonious wholeness and unity of a community. The communal *shalom* is achieved and maintained through the realization of justice and righteousness in a community. As a Hebrew Psalmist sang, "righteousness and *shalom* will kiss each other" (Ps 85:10) in a community where *shalom* prevails. There is no *shalom* in a society, no matter how peaceful and well-ordered on the surface, if justice is warped for the benefit of the powerful while the poor and powerless are treated unfairly, their rights are disregarded.

In proclaiming that Jesus Christ is the Prince of Peace, it is not simply an affirmation of faith but also a clear call to action. As faithful followers of the Prince of Peace, Christians are called to be "*shalom* makers." In the Sermon on the Mount, Jesus says, "Blessed are the peacemakers, for they will be called children of God" (Matt 5:9). From this pluralist Christian perspective, *shalom* is not only a gift of grace, restored for all human beings through Jesus Christ, but also a task and responsibility entrusted to all who are rightly called "children of God."

Peacemakers are not simply peaceable and peaceful persons; they are those who actively and earnestly endeavor to "make" peace, *shalom*, here and now. The church and Christians are called to be signs and instruments of *shalom* in this world still torn with strife and violence, warped with injustice and oppression, and divided with enmity and hostility.

Wherever *shalom* is broken and lost—such as in the Nigerian communities—that is where many pluralist Christians say their work begins.

To be "*shalom*-makers" it is imperative that Christians make their *shalom* with God. But how is this possible? One way is through believing that *shalom* is also a gift from God in the form of a child, as presented in the following passage from the prophetic writings of the Hebrew Bible: "For to us a child is born, to us a son is given, and he will be called, 'Wonderful Counsellor, Mighty God, Everlasting Father, Prince of Peace [*sa shalom*]'" (Isa 9:6). Although Christians often apply this text to Jesus, a pluralist Christian interpretation can also include all human beings as children of God that are responsible for *shalom*-making.

POLITICAL INTERPRETATIONS

The current violence in Nigeria is often interpreted as the result of a long history of power dynamics amongst the political elites and their difficulties at sharing power. The way politics has been managed has also negatively affected interreligious relations. This started in 1914, when the British brought together North and South Nigeria as one entity, though in practice, they managed the territory as two separate colonies. The North, under the Sultan of Sokoto, was allowed to be ruled by the traditional mix of local customs and *shari'a* law, while grooming the military elite from their ranks. The South, on the other hand, was favored in terms of education and industrialization. As a result, the North remained relatively impoverished.

After World War II, with the advent of decolonization, the British and the Nigerians moved in the direction of creating a unified country. Paden calls this a "fateful decision." The British used the Qur'anic paradigm of "the people of the book" to bring together the two regions. With time, it seemed that the Northern rulers had absorbed this paradigm, and Christians and Muslims came to feel that they had more in common as followers of an Abrahamic faith than they had with the devotees of traditional African religion. Paden puts it this way:

> During the early independence era, there was close cooperation in the North between Muslims (whether emirs, civil servants, or teachers) and their Christian counterparts (whether chiefs, civil servants, or teachers). During this period, the premier of the Northern Region, Ahmadu Bello, initiated the Northernization

policy in which Muslim and Christian Northerners were promoted rapidly, both at the regional and the national levels.[34]

According to David Johnston in "Reconciliation Possible in Nigeria":

> This policy generally continued, though three events occurred that revived old tensions and created new wounds. The first was the 1966 coup, in which junior officers, mostly from the Christian Southeast, killed "key Northern Muslim leaders, including Bello." After a countercoup, however, the Northerners selected from their midst a Christian officer, Yakubu Gowon, as chief commander of Nigeria's army. The second stress on the "people of the book" paradigm was the decision made by military ruler Ibrahim Bagangida in 1986 to have Nigeria enter the Organization of Islamic Conference (OIC). As a reaction, officers from the area known as "Middle Belt," attempted a coup to overthrow Bagangida, but failed. Tensions, needless to say, persisted. The third great stress to the system had been building for a long time. On several occasions, there had been talk at the federal level about "adopting *shari'a* law." But starting in 2000, twelve states in all (out of a total of thirty-six), with great fanfare, declared *shari'a* the law of their state. In practice, it only meant the establishment of *shari'a* courts that were to adjudicate cases of crimes specified in the Qur'an and Sunna, the *hudud* laws, or simply penal law.[35]

Continued conflicts created suspicion, destruction, and hatred between Muslim and Christian citizens. Many lives were lost and much property was destroyed. The conducive environment required for development of the country was not only jeopardized; it ended up going backwards by several decades. Naturally, the causes were not easily known because trading of blame and accusations between Muslim and Christian groups. In a nutshell, while Muslims accused Christians of consistently attacking Islam and Muslims, Christians accused Muslims of deliberate Islamization of Nigeria and denying Christians their rights. The polarization reached the extent that both Muslims and Christians watched the activities of governments with great suspicion. Every appointment, every policy of the government was viewed with suspicion by one group or the other, not for its contribution to development, but whether it was more in favor of the other religious group. This easily led to rising tensions in

---

34. Paden, *Faith and Politics in Nigeria*, 22.
35. Johnston, "Reconciliation Possible in Nigeria," 8.

the polity. A peak was reached when, in 1996, the government of General Ibrahim Badamasi Babangida changed the Nigerian status in the OIC, from its earlier status as an observer, to a full member. The observer status Nigeria had until then enjoyed was possible with the approval of a Christian head of state from Northern Nigeria, General Yakubu Gowon, during his tenure (1966–1975). What appeared to be a simple matter degenerated into threats of religious war because Christians alleged that this was yet another clandestine move to Islamize Nigeria. Arguments that it was for economic reasons and that many minority Muslim African countries were members only flared up tensions. The Christians mobilized individuals and organizations, especially the press, insisting that by joining the OIC, Nigeria was—by implication—an Islamic state.[36] An additional contributing problem was the issue of defining the population by the respective religious followers. To close that controversy, in 2006, the latest census in the country abolished the columns for religion and tribe.

Moreover, the issue of *shari'a* has remained a volatile one. While Muslims demanded that *shari'a* court be recognized by the constitution up to the federal level, Christians countered that Nigeria was a secular state and that having parallel laws is inimical to the country's unity. The Muslims, on the other hand, insisted that the new elites (those with a Western educational background) had turned Nigeria into a Christian state. They claimed that despite their majority and Islamic roots, their country had become secular—or even Christian.

The polarization did not stop with the religious hierarchy; it affected students, the civil service, and above all, the military. On April 17, 1990, a Christian group of military officers, led by Colonel Gideon Orkar, tried to topple the regime of General Babangida. Even though the coup was aborted, the leadership transmitted its message. While the military were supposed to protect their country's borders, this group instead excised the predominantly Northern Muslim states from the Nigerian federation. Citizens of the affected states were immediately asked to leave other parts of Nigeria because they were no longer Nigerians. The Sultan of Sokoto, officially recognized as the leader of the Muslims in Nigeria, was dethroned by the coup plotters.[37] This particular episode demonstrated the danger of religious polarization, which separates close friends, neighbors, colleagues. The Nigerian nation-state came close to breaking apart,

---

36. Abdulkarim, "Religion, Peace, and National Development," 3.
37. Abdulkarim, "Religion, Peace, and National Development," 4.

politically and militarily. In the meantime, economic and social development was greatly hampered.

In addition, the introduction of sections 38 (1) and 10 into the Nigerian Constitution, which guarantee freedom of religion and prohibit the declaration of religion by the states respectively, has done little to attenuate the frequency of religious conflicts. Veneration of the two dominant religious groups has only heightened the underlying tensions and rivalry. Thus, conflicts between Nigerian Christians and Muslims continue. Furthermore, Sections 260 (1) and 275 (1) of the Nigerian constitution make provision for the establishment of *shari'a* court in federal capital territory and for any state that requires a *shari'a* court of appeal. This is so despite the fact that the same constitution guarantees the freedom of religion to all citizens. By adopting *shari'a* law, even if only in parts of its territory, the Nigerian nation state is no longer purely secular. We can therefore ask how a non-secular state can protect the rights of all of its religious citizens, going beyond any one religious system that may be biased against other ones.

In general, religious leaders tend to favor their own religion. This tendency runs the risk of making any form of government that claims religious legitimacy to be more susceptible to abuses when it comes to minority religious rights as well as to rights of expression, be they religious or of a different perspective within a religiously powerful community. That is why imposition of *shari'a* law in the Northern part of the country is causing so much tension and conflict, raising serious challenges to national integration.

Religion has become a major topic of national political debates, with each religious community pushing increasingly in opposite directions, creating adversarial agendas. In Northern Nigeria, clashes between Muslim groups—mainly ethnic Hausa and Fulani—and Christian and traditionalist communities have become a monthly affair, with devastating consequences. In this charged environment, where religion functions as the primary idiom of political identity, conflicts over resources, cattle, land, and political offices have often taken on a religious coloration, with Muslims pitted against Christians. Christian ethnic groups in Southern Nigeria have been drawn into these religious conflicts, with their members in Northern Nigerian cities frequently targeted by Muslim mobs. Muslim Northern Nigerians have sometimes been targeted in revenge killings in Southern Nigeria.

SOCIO-ECONOMIC INTERPRETATIONS

Nigeria is the fifth largest oil producer in the world, and oil dominates the economy. The military governments in power between 1966 and 1999 failed to develop the economy in other areas. This, along with economic mismanagement and corruption, has contributed to Nigeria's poor economic performance and rising poverty. There is a highly unequal distribution of wealth in Nigeria with 66 percent of the population falling below the poverty line of $1 a day. This puts it among the twenty poorest countries in the world.

Under thirty years of military rule, Nigeria witnessed military uprisings, the economy suffered greatly, and the military rulers did not help the gradual recession of the economy. The volatile political situation in Nigeria during its military days discouraged foreign investors from investing in the country. The frequent coup d'états and the shaky financial state of the country (due to the looting of the treasury) paved the way for illiteracy and unemployment. As of June 2002, statistics showed that a disturbing 39–51 percent of the entire population is illiterate. This figure translates into the fact that out of the one hundred and forty million people in Nigeria, less than sixty six million are in the workforce. The issue of illiteracy becomes a troubling one when there are literally hundreds of thousands of unemployed and probably able-bodied men and women roaming the streets with nothing to do and no way to survive. "The national unemployment rate, estimated by the Office of Statistics as 4.3 percent of the labor force in 1985, increased to 5.3 percent in 1986 and 7.0 percent in 1987, before falling to 5.1 percent in 1988,"[38] as a result of measures taken under the Structural Adjustment Program. Most of the unemployed were city dwellers, as indicated by urban jobless rates of "8.7 percent in 1985, 9.1 percent in 1986, 9.8 percent in 1987, and 7.3 percent in 1988."[39] Underemployed farm labor, often referred to as disguised unemployed, continued to be supported by the family or village. Therefore, rural unemployment figures were less accurate than those for urban unemployment. Among the openly unemployed rural population, almost two-thirds were secondary-school graduates.

Despite the vast wealth created by the exploitation of huge petroleum resources, the benefits have been slow to trickle down to the majority of the population who, since the 1960s, have increasingly been forced

---

38. Country Studies, "Nigeria Labor," 1.
39. Country Studies, "Nigeria Labor," 1.

to abandon their traditional agricultural practices. Annual production of both cash and food crops dropped significantly in the latter decades of the twentieth century: cocoa production dropped by 43 percent (Nigeria was the world's largest cocoa exporter in 1960), rubber dropped by 29 percent, cotton by 65 percent, and groundnuts by 64 percent. In spite of the large number of skilled, well-paid Nigerians who have been employed by the oil corporations, the majority of Nigerians have become poorer.

In addition, the government and individuals do not respect human rights. Abuse of human rights includes the abuse of religious rights, which is among the causes of religious riots in Nigeria. The high level of corruption in the Nigerian government has helped to foster religious riots. Public office holders seek any available means of embezzling public funds. Some of them use religious riots as a means of making money because after the riots, damages will be paid and investigation panels will be set up. These panels overestimate the costs, failing to provide an in-depth analysis or find the cause of the problem.

The high levels of crime and youth unemployment are also contributing to the fueling of violence in Nigeria. If they were employed, the youth would not have time to take advantage of religious riots as opportunities to make money by stealing under the pretext of a riot. High crime levels in Nigeria allow youth to use every opportunity as an excuse for engaging in criminal behavior.

The lack of good governance and ethnic divisions add to the problems of violence. Since independence in 1960, the leadership of Nigeria has changed nine times. Despite the changes in government, Nigeria has remained corrupt and ineffective. Abuse and misuse of power and authority by Nigerian rulers has not been due to any national lack of capacity for good governance. Nigerian leaders have not been ineffective and tyrannical because they are incompetent or ignorant, nor has the lack of administrative or intellectual expertise to formulate and properly execute growth enhancing policies been the major problem.

Nigeria, unlike Kenya, lacks a good security network that can stop religious riots before they escalate, but it usually takes hours—at times even days—before the Nigerian police arrive at riot scenes and the damage is already done and many lives lost. Unfortunately, death counts usually continue to rise even after the police have been deployed to the ground, and it may take military intervention to stop religious riots. This shows a lack of good security and lack of equipping of our forces.

INTERRELIGIOUS DIALOGUE AND INTER-ETHICAL DIALOGUE PROBLEMS

In Nigeria, the interreligious dialogue and inter-ethical dialogue are also causes of religious violence. The bitter wrangling among people of living faiths is not without its diverse problems. For this reason, discussions, consultations, meeting memorandums, and statements on dialogue often ignore various factors, which make this necessary venture a difficult—though not an impossible—task. I am aware that this task (i.e., dialogue) entails a critical and self-critical assessment of our religious traditions so as to bring into full light what in them is conductive to the achievement of community without minimizing the beliefs, doctrines, and rites which establish the particularity of each tradition. But before I come to claim these resources, I must admit that there are many obstacles in my way. It is one of the tragedies of humanity that it can be precisely the striving for world community, expressed in various beliefs, which prevents the realization of this community here and now. A common way must be found, while honoring the absolute claims of each concerning the world order.

I am fully conscious of elements in our traditions that, because of their particularistic thrust, have had a divisive impact in history, propelled people into mutual distrust, and generated hate and persecution. These elements block advance towards life-in-community. Some of these derive from our own time, some of these derive from our individual beliefs, and others are generated by actual social and political life-situations of religious people and religious communities. Even as I try to overcome such obstacles to community building, every religion and ideology must be allowed to draw upon its own social community. In this context, I found helpful the recognition of particularity as a universal empirical fact, affirmation that our dialogue can only be inhabited, and the warning that temptation to self-justification and self-advancement may become too strong. Minorities may be afraid of being overwhelmed or absorbed by the larger community that they encounter in dialogue. Dissenting groups may be afraid of entering into dialogue with exponents of the ideology of the ruling group.

Ethnic or racial groups may sometimes need to refuse dialogue in order to affirm their distinctive identity. In other cases, an invitation to dialogue may be an occasion for affirmation of the identity of a generally unrecognized group. Some fears may be expressed in terms of rationalization. Two such fears commonly found among Christians are that dialogue may lead to syncretism and compromise of the Gospel and that entering into dialogue with people of other faiths and ideologies may be a betrayal of mission. On the other hand, people of other faiths and ideologies may fear that the Christian concern for dialogue may be a sinister and veiled form of evangelism, cultural imperialism, and even an instrument of economic colonialism. The expressed fear may be genuine or may hide other genuine fears. There is need for this to be examined.

On some occasions, dialogue is impossible because the other party does not care for having a dialogue or might even consider dialogue an effort to undermine its political power, eventually leading to a plural society that it is not willing to accept. On many occasions, however, dialogue with ideologies is difficult because Christians (and possibly any other religious adherent) themselves are not aware of their own ideological assumptions or of any tension between their faith and the ideological domination in their society.

DISPARITY BETWEEN THOSE TAKING PART IN DIALOGUE

We must begin by emphasizing one major difficulty: the enormous difference between those taking part in dialogue as well as those with different levels of studies within their respective traditions. There can be no doubt that this obstacle is the hardest to overcome in the immediate future as, even with the finest dispositions and the best will in the world, one cannot just instantaneously produce, as if by enchantment, people fully qualified and capable of taking part in dialogue. It goes almost without saying that many parts of the world where Christians—as well as Muslims—live as a majority today are poorer regions of the world, facing serious problems of underdevelopment, which is not only material but also, perhaps above all, intellectual. There is no risk of dialogue coming to an end but rather that it never really begins. Insufficient grounding in one's faith as well as knowledge coupled with insufficient understanding of the beliefs and practices of other religious traditions result in a lack of appreciation of their significance and misrepresentation. It is this possibility, far more than difficulties over principles or methods of approach to dialogue, which explains the hesitation, the reticence, the lack of trust, and even, generally speaking, the present sterility of many dialogical encounters or efforts at holding them.

UNEQUAL THEOLOGICAL DEVELOPMENT

Unequal theological development may be a problem both within and across religious communities as well as dialogue groups. These differences in development are due to different historical trajectories. For example, in general, Christianity has been influenced by the more recent confrontation with modernity over the last two hundred years or so. This confrontation also exists for Islam, but due to colonialism and imperialism, the relations Muslims have entertained to modern challenges have been more recent and in a power dynamics of exterminal domination rather than internal transformation—as is the case of European/Western Christianity.

Christian theology has been able to profit from its confrontation with various intellectual systems, both philosophical and ideological, that arose within the Modern West. The most challenging of these, such as communism and secularism, have been the most salutary for its development, by subjecting it—under the pressure of contestation and criticism—to a fruitful tension. Through these confrontations, Christians have been forced to understand their own values better, work out answers, and undertake (at times) agonizing revisions, in the course of which, Christianity has also and perhaps most importantly been enriched by elements that have proven to be compatible with its own internal dynamism. Christian thought has thus been reinforcing its attachment to what is purest and most authentic in its tradition; it has adapted itself to each age and continues daily to progress in this direction. These efforts, noticeable from the nineteenth century onwards, resulted in the breakthrough of the creation of the World Council of Churches in 1948. This, of course, did not take place without a certain amount of drama, of heartbreak, and even of crisis. But after it all, the church feels more committed, better armed, and more ready for dialogue.

CONCLUSION

Frequent religious violence in Nigeria has not only inflicted hardship on people but it has also denied them the opportunity of experiencing the full benefit of encounter with the religions of others, enrichment through other's understanding of the Divine, understanding born out of mutual respect, and critical self-examination that deepen one's religion conviction. Both understanding the deleterious effect of violence on interreligious relations and the growing realization that multireligious efforts can be more powerful than those of a sole religious community open the way to the type of interventions which will be discussed in the next chapter.

CHAPTER IV

Preconditions of Peace Education in Nigeria

This chapter focuses on peace education as the pastoral intervention required in a praxeological methodology. First, it discusses the preconditions of peace education in Nigeria, analyzing the principles and theory of peace education as well as various perspectives on peace education: from a Yoruba Religion, Islamic, and Christian approach respectively.

PEACE EDUCATION

Definitions and Concepts of Peace Education

Before defining peace education, it is necessary to comprehend what peace is. In his article "Peace Theory: An Introduction," Johan Galtung compares different linguistic equivalents to the concept of Peace in a variety of cultures, including: *pax, eirene, salaam, shalom, shanty,* and *ho p'ing-p'ing ho*. The Latin *pax* means the absence of war, *absentia bellum*, under the assumption of a set of binding obligations that are to be observed. The Greek-Hebrew-Arabic concepts of *eirene, shalom*, and *salaam* pick up peace ideas that are also found in such concepts as justice, equity, equality, and freedom. The Yoruba *alafia* is "the sum total of all that mankind may desire: an undisturbed harmonious life."[1]

Francis defines peace as "the absence of war, fear, conflict, anxiety, suffering, and violence and about peaceful coexistence."[2] To him, peace

---

1. Rweyemamu, "Religion and Peace," 382.
2. Francis, "Peace and Conflict Studies," 5.

connotes: the absence of war, presence of justice and development; existence of respect and tolerance among and between people; maintaining a balance with the ecosphere; and quite importantly, having inner peace and wholeness. Johan Galtung opines that there could be direct violence referring to physical, emotional, and psychological violence; structural violence, i.e., deliberate policies and structures that cause human suffering; and cultural violence, which manifests itself in cultural norms and practices that create discrimination, injustice, and human suffering.[3] He also categorizes peace into positive and negative peace. Positive peace can be described as the absence of unjust structures, unequal relationships, justice, and inner peace; whereas negative peace can be equated with the absence of direct violence, war, fear, and conflict at the individual, national, regional, and international levels.

Peace education is not limited to formal education but also extended to both informal and non-formal education, which includes the home and various voluntary organizations. Content and forms may be quite different in these education types, depending on contextual conditions. Peace education is very different from most subjects offered in schools. Groups and individuals both project onto the concept of peace education their own particular vision of a desirable society.[4] The meaning of peace education is therefore often ambiguous and shares different elements, making a broad descriptive overview of the discipline impossible.

According to Betty Reardon in "Peace Education: A Review and Projection," peace education is the transmission of knowledge about the requirements, obstacles, and possibilities for achieving and maintaining peace. Furthermore, it involves the development of reflective and participatory capacities for applying the knowledge of peace education to overcoming problems and achieving possibilities. She adds that peace education "is a planned and guided learning that attempts to comprehend and reduce the multiple forms of violence (physical, structural, institution and cultural). Used as instruments for the advancement or maintenance of cultural, social, or religious beliefs and of political economical institutions or practices."[5]

---

3. Galtung, "Cultural Violence," 291.
4. Bar-Tal, "Elusive Nature of Peace Education," 28.
5. Reardon, "Peace Education," 401.

Peace education requires not only providing information about peace and its achievement but also supplying the tools to allow its students to actively assist in the pursuit of that goal. Hudson argues that:

> It is education that actualizes people's potentialities in helping them learn how to make peace with themselves and with others, to live in harmony and unity with self, humankind, and with nature. The principles upon which this statement rests include: (1) the cardinal prerequisite for world peace is the unity of humankind. (2) World order can be founded only on the consciousness of the oneness of humankind. This basic tenet of democracy rests on the principle of human dignity, which is very much inherent in the dimensions of peacebuilding efforts.[6]

Furthermore, with the proliferation of programs, peace education has become quite diverse and difficult to define. Programs around the world differ widely in terms of ideology, objectives, emphasis, curricula, contents, and practices. Johnson and Johnson assert that the multitude of definitions of peace education may be grouped into the following: cognitive, affective, and behavior definitions. They define peace education as "teaching individuals the information, attitudes, values, and behavioral competencies needed to resolve conflicts without violence and build and maintain mutually beneficial, harmonious relationships."[7] According to Navarro-Castro, there are various forms or facets of peace education practices: Disarmament Education, Human Rights Education, Global Education, Conflict Resolution Education, Multicultural Education, Education for International Understanding, Interfaith Education, Gender Education, and Environmental Education. Each of these focuses on a problem of direct or indirect violence. Each form of peace education practices also includes a particular knowledge base as well as a normative set of skills and value-orientations that it wants to develop.[8] In "Peace Education: The Concept, Principles, and Practices around the World," Harris asserts:

> Peace education has been practiced by generations of humans who want to live in peace. Peace education tends to draw out of people their natural inclinations to live in peace. Peace educators educate people about the processes that promote peace,

---

6. Huston, *New Tools for International Understanding*, 96.
7. Johnson and Johnson, "Peace Education in the Classroom," 226.
8. Navaro-Castro, "A Pathway to a Culture of Peace," 35.

using teaching skills to build a peace culture. They are interested in all different aspects of violence, from the interpersonal to the geopolitical. They see that education provides an important strategy to achieve peace because it provides awareness about different peace strategies, including peacekeeping (or peace through strength), peacemaking (or peace through communication), and peacebuilding (or peace through a commitment to nonviolence).[9]

Peace education has a great role to play in the twenty-first century, as it shapes new global citizens who embrace peace. Multiple global efforts toward creating a more peaceful world have been undertaken recently as we are at the end of the United Nations Educational, Scientific and Cultural Organization's International and Nonviolence for the Children of the World (2001–2010).[10]

Rather than defining peace education in the negative—such as education for the elimination of violence—peace education efforts can also be understood in the positive, as efforts that bridge knowledge and actions, integrating differences in ways that both honor diversity and establish common ground. Peace education works on bringing people together and is about social change. It requires a deep, personal commitment in our hearts and minds to peaceful living, teaching, learning, researching, and institutional transformation. It is relevant because it can provide hope even amid what has been described as intractable conflict.

Goal and Objectives of Peace Education

According to Ian Harris, the goal of peace education is to deal with various types of violence, including physical violence. Physical violence includes direct harm to others, war, ethnic rivalry, juvenile crime, gang attacks, sexual assaults, random killing, psychological violence (psychological forms of violence occur in places of work, schools, and homes, diminishing a person's sense of worth and security), and structural violence (structural violence comes from social institutions that deny certain basic rights and freedoms such as work, health care, water, social security, safe housing, or civil rights to citizens) caused by thoughts, words, deeds, and any dehumanizing behavior that intentionally harms

---

9. Harris, *Peace Education*, 18.
10. Brantmeier, *Spirituality, Religion, and Peace Education*, xiv.

another.[11] In "The Elusive Nature of Peace Education," Bar-Tal proposes that the goal of education is "to diminish or even to eradicate a variety of human ills, ranging from injustice, inequality, prejudice, and intolerance to abuse of human rights, environmental destruction, violent conflict, war, and other evils in order to create a world of justice, equality, tolerance, human rights, environmental quality, peace, and other positive features."[12] A third example is that of Johnson and Johnson, who write that the ultimate goal of peace education is for individuals to be able to maintain peace among aspects of themselves (intrapersonal), individuals (interpersonal peace), groups (intergroup peace), and countries, societies, and cultures (international Peace).[13]

In addition, Bar-Tal states that the objective of peace education implies not only the transmission of knowledge but also, and more importantly, the change of the affective, attitudinal, and behavioral repertoire of the students. The objectives[14] of peace education can only be achieved by imparting specific values, attitudes, beliefs, skills, and behavioral tendencies that correspond to objectives. Imparting values of peace is of particular importance as these values influence specific beliefs, attitudes, and behavioral patterns. Indeed, changes in behavior ultimately signal the achievement of peace education's objectives.[15]

Philosophy of Peace Education

In peace education, the task of the educator is to respect the autonomy of the learners, therefore, there is a difference between preaching and teaching peace. Page affirms: "If we define peace research as normative

---

11. Harris, "Conceptual Underpinnings of Peace Education," 16.
12. Bar-Tal, "Elusive Nature of Peace Education," 28.
13. Johnson and Johnson, "Peace Education in the Classroom," 226.
14. The ultimate goal of peace education is for individuals to be able to maintain peace among aspects of themselves (intrapersonal peace), individuals (interpersonal peace), groups (intergroup peace), and countries, societies, and cultures (international peace). To do so, peace education (among other things) needs to focus on (a) establishing a cooperative, not a competitive, relationship among all relevant parties; (b) ensuring that all relevant parties are skilled in engaging in political discourse and creative decision making that includes an open-minded discussion of diverse views; (c) ensuring that relevant parties seek agreements that are mutually beneficial and that maximize joint outcomes; and (d) inculcating into all relevant parties the values underlying consensual peace.
15. Bar-Tal, "Elusive Nature of Peace Education," 29.

applied research with the aim of emphasizing the importance of a commitment to peace, then it becomes clear that this is not far removed from the aims of peace education itself."[16] Page approaches the philosophy of peace education through engagement in the question of indoctrination. He utilizes philosophy of education methodology, which he suggests is based upon the respect of student autonomy. Autonomy in this context does not mean disregard for inquiry into controversial issues and subject matters.[17]

Page suggests that since violence is pervasive and deeply engrained in human culture, education for peace is a necessary alternative to that violent norm. Peace education is the exploration of peace moments and educational movements[18] as well as a challenge to authority.[19] Peace education connects the political violence to the personal. Since meaning is derived from such violence and conflict, Page rightly questions how we might derive meaning from peace. In addition, he takes up the challenges of peace researchers and educators to engage in philosophical exploration of peace education. Page's stated aim is "to investigate and enunciate ethico-philosophical foundations for peace education."[20]

Theories of Peace Education

In "Peace Education Theory," Harris presents five postulates of peace education that underline five different types of peace education: international, human rights, development, environmental, and conflict resolution education. These postulates are: (1) peace education explains the roots of violence; (2) peace education teaches alternatives to violence; (3) peace education adjusts to cover different forms of violence; (4) peace itself is a process that varies according to context; and (5) conflict is omnipresent.[21]

The peace education work of Danesh in "Towards an Integrative Theory of Peace Education" presents the Integrative Theory of Peace (ITP) based on the concept that peace is at once a psychological, social, political, ethical, and spiritual state with expressions at intrapersonal,

16. Page, *Peace Education*, 4.
17. Page, *Peace Education*, 14.
18. Page, *Peace Education*, 15.
19. Page, *Peace Education*, 16.
20. Page, *Peace Education*, 18.
21. Harris, "Peace Education Theory," 6.

interpersonal, intergroup, international, and global areas of human life. In addition, ITP holds that all human states of being—including peace—are the outcome of the main human cognitive (knowing), emotive (loving), and conative (choosing) capacities, which together determine the nature of our worldview. ITP consists of four subtheories: (1) peace is a psychosocial and political as well as moral and spiritual condition; (2) peace is the main expression of a unity-based worldview; (3) a unity-based worldview is the prerequisite for creating both a culture of peace and culture of healing; and (4) a comprehensive, integrated, and lifelong education is the most effective approach for development of a unity-based worldview.

In "New Directions for Research on Nonviolence," Mayton presents the contributions of four non-violence theorists: Ritter proposed that principled nonviolence that utilizes nonviolent means to achieve nonviolent ends is superior to strategic nonviolence. Burrowes presents another two-dimensional theory of nonviolence that would benefit from empirical validation. Within Burrowes's theory, the principled pragmatic axis and the reformist revolutionary axis form four quadrants of nonviolent action. As for McCarthy and Kruelgler, they suggest that the assumptions of nonviolent approaches to conflict resolution need to be empirically verified as necessary, and if they are not necessary, they should be abandoned. They are critical of the inductive case-study approach and call for a theory-driven program of research, whereby the generalization of specific theories are tested using critically analyzed case studies of historical nonviolent movements.

In "Peace Education, Teaching and Learning, and Spirituality," Brantmeier, Lin, and Miller introduce spiritual themes that are conducive to peace, related to a spiritual tradition or not.[22] Their book explains and illustrates how the concept of interdependence, found in all spiritual traditions (as well as numerous practices and activities that have a spiritual quality), is the key for peace education towards a better future for humanity and our planet. Integrated spirituality is thus the connective, integrative, and harmonizing force found within the lived teaching of great wisdom traditions. They discuss how each religion has its own perspectives on peace education and spirituality.

---

22. Brantmeiter et al., "Peace Education," 8.

TRANSFORMATIVE PEACE EDUCATION

In developing a peace education curriculum for this book, I have been looking for paradigms that can empower educators to play a critical role in peacebuilding through religious practices. Indeed, educators around the world are developing effective strategies to transform education as a powerful force for global peace. The various contributors of the book entitled *Transforming Education for Peace* demonstrate that educators as peacemakers can be and have been instrumental in transforming social forces, the self, and others for the construction of global peace. The contributions illustrate that "peacebuilding is possible in our everyday lives, in our interactions with others, and in our intentions to be understanding, compassionate human beings."[23] In the book *Spirituality, Religion, and Peace Education*, the authors explore the universal and particular dimensions of education for inner and communal peace. It offers a rich overview of the ways in which spirituality can serve as the core of peace education that can also be adopted into interreligious peace education.

"Great Wisdom Traditions and Peace Education," of *Spirituality, Religion, and Peace Education* proffers a series of understandings concerning what some of the great spiritual traditions can offer to check some of the excesses of the dominant contemporary educational system. We are reminded of the spiritual roots of some famous peace educators, activists, and leaders, and learn about lesser known ones. For example, Confucian wisdom provides us with valuable insights for living a virtuous life in our daily interactions. In order to achieve inner tranquility and peace, Sufis (Sufism is a way, a discipline, and a method that teaches the individual to explore and discover the reality of his or her true being. Sufism is the path to self-knowledge toward a state of inner illumination and absolute cognition) bring self-knowledge, i.e., knowledge of the absolute, the divine, the universe, existence, and God as a goal that will free the limitations and boundaries created between self and others, and existence.

In "The Promises and Pitfalls of Peace Education Evaluation," Harris brings out the problem of evaluating peace education. He affirms that even if peace educators persuade students about the dangers of violence and instills in them a desire to do something about those threats, students may not necessarily have the will, the capacity, the knowledge, or the skills to do so, in part or consistently. Therefore peace educators face an important quandary: How can they best assess their effectiveness in

---

23. Brantmeier, *Transforming Education for Peace*, xviii.

bringing peace in the world?[24] He adds: "In spite of [the] efforts and activities of millions of people who have joined an actively supported peace movement, the world has grown more violent with civil crimes, ethnic and religious conflicts."[25] There is a need to evaluate peace education that involves formative ("formative evaluation" concerns the delivery of a peace education program) and summative ("summative" peace education tries to document the impact of instruction on pupils) measures to be able to answer the question: after learning about peace, do people become more peaceful or do they work for peace and hence does the intensity of violence in a given conflict reduce?[26] This evaluation is useful for educators using a variety of peace education approaches—in particular, those who use interreligious peace education.

Peacemaking: from Practice to Theory offers and engages the voices of peacemakers in their experiences and personal stories, providing a depth of understanding that shapes peacemaking's choices and tenacity. Nan recalls that "peacemaking is valued for its real world impact and also as a way of learning peacemaking."[27] Shabnam Hashmi, in "Reaching Out to the Uninitiated: Engaging Youth to Combat Hindu Extremism in India," describes how the Hindu extremists had perfected the spreading of hate: "These exclusionary political forces have consistently and very creatively sowed the seeds of hatred."[28] She also affirms that in the face of inhuman brutalities and gang rape, she was able to organize and distill workshops from highly academic conversations to teach and conscientize young people. This example relates directly to the liberal peace education of Freire, which helps conscientizing its students, and will be particularly useful for religious leaders in an interreligious peace education curriculum.

Freire's major contribution to the field of peace education is the insight that education is necessarily a form of politics. He averred that schooling is never neutral; instead, it always serves some interest and, in turn, impedes others. Freire's magnetism lies in his insistence that schooling can be used for liberation, just as it has been used for oppression. He argued that through liberatory education, people come to understand

24. Harris, "Promises and Pitfalls," 246.
25. Harris, "Promises and Pitfalls," 246.
26. Harris, "Promises and Pitfalls," 246.
27. Nan, *Peacemaking*, 1:1.
28. Hashmi, "Encyclopedia of Politics and Religion," 6.

social systems of oppression and equip themselves to act to change those situations. Educators, then, must reconceptualize their labor as political work and "must ask themselves for whom and on whose behalf they are working."[29]

PEDAGOGY OF PEACE

Pedagogy, according to Sue McGrego, is the act of imparting knowledge to someone.[30] It is made up of two things: (a) what counts as knowledge and (b) what is the most effective way to get this knowledge across to or solicit it from the "learner." Knowledge can come from: (1) personal/cultural, as lived each day, (2) popular culture, press, and the media, (3) mainstream academics, (4) transformative academics, or (5) school knowledge, found in books and curriculum guides. One's pedagogical approach is a key determinant of human relationships in the educational process. It is the medium of communication between teacher and learner and the aspect which *most* affects what learners receive from their teachers (and vice versa).

Peace pedagogy, peace education brings together multiple traditions of pedagogy. Learners should leave the course with a closer appreciation of their own professional understanding of peace education pedagogy. The final theme of peace pedagogy is an imaginative understanding or vision of peace. Danesh considers peace education as a process in which "the conflict-based world views that inform most of our educational endeavors are replaced with peace-based worldviews."[31] Harris and Morrison refer to the affirmation of peace as peacebuilding, a "proactive" stance for developing peace.[32] Lederach, in advocating for learning the ways of peace, poses a key question: "How do we transcend the cycles of violence that bewitch our human community while still living in them?"[33] Hence he calls for the development of moral imagination in which people can envision a peaceful world and the relationships necessary to create such a world.[34] Shapiro conceives of such imagination in

---

29. Freire, *Politics of Education*, 80.
30. McGrego, "Peace and Social Justice," 1.
31. Danesh, "Towards Integrative Theory of Peace Education," 58.
32. Harris and Morrison, *Peace Education*, 11.
33. Lederach, *Moral Imagination*, 4.
34. Lederach, *Moral Imagination*, 29.

her guiding principles of "affirming each human life" and formulating a "language of possibility."[35] As follows, before students can learn how to make peace, they must understand and feel what peace means deeply. For teachers to foster peace-based worldviews, they must first create cultures of peace in classrooms and schools and encourage their students to value the experience of peace. In this book, I drew from Harris and Morrison's distinctions among peacekeeping, peacemaking, and peacebuilding.[36]

A NEW PEDAGOGY OF INTERRELIGIOUS PEACE EDUCATION

Many religious institutions are known for the promotion of peace and peacebuilding. The two major religions in Nigeria (Christianity and Islam) are categorical in their promotion of peace even though in the curriculum training future religious leaders in their respective institutions, there has been very little room for peace education as such. Paradoxically, sometimes these same institutions are involved in disruptive violence. But a careful understanding of the teachings of the two religions would show that they do value peace—though at times inconsistently—as well as promote it, seeking to build peace in the hearts of their followers and society at large. Based on those important sources for peacebuilding, it is important to develop a pedagogical approach to peace education that is suited to Nigerian people in general and their religious leaders in particular.

Better education is a crucial tool and hope for the future of Nigeria, especially in times of crisis. It is the best resource and means for countering the dangerous trends of prejudice, violence, and exclusion that plague our multicultural society. Peace Educator Betty Reardon writes: "Education is that process by which we learn new ways of thinking and behaving, a very significant component of the transition-transformation processes. Education is that process by which we glimpse what might be and what we ourselves can become."[37] Ian Harris gives a brief synopsis of the history of peace education. He states that:

> Maria Montessori was urging teachers to abandon authoritarian pedagogies, replacing them with a dynamic curriculum

---

35. Shapiro, "Pedagogy of Peace," 48.
36. Harris and Morrison, *Peace Education*, 11.
37. Reardon, "Peace Education," 2.

from which they could choose what to study. She reasoned that children who didn't automatically follow authoritarian teachers would not necessarily follow rules urging them to war. She saw that peace depended on an education that would free the children's spirit, promote love of others, and remove the climate of compulsory restriction.[38]

What use is a teaching that does not address the needs of a society? For a peaceful society, peace education is mandatory. Educating people for peace is crucial in the transformative process of such a society. Feminists have contributed to the expansion of peaceful approaches to schooling by urging schools to change their curriculum away from competitive to a caring focus that emphasizes domestic skills.[39] The 186 member states of the 28th General Conference of United Nations Education, Scientific, and Cultural Organization (UNESCO) believed that the major challenge at the close of the twentieth century was the transition from a culture of war and violence to a culture of peace. In November 1998, the United Nations General Assembly adopted one resolution promoting the culture of peace, another declaring the year 2000 as the International Year of the Culture of Peace, and the years 2001–2010 to be the International Decade for a Culture of Peace and Nonviolence for the Children of the World. From that mandate, UNESCO has developed eight areas of action necessary for the transition from a culture of war to a culture of peace.

The first of these is the promotion of a culture of peace through education. Education is the only way to fight violence with nonviolence. In spite of the world being torn apart by wars, inter-ethnic misunderstanding, religious strife, financial devastation, class and caste distinction, and human destruction of the rainforest and the ozone layer, most countries lack an effective educational system that reduces violence. As many educators, practitioners, and religious leaders recognize the seminal influence of religion on the futures of individuals, communities, and societies, I am focusing on interfaith education to shed light on the challenges we face. In " Transforming our World: Critical Pedagogy for Interfaith Education," Puett asserts that: "Interfaith education has an important role to play in the search for new methods of education that will advance broad social transformation, shifting away from a paradigm of dominance, exclusiveness, and violence and toward a new paradigm of

---

38. Harris, "Conceptual Underpinnings," 19.
39. Martin and Noddings quoted in Harris, "Conceptual Underpinnings," 21.

equity, inclusiveness, and peace."⁴⁰ The practices he describes address the pressing issues inherent in the context of this discourse:

> The parameters of the field include a diverse array of practices, not all of which would meet the criteria of "best practices." Best practices of interfaith education are contextual and experiential, aiming to put a "face" on religions, so they are not explored in just an abstract, theoretically objective manner, but are experienced as constellations of values, beliefs, practices, and heritages that give meaning to the lives of people we know. These practices present the complexities and internal diversity within religious traditions. The necessarily self-reflective nature of these experiential practices can create the capacity for profound, personal, and societal growth, which is essential to fostering and sustaining cultures of peace.⁴¹

Because my aim is to use the teachings, doctrines, sacred texts, and oral traditions of Yoruba Religion, Islam, and Christianity to create a culture in Nigeria for social transformation, his argument resonates better than others to me, especially when he affirms that:

> As interfaith educators endeavor to create a culture of peace, to facilitate individual and communal transformation, and to subvert the divisiveness, intolerance, and violence that currently plague our globe, there is a need for pedagogical reflection and for new pedagogies, as well, that explicitly address how we ought to educate for these ends. Interfaith education has an important role to play in the search for new methods of education that will foster broad social transformation. Yet, the field requires reflection on the development of pedagogies for transformation, in order to ensure that the methods used in interfaith education embody the ethic they promote.⁴²

In "New Directions for Research on Nonviolence" Mayton affirms that religions in themselves offer valuable resources for this task.⁴³ Religions—as traditions and bodies of thought, ethics, and practices—persuade adherents to look beyond themselves as individuals and consider their wider connectedness. Religious identities are communal in nature. He asserts a shared humanity and compels a critical examination of our

---

40. Puett, "On Transforming Our World," 264.
41. Puett, "On Transforming Our World," 265.
42. Puett, "On Transforming Our World," 266.
43. Mayton, "New Directions for Research on Nonviolence," 239–51.

obligations to others within and beyond our own communities. Mayton adds: "The key for nonviolence to emerge from all religions is the focal point to the nonviolent teaching within the world view espoused by its followers. The key for religion to affect peace and promote nonviolence in the world is to encourage more moderate and balanced clergy and followers of any religion to impact their believers."[44]

In addition, Mayton posits that: "Even as most societies in today's world function as cultures of violence, there are pockets of peaceful societies in Africa, Asia, and North and South America."[45] These peaceful societies will be studied to understand their modes of operation and what educational learning we can learn from them. He joins others also to affirm "effects to infuse nonviolence instruction into the education curricula needs to continue and the impact empirically studied."[46] He raises several questions[47] that will guide the applied parts of this book. The motivation is to bring nonviolence into the mainstream of our discipline, life, and our world, for, according to him: "It isn't enough to talk about peace. One must believe it. And it is not enough to believe in it. One must work at it."[48] He brings out theories of nonviolence and nonviolent action from the perspective of several disciplines within the social sciences. His placement of each theory of nonviolence into a particular discipline is somewhat arbitrary, as several of them are multidisciplinary, so the classification is primarily based on the primary discipline of the authors. Beginning with philosophical approaches,[49] he moves through

---

44. Mayton, *Nonviolence and Peace Psychology*, 242.

45. Mayton, *Nonviolence and Peace Psychology*, 241.

46. Mayton, *Nonviolence and Peace Psychology*, 246.

47. "1. Is it necessary for leaders and activists in nonviolent struggles to be committed to nonviolence as a way of life or can they view it as a technique? 2. Does the leadership of a nonviolent action need to be highly centralized and charismatic? 3. What are the most productive leadership tasks, organization types, means of recruitment, and communication systems for nonviolent movements? 4. What are the necessary components of a nonviolent movement that induce the intended changes? Is it the self—sufferings and the accompanying moral contradictions it creates in one's adversaries that achieves changes? How much sacrifice are people willing to make to achieve a more nonviolent world?" (Mayton, *Nonviolence and Peace Psychology*, 243)

48. Mayton, *Nonviolence and Peace Psychology*, 249.

49. Holmes presents a theory of nonviolence from a philosophical perspective (see Mayton, *Nonviolence and Peace Psychology*, 32). His theory is based on the assumption that nonviolence involves a significant degree of power and is a forceful concept. He broadly defines nonviolence as a tactic, a way of life, or a philosophy. To set up his discussion of nonviolence further, Holmes distinguishes two types of violence. He

sociological, anthropological,[50] and psychological approaches, and then discusses that of political scientists. Finally, he discusses two theories that are multidisciplinary in nature. He defines nonviolence not as the absence of violence but rather as an action that uses power and influence to reach a goal without direct injury to the persons working against achieving that goal. It is a principled action based on an underlying belief system that desires to understand the truth within a conflict, believes in noncooperation with evil, considers violence as something to be avoided, and shows a willingness to accept the burden of suffering to break the cycle of violence.[51]

Mayton also reminds us of the United Nations manifesto of 2000, which suggests that "to become a culture of peace, a society needs to address human rights, gender equality, democracy participation, tolerance, and solidarity among all their people, participatory communication and the free flow of information, international peace and security, general education and peace education and sustainable development."[52] Ritter proposes that principled nonviolence that utilizes nonviolent means to achieve nonviolent ends is superior to strategic nonviolence. Ritter makes the case that coercive action within the pragmatic use of strategic violence will lead to short-term successes. Only the conversion of the other—in any conflict—would enable a long-term solution.[53] In "Transforming Warfare Training into Peace Education," Zoppi and Yeager reaffirm the importance of education and believe that through understanding, peace can be attained: "In this effort, peace education is to cultivate an in-depth understanding of conflicts and explore peaceful solutions to conflicts. The root of peace is love, whereas the root of war is fear."[54] Also, in assessing the effects of violence, the individual obsession, and the unconscious acceptance of violence, this interreligious peace education will focus on

---

refers to physical violence or violence 1 as actions committed with the intent to do physical harm and to psychological violence or violence 2 as actions intended to do psychological harm.

50. Sponsel argues that anthropology has much to give to the study of peace and nonviolence and, at the same time, peace studies can positively impact anthropology (see Mayton, *Nonviolence and Peace Psychology*, 34). Most of the research and writing within the field of anthropology that is relevant to nonviolence has been in the analysis of tribal and other societies that are primarily peaceful and nonviolent.

51. Mayton, *Nonviolence and Peace Psychology*, 239.

52. de Rivera, "Introduction," 1–8.

53. Ritter, *Two-dimensional Theory of Nonviolence*, 243.

54. Zoppi and Yeager, "Transforming Warfare Training," 286.

societal obsession because it has been affirmed: "Culturally, our society has fostered an obsession with violence without recognizing its origins as fear based. This obsession has directly interfered with peace education efforts to transform military education for warfare into peacebuilding."[55] "If the role of peace educator in the twenty-first century is to facilitate a shift in global consciousness away from war to peace, peace educators must have the ability and mission to not just believe that peace is possible but also to demonstrate it in themselves and for others as a way of being."[56] It is submitted that interreligious educators will strengthen this notion in a multicultural society and community.

PEACE EDUCATION IN THE YORUBA RELIGION

Yoruba Religion is the indigenous faith of the Yoruba people, which was passed down from their origins through oral traditions, art, crafts, liturgies, pithy sayings, proverbs, folklores, stories, songs, and wise sayings to the present age. It has no founder, no scriptures, and does not possess zeal for increasing membership. It has a natural appeal and most of its adherents are born into it. It accommodates all that modern trends bring with it. It is flexible and generates a lot of support for their adherents. *Olodumare* (God) is its central theme.

Every major event in Yoruba lives is attended by elaborate worship. A typical formal worship includes libation, poured to open up the earth, to attract the spirit beings, to attend to the worship, invocation of esoteric names, praises, and formulae are attracts to the beings of worship, and Divination, by which means the message and revelations of the being of worship are made known to people.

In Yoruba Religion, peace is conceived not in relation to conflict and war but rather in relation to order, harmony, and equilibrium. That the order, harmony, and equilibrium in the universe and society are believed to be divinely established is a religious value, and there is religious obligation to maintain them. It is also a moral value since good conduct is required of human beings if the order, harmony, and equilibrium are to be maintained. The promotion and enhancement of life is the central principle of Yoruba traditional morality. The goal of all moral conduct is therefore the fullness of life. Human life is considered full in Africa

---

55. Zoppi and Yeager, "Transforming Warfare Training," 286.
56. Zoppi and Yeager, "Transforming Warfare Training," 296.

when it is marked by spiritual, material, and social blessings; when the network of relations with the spiritual, human, and material beings is as it should be. Fullness of life is also what is meant by peace in African Religions: "Peace is good relationships well lived, health, absence of pressure and conflict, being strong and prosperous."[57] Peace is the totality of well-being: fullness of life here and hereafter, what the Yoruba call *alafia*—that is, "the sum total of all that man may desire: an undisturbed harmonious life."[58] If one is therefore lacking in any of the basic things—such as good health, a wife or a husband, children, means of sustenance of one's family—or if one, though possessing these things, does not enjoy a good relationship with the other members of the community (living or dead), one cannot be said to have peace. Mere material wealth or progress that is not accompanied by an integral moral life is neither regarded as fullness of life nor is it envied in traditional African societies. Any action that is capable of hindering another from attaining the fullness of life is considered a breach of peace. A selfish or unjust person, even when he or she is not violent, is anti-social and is therefore regarded by the Yorubas as an enemy of peace.

Harmony is a fundamental category in Yoruba religion and thought. In the community, harmony entails smooth relationships between persons and other beings. No attempt is made to deny or cancel out differences; rather, all effort is devoted to finding a way in which differences can continue to co-exist harmoniously. In personal life, such harmony consists in the ability to reconcile one's desires with one's means, coordinate one's thoughts, sentiments, and verbal expressions, as well as the ability to discharge one's religious and social duties. One who is able to do this will experience inner peace:

> The goal of interaction of beings in African world-views is the maintenance of the integration and balance of the beings in it [the world]. Harmonious interaction of beings leads to the mutual strengthening of the beings involved and enhances the growth of life. A pernicious influence from one being weakens other beings and threatens the harmony and integration of the whole.[59]

---

57. Rweyemamu, "Religion and Peace," 381.
58. Rweyemamu, "Religion and Peace," 382.
59. Ikenga-Metuh, *Comparative Studies of African Traditional Religions*, 78.

Harmony is central in the prayer for peace: elders speaking with one voice, tranquillity, agreement between the gourd cup and the vessel, and the banishment of every ill word. These are all fundamental requirements for the realization of the peace prayed for. Since human beings come in different shapes, sizes, and with all sorts of different ideas in their heads, traditional Yoruba societies go to great lengths in trying to accommodate the various opinions of their members. Africans are known for their long, drawn-out village discussions in search of consensus. In Yoruba debates, the goal is always to include everyone in any decision that will be binding on all. And in the interest of harmony, the discussion is continued until the last skeptic has been won over. It often happens that in the interest of harmony, the few who do not share the opinion of the many give up their own voluntarily.

Any person who causes a breach in the harmonious co-existence of the members of the community is required to make up for it through just reparation or restitution, depending on the offense committed. In African Religions, peace in the community cannot be separated from justice. In "African Traditional Religion and Peace," Sarpong underlines this inseparable relationship between justice and peace within his context: "Justice produces peace . . . there can be no peace without justice. . . . Peace is honorable . . . peace can never be achieved when you are disgraced or when you disgrace another person. People must relate to one another on equal terms."[60] Peace is not something that happens but rather a situation that arises when justice happens. It is a pleasant state of things that happens when the state of things is just. The unwritten moral code of the Africans contains not only things that are forbidden but also those things that must be done as compensation and in reparation for the injury which immoral conduct inflicts on individuals and on the society at large. Such compensation and reparation are usually based on past experiences. People are usually at a loss when a person commits a sin or an immoral act hitherto unknown in the community.

In Yoruba societies, there are specific periods of the year marked out for the promotion of peace. During this period—which may last for a week or a month—litigations are suspended while quarrels and all forms of violent and unjust acts are avoided for fear of incurring the wrath of God, the deities, and the ancestors. This sacred period sometimes proceeds the planting season and it is believed that any breach which is not

---

60. Sarpong, "African Traditional Religion and Peace," 351–70.

adequately atoned for will lead to a poor harvest. If a person breaks either the spiritual or the cosmic harmony, the lack of peace that ensues affects the entire community. Sometimes individual reparations, in terms of sacrifices, are inadequate to restore the harmony, and all the members of the community are called upon to right the wrong. There is thus a strong sense of the communal dimension of immoral conduct.

Thus, if for centuries, peace education was based on the teachings of religious leaders who taught that people were supposed to promote peace in their lives and in the world as a whole, what new teaching can religion brings to ameliorate the behaviors of their members? The study of the three main religions in Nigeria has helped to understand that each religion has both peaceful legacies as well as roots that have been used in violent ways. In the next chapter, we focus on how interreligious peace education will attempt to improve the current approach described above to teaching.

The Yoruba people of Nigeria are a very tolerant race, and through their religious-tolerance, they offer a great resource in reducing violence in peace education. The Yoruba proverbs are the vehicle with which socio-cultural and philosophical thoughts underlying social values and ethnic or religious issues are transmitted across generations. The Yoruba proverbs are full of peaceful sayings, such as "*Oro tutu niiyo obi lapo, oro-burukuniiyoidaniaako*," meaning, "Good words (peaceful resolution of issues) bring out kolanut from pocket, while confrontation brings about sword from its sheath." Therefore, the Yoruba proverb underscores the need for dialogue, mediation, and negotiation to resolve issues peacefully.

Among the Yoruba people, proverbs are relics, preserved and transmitted over generations. Yoruba proverbs contain themes of co-operation at the family and society levels that are a precondition for peace in the Yoruba worldview. One such Proverbs states: "*Bi ede o dun, biiigbeniiluri*," meaning, "If the home is not settled, the town is like a forest (without any allurement)." This proverb emphasizes the centrality of the family as the basis of socialization and peace education in the indigenous Yoruba education.[61] The Yoruba accord great respect for intelligent and expert use of language, especially the appropriate use of proverbs, and as such, the *agba* (elder) is expected to exhibit/demonstrate this capacity. The capacity for exhibiting this expert use of language is not solely based on age as there are some youth who are witty in the genre of proverbial com-

---

61. Adeyemi, "Indigenous Proverbs and Peacebuilding in Nigeria," 190.

munication and an intelligent use of language. These people are also seen as elders on their own terms. The Yoruba believe that the sagacious usage of spoken word is the harbinger of peace and war, the engine of culture and civility, the hallmark of conversational prudence, and the epitome of intellectual maturity that may be used in matters of conflict.

Furthermore, the Yoruba tradition also provides us with an effective model of conflict resolution in the *agba* (elders). The *agba* were usually relied upon as arbitrators and agents of conflict resolution due to the qualities they possess.[62] *Agba* (elders) are respected individuals, identified by age and other qualities that mark them out in their families, communities, nations, regions, and the world. To be identified as an *agba* (elder), s/he must be fearless person (*alakikanju*); s/he must be knowledgeable and wise but also someone who gives room for criticisms (*ologbon, oloye, afimotielomiran se*); s/he must be tolerant (*alamumora*); s/he must be upright in all ways (*olotito, olododo*); and s/he must not be selfish (*anikanjopon*).[63]

PEACE EDUCATION IN ISLAM

According to Hadhrat Mirza Tahir Ahmad, in "Attainment of Inner Peace," the concept of peace in Islam is two-fold. "Firstly, to be at peace with God and then, secondly, to be at peace with oneself and with the rest of the world."[64] In Islam, the word peace does not only mean to be at rest or to be in a perfect state of understanding with the rest of the world, it also means submission. As Tahir Ahmad asserts: "According to the Qur'anic concept of peace, no peace on earth can ever be conceived, not to mention established, by human effort. It cannot even be conceived theoretically without man finding God, the Creator, without recognizing the hand of the Creator universally at work."[65] Once man recognizes the Creator, the second step is to be at peace with the Creator, and this peace has dual meaning: first, you are not to do anything which creates a distance between you and the Creator. Secondly, you are to practice submission to the will of God. For Muslims, submission to the will of God is the only means of attaining peace with God. Logically, if children are

62. Bamikole, "Democracy in a Multicultural Society," 10.
63. Bamikole, "Democracy in a Multicultural Society," 12.
64. Ahmad, "Attainment of Inner Peace," 1.
65. Ahmad, "Attainment of Inner Peace," 2.

at peace with their parents, it is impossible for them to defy their orders and wishes. If one submits to the authority, will, or desire of a loved one so completely, nothing in the person is at war with the desire, will, or the way of life or the style of another person.

Islam as a religion of peace recognizes other religions and is open to dialogue. In Qur'an, God said: "Let there be no compulsion in religion: Truth stands out clear from Error" (Q 2:56). There are many other verses in the Qur'an that deal with the openness and lack of compulsion in the nature of spreading God's message. One of the favorite quotes in this regard reads: "If it had been thy Lord's Will, they would all have believed, all who are on earth! Wilt thou then compel mankind, against their will, to believe!" (Q 10:99). These verses (and many others) show how much emphasis Islam places on the responsibility of people, Muslim or non-Muslim. In this regard, Muslims are governed by rules that require their relationship with non-Muslims to be based on justice, mutual respect, cooperation, and communication.

In "Peace Education: an Islamic Approach," Köylü affirms that like many countries, majority Muslims countries do not give the necessary importance to peace education. Nevertheless, Köylü reassures us that this does not mean there is no Islamic basis for peace education. Islamic peace education draws on the efforts of a growing body of Islamic peace scholars and practitioners from a range of backgrounds who are re-examining and reinterpreting Islamic resources, traditions, and practices on nonviolence and peacebuilding.[66] Chaiwat Satha-Anand's work, for instance, puts forward the powerful assertion that violence is unacceptable in Islam, especially when combatants and non-combatants are difficult to distinguish from one another, as is the case in modern warfare. Abdul Aziz Said, Nathan C. Funk, and Ayse S. Kadayifci define an Islamic paradigm for transformation based on Sufi (mystical) principles and practices of peace as an "all-embracing harmony perceived through inward renewal and transformation of human consciousness."[67]

In "Islam and Peacemaking," Sheherade Jafari and Abdul Aziz explain the role of religion as a powerful framework of social identification—especially with the rise of Islamophobia and the clash of civilizations between the Western and Islamic worlds. They state that in Islam, peace is not the absence of war but rather a presence of divine guidance

---

66. Köylü, "Peace Education," 59–76.
67. Said and Funk, "Peace in the Sufi Tradition," 21.

and human responsibility; peace and peacemaking are a *fatwa*, a holy edict. They give examples of Islamic teachings that provide practices of reconciliation such as *sulha*, a form of mediation or arbitration and the principles of equality, as well as *tahkim* or arbitration.

PEACE EDUCATION IN CHRISTIANITY

Christian theologians have also developed and spread a paradigm for peacemaking and reconciliation. The Christian concept of peace is revealed in both the Hebrew Bible and in the New Testament. In the Hebrew Bible, peace is inseparable from righteousness and justice. These concepts are embodied in one Hebrew word, *shalom*, which connotes right relationship between two or more parties. This word is usually translated as "righteousness," referring not only to doing morally correct deeds but also to living rightly in relationship with others. Righteousness is also closely connected to justice because the righteous person acts with justice in the civil or judicial sphere. The necessary link between righteousness and peace can be seen, for example, in Isaiah's vision of a future day when a righteous king will reign over Israel and God's Spirit will be poured out upon the people:

> Until a spirit from on high is poured out on us, and the wilderness becomes a fruitful field, and the fruitful field is deemed a forest. Then justice will dwell in the wilderness, and righteousness abide in the fruitful field. The effect of righteousness will be peace and the result of righteousness, quietness and trust forever. (Isa 32:15–17)

With a similar picture in mind, the Psalmist looks forward to a time when God's salvation pervades the nation. On that day, "Unfailing love and truth have met together. Righteousness and peace have kissed" (Ps 85:10). From the biblical perspective, therefore, the absence of conflict is only the bare beginning of peace. True peace includes personal wholeness, corporate righteousness, political justice, and prosperity for all of creation. For Christians, that is the way God intended things to be when God created the garden, paradise. Perhaps no term better describes God's perfect paradise than "peaceful," a world full of wholeness, righteousness, justice, and prosperity.

According to Walker Homolka in *The Gate to Perfection: The Idea of Peace in Jewish Thought*: "Shalom includes an all-around, comprehensive sense of welfare, facilitating and supporting life."[68] Benjamin Davidson, in his *Analytical and Chaldean Lexicon*, describes the basic meaning of shalom as "wholeness," "integrity," "perfection," and "well-being."[69] In addition, according to Joon Surh Park in *Jesus Christ: The Prince of Peace*, shalom means "wholeness in the sense that no component part is missing, impaired or damaged. It means also that all parts are in harmony, order and unity."[70]

From this basic meaning, *shalom* is used comprehensively, in a variety of ways, depending on the context. For example, when *shalom* is used in reference to physical conditions, it means health—in the sense that a body is in a state of wholeness. When *shalom* is used in the context of material condition, it means prosperity, good harvest, and fertility. When *shalom* is used in this sense, the word is often paired with *tobah*, which has the specific meaning of prosperity (Deut 2:6; Ezra 9:12). When *shalom* is used in the context of warfare, it means victory. King David summoned Uriah, the husband of Bathsheba, and inquired how the war prospered (2 Sam 11:7). David's question was literally, "How was the *shalom* of the war?" It is a seemingly contradictory phrase if we understand *shalom* as meaning "peace." When soldiers return from the battle "in *shalom*," it means a victorious homecoming (Josh 10:21; Judg 8:9, 11–31; 1 Kgs 22:27). In *Biblical Basis for Peacemaking*, Peggy Cowan wrote that *shalom* "is often used in reference to personal relationships, and it means "wholeness" of relationship, i.e., a relationship with goodwill and harmony."[71] This is the reason why *shalom* was used as an identification of friend or foe when two parties encountered one another (1 Kgs 2:13). *Shalom* is also used in the same sense on the level of international relations. When two countries are in the relation of *shalom*, it does not simply mean that there is no war between the two; rather, it goes beyond that and means that a relationship of amity, alliance, and cooperation exists between them (1 Kgs 5:12).

Shalom, of course, includes the state of peace in the sense of the absence of war. But such peace is one of many manifestations of *shalom*. *Shalom* does bring peace, and the breakdown of *shalom* often leads to war. However, the cessation of armed conflict does not automatically bring

---

68. Homolka, *Gate to Perfection*, 5.
69. Davidson, *Analytical and Chaldean Lexicon*, 197.
70. Park, "Jesus Christ the Prince of Peace," 1.
71. Cowan, *Biblical Basis for Peacemaking*, 2.

shalom. In the biblical sense, *shalom* is a much more comprehensive and dynamic concept than peace in a narrow sense—as God's gift (Isa 26:3–12) and God's intention (Jer 29:11). It is the completion of God's purpose for creation that is described as a covenant of *shalom* (Num 25:12).

Although given by God, *shalom* is not to be passively awaited, but actively pursued (Ps 34:14). "*Shalom* also involves positive relationships between peoples and persons. Positive relationships within the community means that the needs of all persons are met, and there is material well-being, economic security, and prosperity for all" (Isa 54:13; 66:12; Jer 29:5–7; Ezra 34:27–29; Ps 37:11; 72:3; Hag 2:9). *Shalom* involves the absence of war but also goes beyond it, to include security and lack of fear. The full meaning of *shalom* can only be grasped when human well-being is balanced. After the fall, humankind became separated from the creator, from each other, and from the natural world. The wholeness of God's creation—*shalom*—was broken into chaotic fragmentation. The whole creation waited for the coming of the one who would restore the broken *shalom* to its original wholeness. In summary, "*Shalom* can be defined as the welfare and state of completion of all creatures, arising from a divine will for peace, including their peaceful coexistence in a way of life based on God's commandments."[72] The Christian community reads in the New Testament that "when the fullness of time was come" (Gal 4:4), God sent his Son, Jesus. He is the one who came to heal the broken relations and recover the lost *shalom*: "We have peace with God through our Lord Jesus Christ" (Rom 5:1). Jesus Christ, by his work of reconciliation, restores *shalom* in heaven and earth. Paul says, "Through him [Jesus Christ] to reconcile to himself all things, whether on earth or in heaven, making peace by the blood of his cross" (Col 1:20). In the Letter to the Ephesians, Paul even calls Jesus "our peace," who breaks down the wall of hostility between humankind and God: "He is our peace, who has broken down the dividing wall of hostility, so making peace he might reconcile us both to God in one body through the cross, thereby bringing the hostility to an end" (Eph 2:14–16). With the coming of Jesus Christ, the way was opened for the restoration of the lost *shalom* to humankind. This is the reason why, at Jesus' birth, the angels of heaven sang, "Glory to God in the highest heaven, and on earth peace to those on whom his favor rests" (Luke 2:14). Jesus Christ is the great restorer of *shalom*; thus,

---

72. Homolka, *Gate to Perfection*, 6.

throughout history, the Christian church has proclaimed that he is "the Prince of Peace (*shalom*)."

In Greek, Ειρήνη is the word for peace, meaning the absence of war. The New Testament includes all of the meanings of *shalom*: good relationships among peoples and nations (Mk 9:50; Rom 12:18–19; Eph 2:15; Heb 12:14), healthy relationships within the community, a quality of life in the Spirit or in relation to God, a gift of Jesus, reconciliation effected by or through Jesus, and a quality to be pursued by humans.

Christians believe that having peace with God is living in intimate fellowship with God. Similarly, peaceful (peace-full) human relationships are also characterized by *koinônia* (fellowship). Christ lived a life of peace in a world of violence; his followers are called to do, living a life of unconditional love, a love which casts out fear. Christians are called to "not worry about tomorrow" (Matt 6:34), to live each day like a lily of the field. So long as there are conditions set on peace, there is not even a modicum of the faith which was preached by Jesus. In "Jesus Christ: Model of the Nonviolent Human Being," John Dear asserts that:

> We are commanded by Jesus to practice nonviolence. Humanity is charged with the grace of God; our sin is the conscious choice not to act in the grace of nonviolence. Given our violence, we need to ask the God of nonviolence for the grace to become like God, to renounce our violence and join faith communities of nonviolence to help us live lives of active love. Jesus is the model human being because he is nonviolent. He is just, faithful, and unconditionally loving. He loves enemies; serves people; tells truth; builds community; prays to the God of peace; and risks his life in active nonviolence, even to arrest, torture, and execution. Because of this steadfast nonviolence, God raises Jesus from the dead to uphold his life for all humanity to emulate.[73]

A Christian peace education is based on the teachings of Jesus Christ in his sermon on the mount, his mission described in Isaiah 61, on the personal life of Christ (the Prince of Peace), and on the theology of *shalom*. Therefore, the mission of the church must have the entire dimension and scope of Jesus. It consists in proclaiming and teaching, but also in healing, liberating, and in showing compassion for the poor and the downtrodden. It also involves being sent into the world to love, to serve, to preach, to teach, to heal, to save, and to liberate. In order for

---

73. Dear, *God of Peace*, 101.

peace to reign, the concept of love (*Agape*) in 1 Cor 13:13 is applied in any Christian peace education curriculum.

Agape speaks of unconditional love, which is an attribute of God's own heart, a kingdom value. *Agape* speaks of a love that exceeds passion, friendship and benevolence. *Agape* speaks of a love that goes beyond self, yet is more than an unselfish feeling. *Agape* speaks of a love that acts. *Agape* speaks of a love that loves the unlovable. The Good Samaritan and Prodigal Son explore what it is to love our neighbor, and give insights to *Agape* as a theme of mission. *Agape* is the indiscriminate love beyond discrimination, without obligation, without lines of responsibility and exclusion; it responds to persons, not social categories. *Agape* is bold, suspending social and ecclesiastical norms which justify callous disinterest by penetrating social barricades that hold people in prisons, hospitals, addiction centers, and ghettos of all sorts.

Jesus modeled *agape*. He embodied it by being an advocate for the poor. He violated civil and religious laws in the face of human need. His words and deeds insulted the rich and powerful. The Church will only be faithful to Christ when it is engaged in peacemaking. The Church is obedient to Christ when it equips God's people to be peacemakers. The Church bears witness to Christ when it nourishes the moral life of the nation for the peace of the world.

The church as a reconciler and peacemaker needs to work on four attitudes and four skills of a peacemaker. The attitudes are: humility, commitment to the safety of others, acceptance of conflict, and hope. The four skills are: truthful speech, expectant listening, alertness to community, and good process. While these skills and attitudes can be taught, they also need to be lived. Within these skills and attitudes, the primary changes must begin where pastors and other church leaders are trained.

As a Christian, reconciliation is reflected in the epistle to the Colossians, in 2 Corinthians, and in 1 John. God's love and reconciliation are freely given and are not conditional. It is a difficult religious virtue that Christians are to follow. The Bible also teaches love of enemies:

> But to you who are listening I say: Love your enemies, do good to those who hate you, bless those who curse you, pray for those who mistreat you. If someone slaps you on one cheek, turn to them the other also. If someone takes your coat, do not withhold your shirt from them. Give to everyone who asks you, and if anyone takes what belongs to you, do not demand it back. Do to others as you would have them do to you. (Luke 6:27–31)

In addition, "Reconciliation as social virtue imposes the duty to overcome what separates human beings, what turns one against another."[74] Christians are called to move and grow in this changing world, because, according to Liechty: "We always have to keep in mind, when looking at the past, that the passing of time makes retrieving it impossible, that who we are today is different from who we were in the past, who we were even in the recent past, even yesterday."[75] This is why Schreiter asserts that: "Any return is not a return: it is coming into a new place."[76] This also constitutes a very important teaching of peace education.

In the Memorandum of the Council of the Evangelical Church in Germany (2007), the practical aspect of peace education is described: the practical program for peace education must reflect a realistic image of humanity. Such an image must have three elements: Firstly, it will see human beings as God's creatures. This createdness binds us to all other creatures and is essential to help us understand our relationship to our environment with sensitivity and solidarity. Secondly, human beings are creatures with responsibility. As history shows, we spend our lives in practical rebellion against God and are capable of fathomless evil and cruelty. Overcoming violence is therefore a life-and-death affair. Finally, humanity is made in the image of God. It is because of this that we can hope that the power of sin may be halted effectively and that people may be brought up and educated to value peace, which is an essential condition for overcoming violence. It is the image of God in people that enables them to act in God's way in their treatment of others—with love and a willingness to forgive and seek reconciliation.

CONCLUSION

Concepts, principles, and pedagogies for peace education can be found in Yoruba religion, Islam, and Christianity. Each of these religions provides overlapping perspectives, tools which reinforce and support the foundations and principles of peace education. There is need to construct a model of peace education that will include the various distinct values of these three religions for the teaching and reduction of violence in Nigeria. I will be using the five possible ethical foundations identified by Page

---

74. Isasi-Diaz, "Reconciliation," 75.
75. Isasi-Diaz, "Reconciliation," 82.
76. Schreiter, *Ministry of Reconciliation*, 11.

because he describes how peace education has developed in response to global wars, key thinkers, instruments, and institutions. By encouraging and facilitating the sharing of personal narratives, this trans-formative pedagogy will enhance participants' understanding of their interconnectedness across conflicting groups, and nurture empathy for others. In the next chapter, I will discuss a model of how peace education can embrace these values and be developed into an interreligious curriculum for peace education suitable for and tailored to meet the needs of the religious leaders in a multicultural context.

CHAPTER V

Peacebuilding Intervention and Interreligious Curriculum for Peace Education

This chapter provides the following elements: it explores various definitions of curriculum, introduces the interreligious curriculum for peace education, and presents the content of the interreligious curriculum for peace education (ICPE).

DEFINITIONS OF CURRICULUM

Elliot W. Eisner defines curriculum as "a program that is intentionally designed to engage students in activities or events that will have educational benefits for them."[1] The coverage is grounded in the belief that the appropriateness of any given educational practice is dependent upon the characteristics and context of the school program, and the values of the community served.

Cully asserts that: "Curriculum includes both materials and the experiences for learning. The textbook or manual is the starting point, but enrichment books, filmstrips, recordings, and workbooks are other elements. Some people would include all the experiences of a learner as part of curriculum. Attending Sunday worship is such an experience and could well be integrated into the curriculum."[2] As for Oliva, he

---

1. Eisner, *Educational Imagination*, 31.
2. Cully, *Planning and Selecting Curriculum*, 11.

takes a methodical, comprehensive, step-by-step process of curriculum development based upon a small number of key models and basic concepts. He addresses both the technical details and the human dimension of the art of curriculum planning, the philosophy and aims of education, curriculum implementation strategies, and appropriately evaluating instruction.

According to Harris, who specializes in Church curriculum, curriculum is about "the mobilizing of creative, educative powers in such a way as to 'fashion a people.'"[3] According to her, the five different curriculums used within the church are as follows: *Koinonia*, which is Community; *Leiturgia,* which is Prayer; *Didache,* which is Teaching; *Kerygma,* which is Proclamation; and *Diakonia,* which is service. She also asserts that curriculum has multiple meanings, and in some instances, the meanings are in conflict with one another. She limited herself to five challenging influences that contributed to her understanding of curriculum. Two are from general education and three from church education. These are presented in an essay by Newman and Oliver, who examine the missing community in most people's lives, and suggest that the contexts for education are very limited. They advocate a broader educational context as the only one suitable for genuine learning, with the corollary curricular principle that what occurred in such contexts could and did constitute curriculum.

It is a curriculum that will bring changes and transformations in the claims of each of the two "foreign" religions—Islam and Christianity—which have invariably resulted in a state of antagonism because so many of their practitioners have emphasized their respective doctrines of expansion (i.e., proselytism/mission/*da'wa*) rather than interaction. As seen earlier in this book, both Islam and Christianity have major segments of their respective followers who hold to exclusivist beliefs, which thwarts any attempts at interacting with others. From those perspectives, Christianity claims to be the way, the truth, and the life exemplified by the person of Jesus Christ, the Son of God, while Islam claims to be the only religion handed down from God through the great Prophet Muhammad, the final Prophet of God.

Thus defining curriculum as support materials can lead a church or a mosque into two errors. The first is to believe that a curriculum is bought, not designed. The second is to believe that high-quality materials naturally lead to effective learning. Therefore, in order to avoid these two

---

3. Harris, *Fashion Me a People*, 8.

potential mistakes, and integrating many elements of the above definitions, I propose for the purpose of this book to define curriculum as *the course of learning activities designed to accomplish well-defined goals.*

Developing good curriculum for a church or a mosque is not easy. It is rarely available "out of a box," from a publishing house or a seminary. Good curriculum is the product of a local congregation's fervor to meet the spiritual needs of its community and of the skilled leadership of staff in designing the course. Since we learn all the time through exposure and modeled behaviors, this means that we learn important social and emotional lessons from everyone who inhabits the community—from Christians, Muslims, people of other religions, as well as from people whose worldviews does not include anything religious. Many educators are unaware of the strong lessons imparted to our members through such interactions.

In the next section, we begin the presentation of the Interreligious Curriculum for Peace Education. It is the result of having integrated the literature on peacebuilding intervention and the notion and definitions of curriculum.

INTERRELIGIOUS CURRICULUM FOR PEACE EDUCATION

The interreligious curriculum for peace education is divided into five units. Unit 1 is the overview of the curriculum and comprises: the methodology, philosophy, vision, purpose, structure, goals, and objectives of interreligious peace education, the teaching approach, the general considerations, the resources, the choice of school, the group code, the class schedule, the assessments, and the evaluation. Unit 2 deals with concepts of violence. Unit 3 teaches about the concept of peace education. Unit 4 elaborates on human security. Finally, Unit 5 focuses on interreligious practices. Each of the other four units comprises: an introduction, learning objectives, learning activities, content, conclusion, questions for comprehension, analysis and reflection, and examples of required readings.

Unit I: Overview of the Interreligious Curriculum for Peace Education

Methodological Strategies

The methodology used in this curriculum is twofold: theoretically, it uses a constructive approach; in addition, it uses a praxeological approach, which combines theory and praxis. The development of the interreligious curriculum for peace education is aimed at exploring issues related to Yoruba Religion, Islam, Christianity, and peace education, focusing specifically on the relationship between religious values and principles as well as peace education and conflict resolution. This approach addresses both theoretical and practical terms, utilizing scholarly and case studies to illustrate ideas and concepts.

The Philosophy of Interreligious Peace Education

Interreligious peace education is an urgent necessity, not only because Nigeria is now experiencing deep religious violence but also for the reason that conflict has become a reality of life, occurring at any time due to the clash of interests, ideas, political orientations, economic systems, etc. Violence is often utilized as a way of resolving conflict. However, seeking to end conflict through violence only increases insecurity as it lengthens the cycle of violence; new violence may result in even more destruction. Therefore, the form of education that educates religious leaders about how to manage and transform conflicts, that teaches the skills to resolve conflicts, and that emphasizes the importance of peace will play a crucial role in ending those conflicts and creating stable relationships.

The hope of ending violence, oppression, discrimination, and injustice in various aspects of life that impede individuals and society can be achieved through realizing the meaning and essence of peace values. The interreligious curriculum for peace education is expected to function as a general guideline in the process of nurturing religious leaders to develop paradigms, attitudes, and behaviors that can promote appropriate values and methods of managing conflict without violence. The real meaning of interreligious peace education is not solely related to the aspects of attitude-building reflected in the leaders receiving this course, but they should cultivate behavior that conforms with the cognitive and affective aspects of the program. The religious leaders' daily conduct must reflect their education in peace.

This curriculum stresses subject-centered approaches as well as student-centered. The subject-centered approach refers to the choice of the materials (theme and topics) relevant to interreligious peace education. These materials were all accumulated from Yoruba Religion, Islam, and Christianity. The student-centered approach involves the consideration of the students' conditions, including how to incite their motivation and interest to pursue the interreligious peace education contained in this curriculum. It treats pupils as subjects who have the capacity to think and behave through an interactive and democratic learning process.

This philosophy is to undergird religious leaders as they lead, teach, and act with their community members and increase their commitment to interreligious peace education, at all levels of religious education. This curriculum seeks to elucidate how peace is a settled disposition and how it enhances the confidence of religious leaders as agents for peacebuilding, informing them of the consequences of violence and social injustice. It also teaches them the value of peaceful and just social structures as well as to work to uphold or develop such social structures, encouraging them to love the world as well as to imagine and enact a peaceful future.

The Vision of Interreligious Peace Education

The vision of interreligious peace education is to educate religious leaders about what creates and sustains a peaceful society through programs centered on conflict resolution. This approach focuses on the social-behavioral symptoms of conflict and trains religious leaders to resolve inter-personal disputes through techniques of negotiation and mediation.

It also includes learning to manage anger and improve communication through the acquisition of various skills, such as listening, turn-taking, identifying needs, and separating facts from emotions. Its goals are to:

(1) Significantly reduce the human cost of religious violence in Nigeria;

(2) Help build a more effective, interreligious community;

(3) Promote harmony and the spirit of common personhood amongst all the people of Nigeria, transcending religious, linguistic, and regional or sectional diversities;[1] to renounce practices derogatory to the dignity of a person; and

(4) Provide curriculum and tools religious leaders can use to transform their fellow faith community members.

Purpose of the Interreligious Curriculum for Peace Education

The purpose of the interreligious curriculum for peace education is intended to bring a new approach in the training of religious leaders who are called to participate more directly in solving problems of religious violence. There is a myriad of approaches to try to solve religious violence, but ultimately, the roots of this problem are related to human consciousness because war begins in the minds of people. Since religious worldviews, among others, directly influence human consciousness, there is a growing need to improve the teaching on peace for religious leaders in particular and be more creative, genuine, and compassionate in finding sustainable solutions to these problems. If education is probably the strongest defense against human violence, then it is possible to argue that interreligious peace education is the spiritual soul of education, as it can create the inner conscious shield for human survival on planet earth. It is only through interreligious peace education that religious leaders can install peace in human minds as an antidote to religious violence.

Interreligious peace education has an important role to play in the search for new methods of education that will advance broad social transformation, shifting away from a paradigm of dominance, exclusiveness, and violence towards a new paradigm of equity, inclusiveness, and peace. The curriculum is designed to provide more theoretical, background

---

1. Verkuyuten, "Disourses about ethnic group (de-)essentialism: oppressive and progressive aspects," 371–91.

information at the beginning and more practical focus towards the end (although practical examples are interspersed throughout the program). This curriculum is intended to bring interreligious peace education to religious leaders in order to train leaders who will affect their community at the grassroots level.

The Structure of the Interreligious Curriculum for Peace Education

This one year curriculum is divided into 5 units, with each unit being subdivided into many chapters for a total of 18. See summary chart on page 118. The first unit introduces the objectives and aims of the curriculum, determines the teaching approach, builds in an assessment component, and establishes a system of curriculum evaluation.

The second and the third units are to be taught in the first semester. The second unit is comprised of 5 chapters and explores the theories and concepts of violence, enumerates texts and stories in which religion has been a contributing factor to violence, teaches methods to break cycles of violence, and brings preventive measures to violence. The third unit defines peace education, has 4 chapters, and explains its principles and concepts, elaborates on an integrative theory of peace, peacebuilding, and religious texts and stories on peace.

The fourth and fifth units are scheduled for the second semester. The fourth unit deals with human security, is comprised of 4 chapters, and examines the relationship between 3 religions, the components and teachings of human security, and defines the basic principles of human existence and peaceful development. The fifth unit (practices) is comprised of 5 chapters and focuses on various practices of reconciliation, teaches how to build community, advances the interreligious practices from 3 religions, and advocates methods of physical and spiritual healing of wounds. The unit facilitates intervention towards a better training of religious leaders in Nigeria and its five important aims.

The Goals and Objectives of the Interreligious Curriculum for Peace Education

> ➤ Goals of the Interreligious Curriculum for Peace Education

Interreligious peace education tries to arouse the religious leaders' creativity in resolving conflict without violence so that conflict can have positive impacts for life. The goal of interreligious peace education is to provide Yoruba Religion, Islamic, and Christian peace education resources to religious leaders. It has a student-focused learning where the religious leaders will acquire, develop, and use the interreligious peace education principles, theories, knowledge, and skills for their empowerment and transformation. The goal of interreligious curriculum for peace education is also to reveal what the creeds and holy books of the world's religions teach about spiritual systems that reject violence, the individualistic pursuit of economic and political gain, and call their followers to compassion for every human being. It also seeks to lead religious leaders to an awareness that the followers of religions across the world need to be in and to grow in dialogical relationships of respect, understanding, and engagement between people of different religions.

> **Objectives of the Interreligious Curriculum for Peace Education**

The general learning objectives of the interreligious curriculum for peace education are categorized by knowledge objectives, skill objectives, and attitude objectives.

✓ The knowledge objectives:

Religious leaders will be able to develop and use the following knowledge:

- Acquire knowledge of prevailing violence and peace norms and stereotypes; knowledge and sensitivity regarding issues that deal with violence and peace, power and justice, gender and race, ecology and environment, conflicts, etc.
- Have a deep understanding of the relationship between religion and violence and enable leaders to speak to this relationship.
- Broaden awareness of the relationship between religion and peace education.
- Be equipped to contribute to the work of transformation in their community.
- Engage religious leaders in translating theoretical foundations of peace education and the principles of Yoruba, Islamic, and Christian principles into practice.

- Develop a sense of possibility that enables them to become agents of transformation and social change.

   ✓ The skill objectives:

Religious leaders will be able to acquire, develop, and use the following skills:

- Development of communication skills, including attentive and active listening, restating the events of a story, refraining from creative liberty (i.e., changing the actual events of the story), and paraphrasing concepts back to the speaker.
- Acceptance of differences as normal; viewing difference as something interesting that promotes curiosity rather than fear.
- Being an attentive and compassionate listener; and identifying a stereotype and having the skills to debunk it.
- Critical thinking and problem solving/conflict resolution, empathy, assertiveness, sharing, and cooperation to help others learn about peaceful conflict resolution.
- Attitude of self-respect and self-esteem, respect for others, open-mindedness and vision, environment concern, commitment to justice, etc. Develop their ability to work together as a group (teamwork).
- To develop practical resources to help engage members of their community in working towards peace.
- Interreligious peace education skills and the knowledge necessary to live peacefully.

   ✓ The attitude objectives:

Religious leaders will be able to acquire, develop, and use the following attitudes:

- Willingness to take action with indicators such as: knowing one's community and control over things in one's own environment (e.g., personal and natural), identifying range of choices in the face of conflict, choosing constructive and collaborative action, and expressing satisfaction with having taken action and achieving the desired outcomes.

- Working out strategies which are effective in handling violence and establishing peace within and outside the community.
- Sensitizing the community or the organization with sources of violence within.
- Developing pro-peace attitudes, skills, and competence.
- Respect for people and their cultures to be able to motivate the other to search for peaceful conflict resolution in their lives.

For these learning objectives, typical teaching and learning methods will be lectures, seminars or tutorials, and problem-based learning that make use of dialogical methods when appropriate. Assessments would aim to assess that the learners understood and could recall the key features of interreligious peace education accurately.

The Teaching Approach

Peace education embraces the notion of empowerment via education. Empowerment refers to the individual and group as independent thinkers and actors informed by principles of peace. Such empowerment is possible if the concept of learning, especially in the field of peace education, is understood and applied to engage teachers and students, drawing on their experiences and engaging them in constructive pedagogies which challenge them to discover and use their potential to promote peace.

The pedagogy of this curriculum is participatory, dialogical, collective, interactive, and self-reflective approaches. These approaches directly nurture the basic human need for recognition and build on individuals' potential to contribute and to be effective members of their communities. These approaches also ensure that relevant real-life experiences that matter to the learning community are explored and addressed. By doing so, the learning becomes relevant to the lives of the learner, and provides them with a space to learn and share peaceful approaches.

The interactive and participatory approaches do not exclude the use of other pedagogies that rely on the knowledge and experience of the educator, but they do provide the educator with creative approaches to deliver her/his knowledge and experiences in ways that can best inform and enrich the learning community. The dialogical approach means that every effort will be made to foster an environment in which each voice is heard and every person treated with respect.

This approach is also an equal (horizontal) teacher-learner relationship, in which everyone teaches and learns simultaneously from one another. This includes valuing the knowledge and experience that all participants bring to the learning environment. It allows all participants the opportunity to share their knowledge and experience. This also means keeping open to learning from others and remaining flexible to new ideas. Most class sessions include an interactive lecture and time for discussion in smaller groups. Finally, self-reflection exercises, which develop the practice of being introspective and curious about one's own nature, include such elements as noticing one's own reactions, actions, and their consequences. This self-reflection is encouraged not only for students but also on the part of the teacher.

General Considerations

> ➤ **Set-up:**

The setting of interreligious peace education is important to consider. As a facilitator, I might not have much control or choice about where the class is taking place. However, there are details that I can control that can promote a more equitable classroom setting. For example, if I am in a traditional classroom—with a blackboard and rows of desks facing forward—I will consider making a circle with the desks so that everyone will be part of the circle rather than standing alone at the front. This gesture can do a lot to promote dialogue and more equitable relationships in the classroom.

> ➤ **Resources:**

Religious leaders experiencing conflict, violence, and Yoruba Religion, Islam, and Christian practices and theory as well as those lecturers comprises valuable resources for this course. The frame is designed so that lecturers can freely add relevant resource materials. In addition to the readings, there are other resources that will be used such as videos, group activity materials, poetry and prayers, international peace symbols, and many more.

➤ The Choice of School:

The curriculum will cover a period of one intensive year in the Department of Religious Studies at the University of Ibadan (one of the oldest universities in Nigeria offering Islamic, Christian, and African Religious studies in her Religious studies department). It is posited that the development of an interreligious curriculum for peace education for religious leaders will reduce the growing religious violence in Nigeria by addressing the tensions between Christian and Muslim populations and by enabling peacemakers to create interreligious islands of peace amid the violence. The religious leaders studying at the University of Ibadan are trained to participate actively in preventing potential conflicts. The selection of University of Ibadan as our pilot project is based on the understanding that this curriculum can be easily adapted to the graduate program and has the potential to be opened to interreligious peace education training.

➤ Group Behavior

The group comprises of religious leaders who may have different expectations about how the group ought to behave and interact. This is particularly relevant in regards to communication styles, as people coming from different backgrounds, religions, and cultures might have different expectations about what is appropriate and what learning looks like. To address those challenges squarely, the first session of the course includes a brainstorming about such expectations, leading to the development of the students' own "Group Charter." It is helpful to think of it as a charter, rather than "rules" that are to be either abided by or broken. Once a charter is in place, the individual members will self-monitor and remind each other if they are not following the guidelines. I will allow the guidelines to come from the members rather than imposing them upon them. If the group is having trouble thinking of guidelines, I will use "the Guide for Interfaith Celebrations."[2] I can also make a suggestion (for example, "only one person speaks at a time" or "no cell phones during class"), but also I will try to allow the bulk of the guidelines come from within the group. Creating a charter like this is an important step in creating a safe learning environment. This is not only useful for this workshop but also will be a useful exercise for educators to take to their classrooms and communities.

---

2. Brodeur, "Description of the Guidelines," 1.

> **Class Schedule:**

In the department of religious studies, the regular studying period of lectures and classes is fifteen study weeks in a semester. Each course comprises three hours per week. It is assumed that classes end ten minutes early in order to allow for movement to the next class. For effective implementation and success of such an interreligious peace education course, I suggest that the fifteen weeks study should be replaced by a full day lecture, twice in a month, for four months, plus weekend workshop activities in both the church and the mosque.

Assessment

To be able to achieve the learning objectives, periodic assessments are needed throughout the course—and not only at the end—such as class discussions, class presentation, and essays. The essays for the first semester are on religious conflict, while the second semester will be on interreligious peace education practices.

> **Religious Conflict Analysis Paper:**

This assignment asks students to complete a religious conflict analysis relevant to their context or community. The content of their analyses will be as varied as their contexts and the conflicts themselves. But generally, they should aim to identify the extent to which people, problems, and/or processes are at issue.

> **Interreligious Peace Education Resources Paper**

This assignment invites students to envision and/or identify peacebuilding resources available in their contextual education site. They may think of this as a form of asset-based community analysis by using a variety of peacebuilding responses and practices. They are welcome to contextualize any of these and also encouraged to think afresh based on the realities of their own context.

> **Reflection Papers**

In this informal evaluation, three types of evaluations are to be considered:
- Critical reflection weekly paper: the purpose of this essay is to invite students to critically reflect on the course material and their previous experiences by responding to these questions: (1) What have

you learned about the way you respond to conflict? (2) Some weeks after the fact, how do you assess your analysis of conflict? (3) How hopeful do you feel about the peacebuilding resources you identify? (4) Draw on your experiences in your community to raise one or two questions about religious peacebuilding work. The last session will be discussion of the essays and questions students pose.

- Reflection mid-semester paper: where the student discusses what the student notices, feels, and does, both in self-evaluation and the evaluation of others. He also analyzes why and what made him angry.
- End of the year evaluation: where the student evaluates how useful are the exercises over learning.

Curriculum Evaluation

It is important to provide a confidential mechanism to solicit feedback from the religious leaders in training. The evaluation is viewed as a comprehensive, integral, systematic, and continuous activity. It involves evaluation of self, the group, and the curriculum. The results are valued and will be genuinely used to improve programs and processes.

In *Handbook for Curriculum Assessment*, Peter Wolf asserts: "Curriculum assessment is a process of gathering and analyzing information from multiple sources in order to improve student learning in sustainable ways."[3] This curriculum assessment can serve several major purposes: (1) to identify aspects of a curriculum that are working and those that need to change; (2) to assess the effectiveness of changes that have already been made; (3) to demonstrate the effectiveness of the current program; (4) to meet regular program review requirements; (5) to satisfy professional accreditations.[4] According to Wolf, the information gathered as part of a curriculum assessment can be used to inform curriculum changes in several areas, including:

> Curriculum/Course Design

> Curriculum/Course Delivery

---

3. Wolf, *Handbook for Curriculum Assessment*, 3.
4. Wolf, *Handbook for Curriculum Assessment*, 3.

- Assessment
- Learning Environment
- Other

The Curriculum assessment efforts are generally effective when:

- **Viewed as a comprehensive, integral, systematic, and continuous activity**
- **Viewed as a means for self-improvement**
- **Measures are meaningful**
- **Multiple sources of measures are used**
- **Results are valued, and are genuinely used to improve programs and processes**
- **Involves the participation and input of faculty, staff, and students**
- **Focuses on the program, not on individual performance of educators**

It is one thing to suggest that curriculum assessment should ideally take place in all stages of the curriculum, but it is another thing entirely to know how and when to do it. One model in particular has proved its worth time and again. Kirkpatrick's four "Levels of Evaluation," which originally was conceived for training environments, provides a clear and concise framework to understand the "how" and the "when" of curriculum assessment. According to Kirkpatrick, evaluation should always begin with Level 1, and then, as time and budget allows, should move sequentially through Levels 2, 3, and 4.[5] Information from each prior level serves as a base for evaluation at the next level. Though not all levels are always measured, each successive level represents a more precise measure of the effectiveness of the training program, but at the same time requires a more rigorous and time-consuming analysis.

---

5. Winfrey, *Kirkpatrick's Four Levels of Evaluation*, 1–3.

Unit II: Violence

The second unit explores the concepts and theories of violence, enumerates texts and stories in which religion has been a contributing factor to violence, teaches methods to break cycles of violence, and brings preventive measures to violence. This unit is comprised of five chapters: (1) Concepts of Violence; (2) Theories of violence; (3) Sacred Texts/ Stories Fostering Violence; (4) Breaking the Cycles of Violence; and (5) Prevention of Violence.

Chapter 1: Concepts of Violence

Introduction

Violence is a major problem in society and is a threat to everyone. There are many factors that contribute to this grave and distasteful activity happening in our homes, community, society, and country. A common understanding of the causes of violence can help participants develop more effective responses to it.

Learning Objectives

At the end of this chapter, participants will be able to:

1. Define violence and various forms of violence.
2. Understand violence and conflict.
3. Understand the root causes of religious violence in the Nigerian society.

4. Understand group dynamics.
5. Explore the sources and dynamics of violence and how it relates to religion and religious values.
6. Understand the dynamics of power and control within a relationship and to determine when behavior becomes abusive and harmful.
7. Understand their sensitivities and the sensitivities of the topic.
8. Broadly outline justice system responses to violence.

Learning Activities

Self-introduction by participants, divide the class in groups, each group is comprised of different religion. Give them national newspapers and online news sites related to religious violence and ask them to answer the following questions after reading:

1. What are local community attitudes to religious violence?
2. What elements should be absent for peace to occur?
3. Can you think of instances when conflict might be positive?
4. Can you think of an example in your life where a conflict resulted in a positive outcome?
5. How does personal violence take place in your community?
6. Where does structural violence take place? Does personal violence become institutionalized or structural violence and how?
7. What is the role of a religious leader in personal or structural violence?
8. When does violence have religious causes? When is it caused by other things? How are these causes related or unrelated?

Content

1. Definitions of Violence

Violence is commonly understood as a pattern of behavior intended to establish and maintain control over family, household members, intimate partners, colleagues, individuals, or groups. Violence can also be defined as the intentional use of physical force or power, threatened or actual, against oneself, another person, or against a group or community that either results in or has a high likelihood of resulting in injury, death, psychological harm, abnormal development or deprivation.[1] This includes: physical, sexual, and psychological abuse (such as the significant abuse of power arising from a dependent relationship, threats, intimidation, and neglect). Garver considers the core meaning of violence to be the act of violating a basic right of the human being.[2] For Garver, the two basic human rights are the right to one's body and the right to autonomy. Violation of these rights implies that violence has been done.

2. Types of Violence

The World Health Organization (1996) has developed the following typology, which divides violence into three categories, based on the relationship between the perpetrator/s and the victim/s: self-directed violence, including suicidal behaviour and self-harm; interpersonal violence, including violence inflicted against one individual by another—or by a small group of individuals—and can be categorized as: (1) family and intimate partner violence, involving violence between family members and intimate partners (including child abuse and elder abuse), often taking place in the home; (2) community violence, involving violence between people who are not related, and who may or may not know each other (acquaintances and strangers), generally taking place outside the home in public places; and (3) collective violence, including violence inflicted by large groups such as states, organized political groups, militia, or terrorist organisations.

> ### Tilly's Types of Violence[3]

Individual aggression (single-perpetrator rapes, assaults, etc.); brawls (street fighting, small-scale, batteries at sporting events, etc.); opportunism (looting, gang rape, and piracy); scattered attacks (sabotage, assault of governmental agents, and arson); broken negotiation (demonstration, governmental repression, and military coups); coordinated destruction, (terrorism, genocide, and politicide); and violent rituals (lynching, public executions, gang rivalries, etc.).

---

1. World Health Organisation, "Violence," 5.
2. Garver, *What is Violence*, 817–22.
3. Tilly, *Politics of Collective Violence*, 14–15.

> **Garver's Four Types of Violence**[4]

Personal overt violence (overt physical assault of one person on the body of another, e.g., assault, mugging, rape, murder, and police brutality); overt institutional violence (people obeying orders: the extreme manifestation being war, but the category includes both riots and "war campaigning" policies of law-enforcement agencies); quiet personal violence (a human being deprives another person of their autonomy, dignity, or right of self-determination through the manipulation of symbols); psychological violence (one person driving another to suicide); and finally, quiet institutional violence, which operates when people are systematically denied access to social options open to others.

3. Definitions of Various Forms of Violence

The Government of Newfoundland and Labrador[5] defines the various types of violence as follows:

> **Physical Violence**

Physical violence occurs when someone uses a part of their body or an object to control a person's actions. Physical violence includes but is not limited to: (1) using physical force, which results in pain, discomfort, or injury; (2) hitting, pinching, hair-pulling, arm-twisting, strangling, burning, stabbing, punching, pushing, slapping, beating, shoving, kicking, choking, biting, force-feeding, or any other rough treatment; (3) assault with a weapon or other object; (4) threats with a weapon or object; (5) deliberate exposure to severe weather or inappropriate room temperatures; and (6) murder.

> **Sexual Violence**

Sexual violence occurs when a person is forced to take part in sexual activity unwillingly. Sexual violence includes but is not limited to: (a) touching in a sexual manner without consent (i.e., kissing, grabbing, or-fondling); (b) forced sexual intercourse; (c) forcing a person to perform sexual acts that may be degrading or painful; (d) beating sexual parts of the body; (e) forcing a person to view pornographic material or forcing participation in pornographic filming; (f) Using a weapon to force compliance; (g) exhibitionism; (h) making unwelcome sexual comments

---

4. Garver, *What is Violence*, 817–22.
5. Newfoundland and Labrador, "The Violence Prevention Initiative," 1–2.

or jokes and/or leering behaviour; (i) withholding sexual affection; (j) denial of a person's sexuality or privacy (watching); (k) denial of sexual information and education; (l) humiliating, criticizing, or trying to control a person's sexuality; (m) forced prostitution; (n) unfounded allegations of promiscuity and/or infidelity; and, (o) purposefully exposing the person to HIV/AIDS or other sexually transmitted infections.

➤ Emotional Violence

Emotional violence occurs when someone says or does something to make a person feel stupid or worthless. Emotional violence includes, but is not limited to: (a) name calling; (b) blaming all relationship problems on the person; (c) using silent treatment; (d) not allowing the person to have contact with family and friends; (e) destroying possessions; (f) jealousy; (g) humiliating or making fun of the person; (h) intimidating the person or causing fear to gain control; (i) threatening to hurt oneself if the person does not cooperate; (j) threatening to abandon the person; and, (k) threatening to have the person deported (if they are an immigrant).

➤ Psychological Violence

Psychological violence occurs when someone uses threats and causes fear in a person to gain control. Psychological violence includes, but is not limited to: (a) threatening to harm the person or her/his family if she or he leaves; (b) threatening to harm oneself; (c) threats of violence; (d) threats of abandonment; (e) stalking/criminal harassment; (f) destruction of personal property; (g) verbal aggression; (h) socially isolating the person; (j) not allowing access to a telephone; (k) not allowing a competent person to make decisions; (l) inappropriately controlling the person's activities; (m) treating a person like a child or a servant; (n) withholding companionship or affection; or (o) use of undue pressure to: sign legal documents, not seek legal assistance or advice, move out of the home, make or change a legal will or beneficiary, make or change an advance health care directive, give money or other possessions to relatives or other caregivers, or do things the person doesn't want to do.

➤ Spiritual Violence

Spiritual (or religious) violence occurs when someone uses a person's spiritual beliefs to manipulate, dominate, or control the person. Spiritual violence includes, but is not limited to: (a) not allowing the person to follow her or his preferred spiritual or religious tradition; (b) forcing a spiritual or religious path or practice on another person; (c) belittling or making fun of a person's spiritual or religious tradition, beliefs, or practices; and (d) using one's spiritual or religious position, rituals, or practices to manipulate, dominate, or control a person.

➤ Cultural Violence

Cultural violence occurs when a person is harmed as a result of practices that are part of her or his culture, religion, or tradition. Cultural violence includes but is not limited to committing "honor" or other crimes against women in some parts of the world, where women especially may be physically harmed, shunned, maimed, or killed for: (a) falling in love with the "wrong" person; (b) seeking divorce; (c) infidelity or committing adultery; (d) being raped; (e) practicing witchcraft; and (f) being older. Cultural violence may take place in some of the following ways: (i) lynching or stoning; (ii) banishment; (iii) abandonment of an older person at hospital by family; (iv) female circumcision; (v) rape-marriage; (vi) sexual slavery; and (vii) murder.

➤ Economic Violence

Economic violence occurs when financial extortion, wages of elderly, confiscating, paying below a living wage, requiring long hours of work, unsafe work situations, or forcing employees to use or buy company materials at exorbitant prices are practiced.

➤ Violence and Conflict

What is conflict? Conflict is from the Latin word *conflictus,* which means striking together with force. It occurs when one's actions or beliefs are unacceptable to—and hence resisted by—the other.[6] Conflicts occur in dyads, groups, or larger societal structures. Why do conflicts arise? At the national or global level, they may be caused by territorial disputes, ethnic and religious animosities, ideological and power struggles, social injustice, search for statehood, trade and market competitions, and contests over economic resources, among others. In the complex of interrelations within our immediate setting, conflicts may be caused by misunderstanding, misperception, and miscommunication; difficult behaviors; unmet expectations; incompatibility of ideas, opinions, beliefs, values, goals, and interests; distrust; competition over material resources;

---

6. Forsyth, *Human Aggression,* 15.

coercion; defense of honor; desire for revenge; need for attention and appreciation; intolerance; a lack of empathy; and power struggles in group situations, among others.

For Mitchell, a conflict is any situation in which two or more parties (however defined or structured) perceive that they possess mutually incompatible goals.[7] Any conflict consists of three components:

- ✓ Incompatibility: actors or parties think that the realization of one or more of their objectives is blocked by the other party's attempt to reach its own respective goal. Mitchell's conflict triangle model takes the occurrence of goal incompatibility as the starting point from which a conflict becomes manifest and each of the three elements begin to interact. Goals are defined as consciously desired future outcomes, conditions, or end states, which often have intrinsic values for members of particular parties.

- ✓ Conflicting attitudes: those psychological states (common attitudes, emotions, and evaluations as well as patterns of perception and misperception). There is a difference between emotional orientations (feelings of anger, distrust, resentment, scorn, fear, envy, or suspicion of the intentions of others) and cognitive processes (such as stereotyping or making fun of someone/some group)

- ✓ Conflict behavior: conflict behavior consists of actions undertaken by one party in any situation of conflict aimed at the opposing party with the intention of making that opponent abandon or modify its goals.[8] It can take on a wide variety of forms in addition to "physical damage to people and property." Conflict behavior includes all actions undertaken by one conflict party aimed at the opposing party with the intention of making that adversary abandon or modify its goals. Databases of conflict range from demonstrations and strikes to self-destructive strategies—such as hunger-strikes or suicide—but can also include more subtle forms of "everyday resistance" such as sabotage, disobedience, or non-cooperation. Violence is often conceptualized as a degree of conflict: as something that occurs automatically when conflict

---

7. Mitchell, *Structure of International Conflict*, 17.
8. Mitchell, *Structure of International Conflict*, 29.

reaches a certain temperature, the measurements for which are not yet precise and agreed upon.

4. What Prevents People from Resolving Conflicts?

There are many factors that hinder people from resolving conflicts. One of them is the experience of strong emotions such as fear, pride, anger, and the desire for revenge. When these powerful emotions are present, it is difficult to process information objectively. Indifference or apathy is another obstacle to conflict resolution. People sometimes show a lack of concern or interest, whether deliberately or not, for the situation. Others feel helpless or hopeless, perhaps, because the situation is discouraging or the other party is a person of authority. The lack of communication between disputants—or the absence of it altogether—may also be a hindering factor in conflict resolution. There are also situations when conflicts are not resolved because of provocations from sympathizers who, whether intentionally or not, "fan the fire" and aggravate the situation. There are also situations when people perceive the problem-solving process tedious and stressful and hence shun it. Dialoguing with an adversary also requires a great amount of courage and we often find ourselves lacking in audacity to face the "enemy."

5. Group Formation and Violent Action

Any meaningful study of violent conflict should consist of a systematic analysis of identity group formation, dynamics of interaction, and collective action. This is not to say that identity or identity differences are causing violent conflict; rather, identity boundary drawing is a central aspect of the mobilizing of support for armed conflict in the world. Violent conflicts are complex phenomena that foster interaction among actors with distinct identities, needs, and interests. Three questions arise when we take this process of group formation and violent action seriously: what makes a group? Why and how does a group resort to violence? Why and how do they (not) stop?

6. Identity and Violence

Identity, broadly defined, is the answer to the question, "Who or what are you?" The enormous range of answers to this question call for more precision. Are we free to define who we are? How do context and structure, roles and norms, and discourses and symbolic orders impact our self-understanding? Why is it that some identities come to dominate others?

➤ Explain key factors to understanding identity

Identities are real (perceived, imagined).

Identities live through language (both rational and symbolic narratives).

Identities are dynamic (degrees of fluidity).

Identities are relational (not individual).

All identities function similarly.[9]

➤ Explain 10 Key Drivers to Understand Multiple Identities & Power Dynamics

All societies have a hierarchy of identities

Many identities seek to reproduce themselves

Many identities seek to protect their interests

Many identities exist through institutions

Many identities are networked

All identities have implicit boundaries of reference

Normative identities become subconscious

Normative identities carry privileges

Identity similarities attract & identity differences divide

Divisions lead to exclusions, which, in turn, can lead to radicalizations and various forms of violence (outer, inner, apathy).[10]

➤ Understanding the key Conceptual & Practical Solving Tools

Emphasize face-to-face encounters are essential for human transformation

Change the boundaries of reference to realign identity dynamics (creating new spaces, new institutions, and new networks)

Work at the interstices of identities: Balancing similarities & differences

Emphasize common and broader shared identities rather than narrower dividing ones. Notice tensions as source of dynamic growth before they turn into conflicts![11]

7. Conflict Analysis

Conflict mapping is a technique that is used to show the relationships of the conflict actors to each other and to the prioritized conflict. Conflict maps clarify where the power lies and where an organization is situated

---

9. Brodeur, "Identity and Power Dynamics," 1.
10. Brodeur, "Identity and Power Dynamics," 1.
11. Brodeur, "Identity and Power Dynamics," 1.

among the conflict parties. These maps are helpful in identifying potential allies and opportunities to intervene.

Basic questions that will help to map conflict:

➤ **Who are the main parties?**

➤ **What is happening between them?**

➤ **What is happening within them? (Distinguish positions, interests, needs, fears)**

➤ **Who are the secondary parties (or stakeholders)?**

➤ **What is happening between them all?**

➤ **What is happening between the parties and the external environment?**

➤ **Where are you on the map?**

In order to understand the causes of violence, there is need to reflect on why there are so many conflicts and violation of human rights among religions in Nigeria. The causes of violence are: systematic injustice, no rule of law, law as applied discrimination, religious bigotry, and poverty. Oppressive structures—such as patriarchy and legal structures that are not applied uniformly—become obstacles to the attainment of peace. Such obstacles are found in all institutions in a society: the family, politics, church, school, and economics.

This understanding of causes of violence will start with personal or communal examples. The following questions will be answered by the participants: is there violence in your community? What kind of violence? Have you or one of your friends ever had to deal with violence yourself, physical or mental? How did you deal with it? What can you do to stop violence in your community and create a more peaceful environment for everyone in your community? Role play can be used. How can you implement some points of peace into your mosque and church? Have you had the experience of religious violence? What are the implications in our lives and in our community? Bring newspapers reporting violence and it is implications. Do exercises on conditioning: "Are we conditioned to be a violent community?"

8. Reasons for Violence in Nigeria

Much religiously inspired violence is often motivated by social injustices, unresolved frustrations, endless suffering, powerlessness, and hopelessness. Similarly, politicization of religion emerges when secular regimes fail to establish the rule of law or when injustice lingers for too long. It builds hatred and thereby becomes the source of violence among people. The rationale of initiating violence is not always geared to defeat the enemy but also to gain psychological victory and publicity. Religious violence is often provoked by the greed that promotes various forms of inequalities and institutionalized injustices in the economic, political, ethnic, and religious spheres in the society. Consequently, the situation leads to feelings of hopelessness, hatred, prejudice, and the desire for vengeance.

The first reason is related to **economics**. Despite the vast wealth created by the exploitation of impressive petroleum resources, the benefits have been slow to trickle down to the majority of the population who, since the 1960s, have increasingly been forced to abandon their traditional agricultural practices. In spite of the large number of skilled, well-paid Nigerians who have been employed by the oil corporations, the majority of Nigerians have become poorer. There is a highly unequal distribution of wealth in Nigeria with 66 percent of the population falling below the poverty line of one dollar a day. This puts it among the twenty poorest countries in the world.

The second reason is the **lack of good governance** and **social structures** that deal effectively with political, social, and economic inequalities in Nigerian societies. This has resulted in a culture of intolerance, where people lack mutual trust and respect. Nigerian leaders have acted in their own selfish interests, in total disregard for existing rules and laid-down procedures.

Socioeconomic causes can lead to religious violence. Explain the roots of religious fundamentalism: human security, including such psychological factors such as fear of scarcity, lack of economic stability, and the absence of an appropriate sense of belonging.

Religion as a powerful instrument in the hands of those who use it. It is a negative power when it is used to oppress and exploit others. Immediate and visible factors that generate religious violence are:

- ✓ Religious intolerance
- ✓ Fundamentalism
- ✓ Disparaging preaching and stereotyping
- ✓ Proselytizing
- ✓ Government patronage, religious preferentialism and marginalization
- ✓ Sensationalism in media reportage
- ✓ The use of religious symbols. The use of religious symbols is increasingly becoming a source of religious conflict and violence in Nigeria
- ✓ The lack of recognition of one another
- ✓ Campaigns of hatred and blackmail
- ✓ The lack of genuine desire to understand each other's belief and culture
- ✓ Extremism

Questions for Comprehension, Analysis, and Reflection

1. What are the types of violence you can identify within your context?
2. Name the causes of religious violence in your community.
3. Can we have a community free of violence?
4. What are the needed actions religious leaders must take to create a non-violent community?

Conclusion

There are many reasons for the increase of violence in Nigeria. Most of them are not religious in nature. Yet, at times, there are interpretations of religion—especially amongst Christians and Muslims—that foster an understanding of one's religious tradition in such a way that it leads to religion being used for violent ends. There are conflicting interpretations within each religious community, as well as across them, as to whether or not it is acceptable to promote or use violence in the name of religion. Those conflicts of interpretation are at the heart of the problem as much as economic and political reasons.

Examples of Required Readings

Anderson, Paul N. "Religion and Violence: From Pawn to Scapegoat." In *Sacred Scriptures, Ideology, and Violence*, edited by J. Harold Ellen, 265–283. Vol 1. of *The Destructive Power of Religion: Violence in Judaism, Christianity, and Islam*. Westport, CT: Praeger, 2004.

Appleby, Scott R. *The Ambivalence of the Sacred: Religion, Violence, and Reconciliation*. Lanham, MD: Rowman & Littlefield, 2000.

Cavanaugh, William. "Does Religion Cause Violence?" *Harvard Divinity Bulletin* 25.2/3 (2007) 22–35.

Ellens, Harold. "Introduction: the Destructive Power of Religion." In *Sacred Scriptures, Ideology, and Violence*, edited by J. Harold Ellens, 2–9. Vol. 1 of *The Destructive Power of Religion: Violence in Judaism, Christianity, and Islam*. Westport, CT: Praeger, 2004.

Juergensmeyer, Mark. "Is Religion the Problem?" *Hedgehog Review* 6.1 (2004) 21–33.

Juergensmeyer, Mark. *Terror in the Mind of God: The Global Rise of Religious Violence*. Berkeley: University of California Press, 2000.

McCutcheon, Russell T. "Myth." In *Guide to the Study of Religion*, edited by Willi Braun and Russell McCutcheon, 190–208. New York: Cassell. 2000.

Sen, Amartya. "The Violence of Illusion." In *Identity and Violence: The Illusion of Destiny*, 1–17. New York: Penguin, 2006.

Witte, Griff. "Violence: Its Source Is Not Always What It Seems." *Nieman Reports* (2007) 6.

Chapter 2: Theories of Violence

Introduction

This chapter provides various theories of violence by exploring the most prominent theories of violence in general rather than those of violence in particular. It maintains that the individual and collective pathways to violence require nothing less than a theoretical framework that incorporates a reciprocal integration of interpersonal, institutional, and structural violence.

Learning Aims and Objectives

At the end of this chapter, the participant will be able to:

1. Understand, identify, and evaluate different theories of religious violence.

2. Explain how the theory of violence used dictates the response to religious violence.

3. Identify religious violence as intentional, learned behavior designed to achieve power and control over another.

4. Acquire critical tools for evaluating theories, rhetoric, and evidence about religious violence.

5. See the limits of their respective applications as part of learning about the challenges facing peace, peacebuilding, and peace education itself.

Learning Activities

Lead a brainstorming session about theories of violence. Ask each of the participants to share their ideas randomly or in turn. The ideas are not criticized or discussed, but participants may build on ideas voiced by others. The questions for brainstorming are:

1. What common explanations have you heard about why religious violence occurs?

2. What explanations can you imagine people might give for why religious violence occurs?

3. Write down each answer as they are offered on a flipchart or chalkboard without any comments, notes, or questions for 5–7 minutes. After discussing the ideas, post the list on the wall or leave the list on the chalkboard so it is visible throughout the training.

Content

1. Theories of Violence

Clearly articulate and explain the following theories of violence.

➤ **Social Theories**

Social theories of violence can be grouped into several categories. The following categories will serve to illustrate and explain this approach.

Social and political change

Families, communities, and nations often evolve in ways that benefit some of their members and work to the disadvantage of others. Societies have created a variety of mechanisms—including elections, courts, and mediation—with the intent of facilitating change and eliminating injustice. But such mechanisms have their limitations. For example, courts create a need for either education or money to guarantee a fair hearing of a grievance. Violence is often explained as the only alternative for individuals and groups who do not see a nonviolent way to break out of a position of disadvantage.

Social Stability

Many of the mechanisms that serve the goal of social change have been created by a powerful elite with the goal of ensuring that change happens gradually and does not threaten their privileges. In this case, violence is seen as a natural response when a social hierarchy is threatened.

Socialization.

Children must be taught the expectations of their social group and must be helped to acquire the skills and understandings to take their place in the group. Violence may result when children do not acquire the necessary skills to handle interpersonal relationships, manage their own lives, and become economically self-sufficient. Effective socialization requires more than just the presence of adults who can teach skills. Farrington, for example, found deficiencies in the parenting experiences of violent adolescents; their childhood was characterized by harsh discipline, lack of nurturance, and poor supervision.[12]

Stress Management

Since there can be no such thing as a stress-free society, every social group must manage stress; companionship, play, and sex are among the aspects of social life that can serve a stress-management function. Linsky, Bachman, and Straus documented a connection between stress levels and the level of violence.[13] When stress management fails—either through decreasing effectiveness of familiar approaches or through increases in stress beyond the group's capacity—it seems that violence is among the likely outcomes.

Conflict Theories

Conflict theorists suggest that conflict is a positive force in society and that human groups must handle conflicts in productive ways. Sprey described the informal mechanisms that traditional community and family structures offered for the management of conflict.[14] For example, in the extended/multigenerational household, any conflict between intimates could be mediated by others who were not as intensely involved. Neighborhoods also offered ready access to others who could assist with a family (or other) dispute. Lacking the support of concerned others, disputants may use violence in an attempt to achieve resolution.

Social Control

Social control is another essential function. A society needs ways to ensure that its members do not harm each other. Violence, from this perspective, demonstrates failures in the control process. Research supports this theory: Shaw and McKay identified a high correlation between

---

12. Farrington, "Childhood Aggression and Adult Violence," 5–29.
13. Linsky et al., *Stress, Culture, and Aggression*, 22–72.
14. Sprey, "On the Management of Conflict in Families," 110–19.

ethnic heterogeneity, low socioeconomic status, residential mobility, and delinquency.[15] They theorized that neighborhoods lacking stable, cohesive networks of informal social control experience more problems with youth gangs and violence. Formal social control is also associated with violence; Wilson has pointed out that law enforcement is inconsistent in "ecological niches" characterized by drug sales and high crime.[16]

FUNCTIONALIST CONTRIBUTIONS

Functional analysis has identified many factors that may help to explain contemporary violence. Many people consider violence to be a necessity that comes into play when the various mechanisms of society do not address social needs. High stress levels, rapid technological, social, and economic change, and conflict between social groups make sense as contributors to violence. These understandings of violence have the advantage of leading directly to action; if a society knows what is broken, it can organize attempts to fix it. On the other hand, a functionalist approach can point to so many possible areas of change that the result is essentially a "laundry list" of problems and proposed solutions. The theory does not explain how to set priorities or coordinate interventions.

1. Constructionist Theories

Constructionist theories of violence focus on discourse themes—shared meanings—that either justify violent acts or else redefine violence so that it is acceptable behavior. Three such discourse themes are:

Gender and Family Violence

Violence is strongly associated with gender; males not only commit more violent acts, they are also the primary consumers of entertainment with violent themes.[17] The constructionist theory of gendered violence suggests that men perpetuate this pattern in their discourse.[18]

The Violent Society

15. Shaw and Mackay, *Juvenile Delinquency and Urban Areas*, 487–88.
16. Wilson, *Truly Disadvantaged*, 12–27.
17. Kruttschnitt, "Gender and Interpersonal Violence," 293–376.
18. Blumenthal et al., *Justifying Violence*, 35–65.

In contemporary society, the young are still being trained to be killers; video games have enabled the child in the 1990s to develop perceptual skills and eye-hand coordination in preparation for space wars as well as street warfare. But these young people are also growing up in a world where cooperative efforts are increasingly valued and violence is increasingly punished. As the number of arrests for violence is increasing, the number of individuals imprisoned for violence also increases. But the ideal remains the same. Toughness is valued, and the young know what really matters. The societal response—meeting violence with violence—does nothing to alter the theme.

Economic and Racial Segregation

Violence also seems to be more common among groups who are excluded from the mainstream.[19] A constructionist theory of such marginalization calls attention to differing views of opportunity and success. Among those who see themselves excluded from well-paying employment, success through nonviolent means seems to be based on luck.

2. System Theory

Systems theorists view all social interactions as somehow patterned in ways that regulate violence—along with all other forms of behavior. System levels are nested, and each level operates according to its own rules. Feedback processes enable each level to assess its effectiveness and to make the necessary modifications to continue functioning. Systems are always in a state of change, but the changes do not disturb the stability of the system. Understanding the processes, however, is not sufficient for planning and implementing more permanent change. Systems theorists believe that direct efforts to change any system element will fail; the system will restore the missing piece or replace it—often in a more exaggerated form. Making a long-term change in a system problem—such as violence—requires a coordinated approach that includes an understanding of how violence fits into the system. A complete systems analysis of violence[20] would locate sources of violence: (a) in the individuals; (b) in dyadic interactions as varied as infant/caregiver and teacher/student; and

---

19. Reiss and Roth, *Understanding and Preventing Violence*, 23–63.
20. See Straus, "General Systems Theory," 105–25, for a partial example.

(c) in family subsystems, neighborhoods, communities, ethnic and religious groups, and the larger society. Subsystem contributions would be seen as organized in ways that both encouraged violent acts and imposed limits on violence. The various system levels would be seen responding to changing resources, challenges, opportunities, and barriers. Above all, the analysis would demonstrate that various attempts to reduce or eliminate violence seem to have instead activated a "positive feedback loop" in which the problem appears to be getting worse.

3. The Stream of Theoretical Thought

The stream of theoretical thought is biocentric in character. It draws from the frustration-aggression hypo book. The three causal sequences are: the development of discontent; the politicization of discontent; and the actualization of discontent through violent action against political objects and actors.

4. The Ephemeral Gain Theory

The ephemeral gain theory emerges from elements of social psychology literature and an analysis of historical trajectories that are most likely to lead to political extremism. It is a combination of behaviors expressed in Nigeria today, such as: (1) the threat and fear of reversion to an earlier state of subordination; (2) perceptions of injustice leading to anger and blame, including a possible stereotyping of innocents; and (3) humiliation and shame. All three, separately or in some combination, can lead to extremist behavior.

5. The Elite Theory

The Elite theory of conflict is based on the assumption that ethnic wars are functional. Ethnic violence does not result from irrational and spontaneous eruptions of mass anger or frustration, but it is deliberately orchestrated and planned by elites and organizations to increase group cohesion and build a loyal support base. Elite theories of violence emphasize the ways in which leaders who fear losing power or new leaders trying to create own constituency may gamble for resurrection or rise to power by provoking ethnic conflict. Elite theory of conflict argues that ethnic violence is a political strategy to create, increase, or maintain group boundaries and political support.

OTHERS THEORIES

> *Jus* (or *ius*) ***ad bellum***

Jus (or *ius*) *ad bellum* is, the title given to the branch of law that defines the legitimate reasons a state may engage in war and focuses on certain criteria that render a war *just*.

> ***Jus in bello***

Jus in bello, by contrast, is the set of laws that come into effect once a war has begun. Its purpose is to regulate how wars are fought without prejudice to the reasons of how or why they had begun. So a party engaged in a war that could easily be defined as unjust would still have to adhere to certain rules during the prosecution of the war, as would the side committed to righting the initial injustice.

> **The *jus in bellum***

The *jus in bellum* requires a right authority to initiate force, a justifying cause, and a right intention toward the enemy.

> **The *jus in bello***

The *jus in bello* sets limits on who might legitimately be attacked (the idea of non-combatant immunity) and the means that could be legitimately employed (the principle of proportionality). This Western notion of the just war (*jus in bellum* and *jus in bello*) can be applied to Islamic notions of *jihad* (sacred struggle) and *qital* (fighting).

> **Exclusivism in Islam**

For many Muslims, *jihad* is a sacred struggle to establish an Islamic rule by means other than self-discipline, persuasion, and example. They believe that *jihad* as a defensive military action is a collective duty of the Muslim community and *jihad* can be carried out by the *khalif* or *imam*—the religious and political leader of the Islamic community—depending on the period of Islamic history and the school of Islamic jurisprudence (*madhahib*). There are several Qur'anic verses where the word *jihad* has been interpreted as being synonymous with the words war and fighting, (Q 2:215; 8:41; 49:15; 61:11; 66:9). The most commonly cited verse used to justify the equation of *jihad* with violence reads, "Strive (*Jihad*) your utmost in the cause of Allah with your property and your persons" (61:11). The Qur'an also uses *jihad* in chapter 22, "And strive in his cause as you ought to strive" (Q 22:78).

> ➤ **Exclusivism in Christianity**

For many Christians, "Jesus is the only way to salvation." This is based on multiple Bible passages, including: "For God so loved the world that he gave his only begotten Son, so that everyone that believes in him may not die but have eternal life. Whoever believes in the Son is not judged; but whoever does not believe has already been judged, because he has not believed in God's only Son" (John 3:16, 18). This notion has been used for proselytizing, violent conversation, and justifying economic, environmental, and military oppression.

> ➤ **The Yoruba concept of violence:**

Bo ba baa ko pa, tioba baa kobu lese. That is, kill him or destroy him (Physically or spiritually).

Questions for Comprehension, Analysis, and Reflection

1. What is the relevance of the theories of negative peace, positive peace, and structural violence to peace?
2. Think of examples of negative peace and positive peace in your own context. What religious initiatives have there been to promote negative and/or positive peace?

Conclusion

The understandings of these theories of violence, showing the ways in which violent acts are linked, are precious tools for reducing or eliminating violence. In fact, many policymakers, teachers, social workers, and religious leaders familiar with these theories would be expected to be more effective in their daily practices.

Examples of Required Readings

Barak. "A Critical Perspective on Violence." In *Advancing Critical Criminology: Theory and Application*, edited by Walter S. DeKeseredy and Barbara Perry, 115–18. Lexington, 2006.

Hashmi, Sohail H. "Jihad." In vol. 1 of *Encyclopedia of Politics and Religion*, edited by Robert Wuthnow, 425–26. Washington, DC: Congressional Quarterly, 1998. http://www.cqpress.com/context/articles/epr_jihad.html

Hector, Avalos. "Previous Theories of Religious Violence." In *Fighting Words: the Origins of Religious Violence*. Amherst, NY: Prometheus, 2005.

Manus, I. Midlarsky. *Origins of Political Extremism: Mass Violence in the Twentieth Century and Beyond*, 1–69. Cambridge: Cambridge University Press, 2011.

Ozcelik, Sezai. "Islamic Peace Paradigm and Islamic Peace Education: The Study of Islamic Nonviolence in Post-September 11 World." 2007. http://lass.purduecal.edu/cca/jgcg/2007/fa07/jgcg-fa07-ozcelik-ogretir.htm.

Chapter 3: Sacred Texts and Stories Fostering Violence

Introduction

This chapter focuses on many passages in the sacred texts and stories from Yoruba Religion, Islam, and Christianity that foster religiously motivated violence. It uses Kellie's three approaches to reinterpret these sacred texts.

Learning Aims and Objectives

At the end of this chapter, participants will be able to:

1. Familiarize themselves with primary sacred texts and stories that deal with violence.

2. Awaken themselves to the various ways in which violence is viewed in these texts and stories (e.g., holy violence, apocalyptic violence, and violence against bodies).

3. Engender critical reflection on the study of sacred texts and stories, as well as challenge them to reflect upon the ways in which this literature has impacted modern understandings of religion, sacred texts, and violence.

4. Develop their own view(s) of the subject matter through reading primary and secondary sources, in-class discussion, and independent research.

Learning Activities

Ask the participants in group to express their views on the following statements:

1. Religion is the major source of violence. Therefore, if we seek a more peaceful world, we should abolish religion.

2. Religion is not a source of violence. It may be used by manipulative leaders to motivate people to wage wars precisely because it inspires

people to heroic acts of self-sacrifice, but religion itself teaches us to love and forgive, not to hate and fight.

3. Their religion, yes; our religion, no. We are for peace. They are for war.

Write down each answer as they are offered on a flipchart or chalkboard without any comments or notes. After discussing the ideas, post the list on the wall or leave the list on the chalkboard so it is visible throughout the training.

Content

1. Oral Curses and Maledictions in Yoruba Religion

"*Epepojuohun to nu lo, abere so nu a gbeseeresita,*" meaning "The curse is out of proportion to the lost article, a needle is lost, the owner brings out his/her magic wand."[21] The proverb cautions against over-reaction to issues which may cause social disharmony, conflict, or even war.

2. Qur'anic Quotes Supporting the Use of Violence

God promises to "cast terror into the hearts of those who are bent on denying the truth; strike, then, their necks!" (Q 8:12); God instructs his Muslim followers to kill unbelievers, to capture them, to ambush them (Q 9:5); "Strike terror into God's enemies, and your enemies" (Q 8:60); fighting in the way of Allah (Q 2:244; 4:34).

3. Bible Quotes Supporting the Use of Violence

The Lord is a man of war (Exod 15:3). "I will make my arrows drunk with blood and my sword shall devour flesh" (Deut 32:42). We then turn to the full orgy of militarism, enslavement, and race war in the books of Joshua and Judges. Moses himself reputedly authorized this campaign when he told his followers that once they reached Canaan, they must annihilate all the peoples they find in the cities specially reserved for them (Deut 20:16–18).

Jesus said to them, "But now, if you have a purse, take it, and also a bag; and if you don't have a sword, sell your cloak and buy one." The disciples said, "See, Lord, here are two swords." "That is enough," he replied

---

21. Owomoyela, *Yoruba Proverbs*, 1.

(Luke 22:36, 38). Jesus made a whip out of cords, and drove all from the temple area, both sheep and cattle; he scattered the coins of the money changers and overturned their tables (John 2:15). "Do not suppose that I have come to bring peace to the earth. I did not come to bring peace, but a sword" (Matt 10:34). "He has sent me to bring good news to the poor, to proclaim liberty to the captives and to set the oppressed free" (Luke 4:18).

4. Reinterpreting Sacred Texts and Stories Fostering Violence

In many sacred texts and stories, there are passages that seem to condone violence. Many exist in both the Bible and the Qur'an. If a text contains violent imagery or commands, those who take the text as authoritative—because "God Said It. I Believe It. That Settles It."—are prone to act violently. Alongside destructive images and models, there are other texts that express a different and even opposed viewpoint within the same tradition. The Yoruba contrasting proverbs are also enlightening. They stress mercy, reconciliation, and peace. How does one decide which is more determinative? In any given situation, which is more likely to shape our behavior and attitudes? Each of the two traditions has a slightly different approach to understanding its sacred scriptures as authority. Within each tradition exists a wide range of possible responses to images, worldviews, and pronouncements within sacred texts.

> **Using Kellie's Three Approaches to Reinterpret Sacred Texts**

In *The Bible Made Me Do It: Text, Interpretation, and Violence*, Andrew Kellie describes the role of sacred scriptures in shaping violent attitudes and behavior. He points to the fact that texts do not "do" anything in themselves; it is only in the dynamic encounter between the text and a specific reader, in a specific community, or in a particular historical and cultural context that individuals engage, interpret, internalize, and ultimately act on those texts. Some observations and categories from psychological theory may help in our understanding of how sacred texts may come to be interpreted to condone violence, but also assist in reinterpreting these sacred texts.

✓ *Kellie's First Approach: On Object Relations*

In order to develop a coherent ego or identity that is able to relate appropriately to the world, the developing individual engages in processes of integration and differentiation, identifying with desirable traits and rejecting undesirable ones. In the early stages, the psyche employs a strategy of splitting, separating the "good" qualities from the "bad." These elements are integrated through processes of identification and introjection or rejected and projected onto others.[22]

> ✓ Kellie's Second Approach: On Idealization and Religion

How it is that religion is able to be at one and the same time the source of profound human transformation and maturity and a source of hostility and aggression? James W. Jones suggests that part of the answer can be found in the psychological dynamic of idealization.[23] Idealization enables a child to defend against a perceived failure of the mother to provide adequately for his or her needs by splitting the good and bad aspects of the mother and internalizing the bad while projecting the good outward onto the mother. This psychic relationship between the needy and vulnerable self and a wholly good external object provides the psychic energy for later distinctions of the sacred and the profane in religious experience.

Every encounter with the "sacred"—be it sacred experience, sacred mountain, sacred image, or sacred text—is linked to and colored by this archaic experience of idealization. The difference between transformative encounters and destructive encounters lies in whether the individual can move beyond idealization to genuine encounter or whether he or she remains caught in the grip of idealization and projection.

The idealization of a sacred text can offer the opportunity for personal transformation. A new perspective or possibility may be offered through reading and responding to the text. One has the opportunity to step outside one's own perceptions and to be addressed through the text. If the idealization of the text does not move into a more complex and realistic understanding, it may lead to religious fanaticism instead. If one's own text is perfect and all-good—without regard for inconsistencies, varied interpretations, and contextual factors in its development and transmission—then all the weaknesses, negativity, and inadequacy that might otherwise be discernable in the tradition are projected onto others.

Given its deep roots in object relations and incomplete development, archaic idealization affects more than just the relationship with a sacred text. Although the text may be an important component of a religious

---

22. Hamilton, *Self and Others*, 31–50.
23. Jones, "Terror and Transformation," 12.

tradition, it is only part of that tradition. An individual who idealizes the text is likely to bring the same dynamics to the whole life of the religious community—to its ideology, its leaders, and its self-identifications.

✓ *Kellie's Third Approach: On the Way of Action: Personality Theory*

The "Way of Action" (corresponding to the Myers-Briggs Sensing-Thinking type) may be applied, for our purposes in this book, in two characteristic ways that seem the most pertinent in relation to sacred writings: the tendency toward religious self-assertion and the tendency toward religious paranoia. These represent two inadequate responses to the disjunction between desired perfection and lived ambiguity.

The "Way of Action" focuses on identifying and doing the righteous thing, and those inclined to this approach seek to live pure lives in the midst of a less than pure world. Religious self-assertion eliminates doubt and contradiction by asserting that my will and God's will are one and the same; my understanding is God's understanding and my interpretation of God's sacred text is the same as God's voice. God exists to fulfill my needs and desires. If I do what God wants, God is compelled to do what I want. In the shared Jewish and Christian biblical Deuteronomy code, with its promise of direct reward for righteous conduct, this attitude seems to be validated. The same is true in terms of the Qur'an.

Religious paranoia, on the other hand, deals with the disjunction of desire and reality by the now familiar defense mechanisms of splitting and projection. Those on the inside are viewed positively as bearers of truth and righteousness. Those on the outside become the enemy, the agents of the devil, the "Evil Empire" or "Axis of Evil."

However, there is no simple line to be drawn between sacred text and religious violence. As much as religious leaders might want to believe that people base their lives and actions directly on sacred texts, the reality is not that simple. While sacred writings may well be employed by religious (and political) leaders to bolster and defend a course of action or set of attitudes, they do not in themselves generally give rise to those attitudes or actions.[24]

In *When Religion Becomes Evil*, Charles Kimball identifies five factors that may indicate a propensity for religiously-based violence: absolute truth claims, blind obedience, establishing the "ideal" time, the

---

24. Kellie and Rollins, *Psychological Insight*, 21.

end justifying any means, and declaring holy war.[25] None of these factors depends on whether violent images or expressions appear in the group's scriptures. Three of the factors, however, may hint at how sacred scriptures could enter the mix. When a group makes absolute truth claims, it will often make them with reference to sacred writings. Yet it is important that truth is claimed not only for the writings themselves but also for how leaders and authoritative teachers interpret those writings. Teachings considered authoritative may not only depart from other accepted interpretations but also the strength of the group's sense of identity may be reinforced precisely by that departure. We can easily recognize the dynamics of extreme idealization at work, one way to deal with ambiguity and imperfection.

Questions for Comprehension, Analysis, and Reflection

1. What are the types of violence you can identify within your sacred texts?
2. What are the difficulties in reinterpreting sacred texts dealing with violence?
3. What are the needed actions religious leaders must take to create a nonviolent community?

Conclusion

This chapter provides the interpretation of *sacred texts and stories* and describes the role of sacred scriptures in shaping violent attitudes and behaviors. At the same time, it gives its alternatives as the source of profound human transformation and maturity.

Examples of Required Readings

Assman, Jan. "No God but God: Exclusive Monotheism and the Language of Violence." In *Of God and Gods: Egypt, Israel, and the Rise of Monotheism*, 106–25. Madison: University of Wisconsin Press, 2008.
Boyer, Pascal. "Why Doctrines, Exclusion and Violence?" In *Religion Explained: The Evolutionary Origins of Religious Thought*, 265–97. New York: Basic, 2001.

25. Kimball, *When Religion Becomes Evil*, 35.

Brown, Michael Joseph. *What They Don't Tell You: A Survivor's Guide to Biblical Studies.* Louisville, KY: Westminster John Knox, 2000.
Collins, John J. *Does the Bible Justify Violence?* Facets Series. Minneapolis: Fortress, 2005.
Firestone, Reuven. *Jihad: The Origin of Holy War in Islam.* New York: Oxford University Press, 1999.
Kinball, Charles. *When Religion Becomes Evil.* San Francisco: Harper, 2002.
Nelson-Pallmeyer, Jack. *Is Religion Killing Us? Violence in the Bible and the Qur'an.* Harrisburg, PA: Trinity, 2003.
Owomoyela, O. *Yoruba Proverbs.* Lincoln: University of Nebraska, 2005.
Schwartz, Regina. "Inventing Identity." In *The Curse of Cain: The Violent Legacy of Monotheism,* 15–38 Chicago: Chicago University, 1997.
Selengut, Charles. *Sacred Fury: Understanding Religious Violence.* Walnut Creek, CA: AltaMira, 2003.

Chapter 4: Breaking the Cycles of Violence

Introduction

The purpose of this chapter is to provide religious leaders with the foundation for understanding the cycle of violence and how it traps people in relationships. Knowing how the cycle of violence works will aid participants in recognizing and preventing potentially abusive behaviors and actions.

Learning Aims and Objectives

1. Develop a greater awareness of peace in their life
2. Understand the process of breaking the cycles of violence
3. Understand the doctrine of Islamic and Christian violence
4. Acquire more skills to break the cycles of violence
5. Acquire skills and understanding to deconstruct the doctrine of violence
6. Able to use the three stages of conflict effectively: prevention (before conflict), resolution (during conflict), and reconstruction (after conflict).

Learning Activities

Have the group read the Ally Pledge: I promise not to be violent to my friends, my family, my lover, or to anyone else. If I am, I will talk about it in this group. I promise to act as an ally to break the cycle of violence. Create a situation of conflict in the group and see how each participant will adhere to the pledge.

Content

1. Breaking Free

In order to break free from these inherited patterns and thereby end unhelpful or destructive cycles, we must undergo a process that falls broadly into three steps. The steps can occur sequentially or simultaneously. The process can apply to specific issues of conflict or to broader parts of our lives.

> **The first step** is to take responsibility for the active or passive role we play in propagating a conflict.

> **The second** involves creating a space for self-reflection so that we can become aware of nocuous behaviors and beliefs that reinforce that role.

> **The third** is to release the source of grievances we hold on to so that we can be free to replace old habits and thinking with new life-affirming ones, thereby creating "positive cycles" around us and others. Releasing the source of grievance that would otherwise compel us to repeat and pass it on can only be done through a process of understanding and forgiveness.

We cannot force nor be forced to undertake the process that leads us to understanding and forgiveness. We can only become willing to do so, to allow ourselves to bring about this change in the perceptions that underpin our attitudes. To break the chain of fear and how we use it or it uses us.

- ✓ Fear of losing control leads us to try to take greater control—usually control of the future, in order.

- ✓ To feel that we will be safer. The need to dominate comes from fear. Become aware of old wounds connected with power struggles both within and without. Become aware of feeding fears with guilt and the self-attack of not being "strong enough, good enough, acknowledged enough, powerful enough, nice enough, brave enough, rich enough, beautiful enough, etc."—all of which keeps us in "victim mode." Victims usually feel helpless.

- ✓ To escape endless self-attack, strive to get free, and to feel more powerful by attacking someone else who is weaker. Notice fear-mongering and the feelings connected with it, whether it is our own or others who are doing the fear mongering (including our leaders, the press/TV, etc.).

- ✓ Break the chain of humiliation. Those who are humiliated and bullied become humiliators and bullies themselves, particularly when they find someone who appears weaker. We also bully ourselves and become self-created victims, using the voice of whichever authority figure originally dominated us internally, until we can forgive that person or persons. Be aware that every time we humiliate someone, we risk setting off a chain reaction; a time bomb thrown into the future. Humiliation is a particularly strong cause of vengeful behavior. Indeed it is not hard to see from our own lives, from school, family, and war. People, tribes, and nations who have been humiliated often humiliate when they regain power. The memory stays live if it is not healed. Most of the dictators and despots of the world were humiliated as children.

2. Deconstructing Religious Doctrines of Violence

▸ **Deconstruction of Proverbs about Violence in Yoruba Religion**

In response to "*Bo ba baa ko pa, tioba baa kobu lese*" ("Kill him or destroy him physically or spiritually"), the Yoruba people say: "*Epepojuohun to nu lo, abere so nu a gbeseeresita*" ("The curse is out of proportion to the lost article, a needle is lost, the owner brings out his/her magic wand").[26] The proverb cautions against over-reaction to issues which may cause social disharmony, conflict, or even war.

▸ **Deconstructing Jihad**

The response to *jihad* as violence is to emphasize its primary signification with a personal struggle against one's own evil inclinations and passions (*jihad-un-nafs*). *Jihad* has great significance in the lives of Muslims and is a healthy practice for the following reasons:

---

26. Owomoyela, *Yoruba Proverbs*, 1.

- ✓ *Jihad* is a sincere and noticeable effort for good, an all-true and unselfish striving for spiritual good.

- ✓ *Jihad* involves change in one's self and mentality. It may concern the sacrifice of material property, social class, and even emotional comfort solely for the salvation and worship of God alone.

- ✓ *Jihad* involves noticeable effort for righteousness. This means that the effort concentrated in the *jihad* is a step on the true and ultimate path of Islam (submission), the effort imposed on one's self. Thus *Jihad* is solely individual, self-centered, and self-interested. This effort is only the doing of good for salvation and pardon of God (Q 16:111; 3:30).

- ✓ *Jihadis* are to exceed in the sincere act of good deeds and refrain from doing sins (to commit adultery, to steal, to lie, to cheat, to insult people, to gossip, etc.).

- ✓ *Jihad* also includes the striving for and establishing of justice.

Understanding other forms of healthy practices in human struggle that have been mentioned in the Hadith literature are as follows:

- ✓ *jihad-un-nafs*, spiritual struggle for self-purification;

- ✓ *jihad-ul-lisan*; struggle to engage in a civil dialogue by way of the tongue;

- ✓ *jihad-ul-qalam*, intellectual struggle by the use of the pen;

- ✓ *jihad-ut-tarbiyya*, educational striving;

- ✓ *jihad-ud-da'wa*, spreading the message of monotheism and servitude to God with wisdom and goodly admonition;

- ✓ *jihad bi-l-maal*, struggle to part with one's wealth to help in a humanitarian cause;

- ✓ *jihad bi-s-sayf*, military engagement for self-defense and self-preservation when all peaceful methods fail to achieve a resolution to the dispute.

In conclusion, *jihad* in Islam is striving in the way of Allah by pen, tongue, hand, media, and, if inevitable, with arms. However, *jihad* in

Islam does not include striving for individual or national power, dominance, glory, wealth, prestige, or pride. The Qur'an and the Hadith—the Traditions of the Prophet Muhammad—show how the notion of *jihad* differs distinctly from the notion of holy war against unbelievers as is commonly understood today by some militant Islamists (as well as some of their foes). *Jihad*, in its original sense, simply meant striving in the path of God. Such striving could take various forms. Helping the poor and the distressed could equally be a form of *jihad* as could defense of the community from hostile attacks. Indeed, *jihad* as war was originally intended as defense of the faith and the community in the face of aggression. In normal times, relations between Muslims and people of other faiths were intended to be peaceful and violence the exception rather than the norm.

> ### Deconstructing Jesus the Only Way

The way. Truth and Life. No one comes to the Father but through me. Jesus is the one mediator of all humanity. Says Paul: "This is good and it pleases God Our Savior, who wants everyone to be saved and to come to know the truth. For there is one God, and there is one who brings God and mankind together, the man Christ Jesus, who gave himself to redeem all mankind" (1 Tim 2:3–6).

A less argumentative version of exclusivism is Universal Salvation, where the spirit of Christ infuses all religions and therefore all of humanity is saved. The concept that Jesus is the only way to salvation needs to be reconstructed. Lifting up other dimensions of Jesus is necessary. The concept of universalistic salvation is that the grace of Christ operates in and through other faith traditions, whether the adherents of these faiths know and acknowledge Christ or not. God sent Jesus Christ to die for all people (2 Cor 5:14), hence God's spirit brings salvation to all people, regardless of their religious affiliation. Persons holding this belief argue that the followers of other religions do not necessarily have to become Christians and evangelization is not necessary.

One alternative is to encourage following the life and example of Jesus, the Prince of Peace. Today, when all the people in the world are in a frantic search for peace, the Christian proclaims that Jesus Christ is "the Prince of Peace." The Christian church confesses in faith that prophecy to ancient Israel was realized with the coming of Jesus Christ, the Lord. To understand what is meant, I will first turn our attention to the meaning of peace in the biblical sense. When the Christian church proclaims that Jesus Christ is the Prince of Peace, it is not simply an affirmation of faith but also a clear call to action. As faithful followers of the Prince of Peace, Christians are called to be "*shalom*-makers." In the Sermon on the Mount, Jesus says, "Blessed are the peacemakers, for they shall be called sons of God" (Matt 5:9). *Shalom* is not only a gift of grace restored for us through Jesus Christ but also a task and responsibility entrusted to all who are rightly called "children of God." Peacemakers are not simply peaceable and peaceful persons; rather, they are those who actively and earnestly endeavor to "make" peace—*shalom*—here and now. The church and Christians are called to be signs and instruments of *shalom* in this world still torn with strife and violence, warped with injustice and oppression, and divided with enmity and hostility. Wherever *shalom* is broken and lost (such as in the Nigerian communities), that is where we can start to work. But first of all, to be "*shalom*-makers," it is imperative that we make our *shalom* with God. This idea needs to be expanded— how do we make our *shalom* with God? *Shalom* is also a gift from God in a child, as presented by the prophetic writings of the Hebrew Bible in Isaiah: "For to us a child is born, to us a son is given, and his name will be called, 'Wonderful Counsellor, Mighty God, Everlasting Father, Prince of Peace [*shalom*]'" (Isa 9:6). Although Christians often apply this text to Jesus, there are numerous areas in today's world that call for our effort as children of God in *shalom*-making.

It is important for the Christian church to work for the preservation and promotion of peace. At the same time, it is vitally important that the church lead the way for living in peace. Jesus called his followers "to love your enemies, to do good to those who hate you, bless those who abuse you, pray for those who abuse you" (Luke 6:27–28).

Christians are supposed to lead the way for all those persons who are denied their basic rights and are discriminated against because of their color, age, economic status, health/dis-ability, sexual orientation, gender, gender identity, ethnicity, national origin, religion, or creedal background, because they do not live in a world of *shalom*. That is, when a society is fragmented between the privileged and underprivileged, the powerful and powerless, there is no *shalom*. Or when political power is misused and abused for the benefit of the powerful and the freedom of the common people is suppressed and curtailed arbitrarily, there is no *shalom* in that society. By following the Prince of Peace, the Christian church is to be alert to the cries of the oppressed, the victims of political, economic, and social injustice and repression. They should work actively for the building of a society where justice and righteousness are fully realized for all, regardless of their social standing.

As followers of the Prince of Peace, Christians can be good leading examples by reducing all forms of discrimination, inequality, and domination. The domination of man over woman—and, inversely, the submission of woman to man—or the hatred and violence of one religious group against another are not the created order of *shalom* but rather a telling sign of the fallen state of humankind. When Christians proclaim the coming of Jesus Christ as Good News, we celebrate the beginning of the victory of the new creation over the old "fallen" order. As St. Paul says, "If anyone is in Christ, there is new creation" (2 Cor 5:17).

In the life of Jesus, God invites Christians to become lovers of peace. Anyone can practice nonviolence; everyone is called to practice nonviolence. God would not have invited us to this life of peacemaking if it were impossible. As Jesus revealed, God never calls us to violence. Over the centuries, the church has done a great disservice to God and humanity by blessing violence and warfare. The gospel is much stronger when it insists that nonviolence is not just an option, it is a commandment by Jesus to practice it. It is nonviolence to all people, even those who do not see Jesus as the only way, not just those we agree with. Even unto death, there is no greater gift than to lay down ones' life for friends.

Questions for Comprehension, Analysis, and Reflection

1. How are religious doctrines used for religious violence in your community?
2. What are the three stages of conflict and how do you apply them to a specific conflict in your community?

Conclusion

The cycle of violence needs to be broken in several theories and doctrines. Different policies can be implemented to try to decrease religious violence. However, even if the levels of violence in society and in local communities remain high, the cycle of religious violence can be broken by trying to affect the mechanisms of its reproduction.

Examples of Required Readings

Asseily, Alexandra. *Breaking the Cycles of Violence in Lebanon—and Beyond*. Brighton, East Sussex: Guerrand-Hermès Foundation for Peace Publishing, 2007.

Khanam, Farida. "Understanding Jihad." 12 Dec. 2005. http://www.allaahuakbar.net/JIHAAD/understanding_jihad_islam.htm2.

Morris, George. *Shalom: A Vision of a New World*. Nashville: Tidings, 1974. http://www.nationsencyclopedia.com/World-Leaders-

Mouhleb, N. "Jihad in Classical and Modern Islam, 2nd ed." *Journal of Peace Research* 44.1 (2007) 129.

Chapter 5: Prevention of Violence

Introduction

The most important outcome of focusing on violence and defining it clearly is the potential to understand its scale, forms, and causes more precisely and to enhance the scope to intervene and prevent its occurrence or to modify its effects. Prevention activities can be classified by the stage during which prevention takes place (primary, secondary, or tertiary prevention) as well as by its relationship to the population (universal, selective, or indicated interventions).

Learning Objectives

At the end of this chapter, participants will be able to:

1. Understand various prevention activities.
2. Acquire violence prevention and intervention strategies.
3. Plan for a safer and better interreligious community.

Learning Activities

Ask each participant to formulate prevention of violence measures based on their religion. Share their personal experiences in preventing religious violence and name the obstacles in applying those measures.

Content

1. Primary Prevention

The primary prevention of violence aims to stop violent incidents from occurring. Primary prevention is the most effective form of prevention but also the most difficult to achieve. Policy initiatives to address poverty and inequity could be classified as primary prevention activities in relation to violence, as could those directed at controlling the availability of firearms.

2. Secondary Prevention

Secondary prevention aims to minimize harm once a violent incident has occurred, focusing on immediate responses, such as emergency services (e.g., the treatment of sexually transmitted diseases following rape). Secondary prevention could also include intervening in situations of high risk, such as reducing the risk of sexual exploitation in refugee camps (or other internally displaced persons' settings) through better planning of facilities, better training of protection forces, and greater calls for accountability by those charged with the duty to protect victims of violence.

3. Tertiary Prevention

Tertiary prevention aims to treat and rehabilitate victims and perpetrators. Approaches focus on long-term care in the wake of violence, such as rehabilitation, reintegration, and attempts to lessen trauma or reduce the long-term disability associated with violence. Examples include psychological therapies for abused children; screening and support services for victims of intimate partner, domestic, or family violence; and specific recognition of the needs of survivors of torture.

4. Universal Interventions

Universal interventions addressing violence are aimed at the general population or groups within it (for example, those of a certain gender or age bracket) without regard for individual risk.

Questions for Comprehension, Analysis, and Reflection

1. What types of violence are you experiencing in your community and how can we prevent them?
2. Name two violence prevention approaches you have learned. Which one is most appropriate to the religious violence in your community?

Conclusion

Violence prevention education programs can be useful for raising awareness of violence, increasing knowledge of how to identify causes of violence, and avoiding religious actions and concepts leading to violence.

Examples of Required Readings

Fanslow, J. "Beyond Zero Tolerance: Key Issues and Future Directions for Family Violence Work in New Zealand." Wellington: Families Commission, 2005. http://www.familiescommission.org.nz/publications/research-reports/beyond-zero-tolerance.

Krug, E., et al. "World Report on Violence and Health." Geneva: World Health Organization, 2002. www.who.int/violence_injury_prevention/violence/world_report/en/full_en.pdf.

Unit III: Peace Education

The third unit is divided into four chapters. This unit defines the concepts and principles of peace and peace education, elaborates on an integrative theory of peace, and explains peacebuilding from various contexts, including religious texts and stories for fostering peace. While this unit is largely theoretical, it lays the foundation for the more practical elements of an interreligious peace education.

Chapter 1: Concepts and Principles of Peace

Introduction

This chapter considers multiple perspectives and definitions of its central concept of "peace." It develops a holistic understanding and awareness of peace. It further explores and considers the interrelationships between the personal, social, political, institutional, and ecological dimensions of peace.

Learning Objectives

At the end of this chapter, the participants will be able to:

1. Understand different definitions of peace.
2. Understand the breadth and scope of peace.
3. Develop their definition of peace.
4. Understand the concepts of peace from Yoruba Religion, Islam, and Christianity.

5. Integrate the values of peace into everyday life.
6. Acquire the skills of peace and to advocate for them.
7. Internalize these concepts in order to be able to effectively convey them to their members.

Learning Activities

Allow participants the opportunity to analyze their local situations and provide real, pragmatic responses to them. Let them determine what behaviors, attitudes, or situations are unfair in their own community. In groups, allow the participants to come up with a nonviolent solution to the problems they have identified cooperatively. Ask the following questions: (1) What is peace to you? Try to think of a definition or brainstorm a list of words that you think of when you hear the word "peace." (2) What is the relationship between peace and education? (3) What knowledge, skills, attitudes, and behaviors are necessary for peace?

Content

1. Definitions of Peace

Peace has been defined in a variety of ways. It has been defined as: (i) freedom from or cessation of the world of hostilities—that condition of a nation or community when it is not at war with another; (ii) a ratification or treaty of peace between two powers previously at war; (iii) freedom from civil commotion and disorder; (iv) public order and security; and (v) freedom from disturbance or perturbation.[1]

Peace has been defined as the "absence of violence." This is rather a narrow and negative definition. Peace should not only mean the absence of war but also violence in all forms, such as conflicts, threat to life, social degradation, discrimination, oppression, exploitation, poverty, injustice, and so on. Peace cannot be built as long as violent social structures exist in society. Naturally, such structures will lead people to act violently. For instance, an unfair system of resource distribution in a society would lead to the frustration of those who are deprived or get less. Frustration in turn could lead people to violence. Presence of all such obstructive and

---

1. Oxford English Dictionary, "Peace," 1.

indicative factors can be termed negative peace. Peace as the "absence of violence" means the absence of fistfights, firing, carpet bombing, or the use of nuclear war heads. This is a rather inadequate and incomplete definition. Peace is a state of mind. This is beautifully expressed in the Preamble to the UNESCO Constitution: "Since wars begin in the minds of men, it is in the minds of men that the defense of peace must be constructed."[2]

Peace is a way of life. Peace is not just the absence of war; it is a balance of a state of mind in which we feel good about ourselves, our lives, our families, our friends, our communities, and our future. Peace is about how we handle problems and how we get along with others. Peace is about community; it is about working together, encouraging each other, and helping each other to live better, more fulfilling lives. Most of all, peace is about respect for ourselves, each other, and the planet we share.[3]

Galtung's concepts of negative and positive peace. Negative peace refers to the absence of direct violence. An obvious example of negative peace would be a ceasefire or truce. Positive peace refers to a state where the conditions of social, political, and economic justice exist.[4]

In her book *Comprehensive Peace Education*, Betty A. Reardon describes positive peace as constituting the conditions for the existence of justice "in the sense of the full enjoyment of the entire range of human rights by all people."[5] We can see from this conception of justice that the concerns and problems that peacebuilding addresses are wide ranging, including (but not limited to) issues of poverty, social and economic inequity, violence, environment and resource degradation, racism, and gender discrimination.

The last principles of the Earth Charter 16 defines peace as: "The wholeness created by right relationships with oneself, other persons, other cultures, other life, Earth, and the larger whole of which all are a part."[6] This definition illuminates peace as a very active concept; it describes peace not as an end state but as a process we have to work hard at continuously. It also illuminates the depth of the concept of peace in terms of

---

2. UNESCO, *Constitution*, 1.
3. People for Peace Project, *We Want Peace on Earth*, 15–25.
4. Galtung, *Peace by Peaceful Means*, 5.
5. Reardon, *Educating for Global Responsibility*, 26.
6. Dieter and Rasmussen, *Earth Habitat*, 119.

relationships. Maintaining "right relationships" requires significant effort and continuous learning.

The National Peace Academy invites learners to inquire into peace and right relationships holistically, through five interrelated and interdependent spheres that need to be nurtured toward the full development of the peace builder: the personal, the social, the political, the institutional, and the ecological. These five spheres relate and function together as a peace system, each representing a unique, crosscutting, and reciprocally reinforcing sphere of human organization and relationships.

In the personal sphere, we ask what it means to live in right relationship with our self. Dale Snauwaert, in "Care of the Self," describes personal peace as living with "the awareness of one's authentic being, and living from and relating to others from that awareness."[7] How often do we take the opportunity to think about what this means? To understand and live with peace at the personal sphere requires inquiring into how we handle our own internal conflicts and emotions. It also requires inquiring into our own values, principles, and attitude so that we can develop the essential internal capacities that prepare us to live with integrity and wholeness within our self.

In the social sphere, we ask what it means to live in right relationships with others. In the social sphere, we inquire into the manifestation of right relationships of individuals with other individuals and to their collective coexistence. This is the sphere of right relationships that most peacebuilding and conflict resolution practices give attention to. To understand and live with peace within the social sphere, we inquire into our attitudes, intentions, and actions regarding how we manage our interpersonal conflicts and differences so that we are honoring the dignity of others.

In the political sphere, we ask what it means to live in right relationships with various groups of people, communities, and organizations. Here, we need to explore how right relationships are established and maintained when diverse individuals and groups come together to discourse, make decisions collectively, and engage in action to create a world together. This is a very complex sphere of peacebuilding, in which the ethic and practices of diversity and inclusion are put to the test.

To understand and live with peace at the political sphere, we have to inquire into how we engage in collective decision-making processes

---

7. Snauwaert, "Care of the Self," 2.

as well as examine the institutions and mechanisms we establish for assuring peace and justice. Thus, a key question we must ask is: who determines those conditions of right relationships in society—and how are they determined? In this sphere, we also ask what it means to be in community as well as how we can work, learn, and grow as autonomous yet interdependent communities.

In the institutional sphere, we consider how we might "institutionalize" right relationships within and between all forms and systems of organizations to support the development and maintenance of peace systems. We thus examine the ways in which organizations and institutions are organized and the systematic structures and processes through which power is mediated and human affairs are governed.

In the ecological sphere, we ask what it means to be in right relationships with Earth and its ecosystems of which we are a part and on which our survival and quality of life depend. To understand and live with peace at the ecological sphere, we inquire into our attitudes, intentions, and actions regarding how we take responsibility to shift our relationship to the natural environment from one based on control to one based on interdependence and living with and within. Human systems are not separate from but rather integral to all living systems and, as such, human organization affects and is affected by all other ecological systems. Ecosystems are both resilient and fragile, and human life depends upon our respect for and stewardship of the entire planet.

Peace, then, can only be cultivated through the training of the mind to control our desire, balancing between deserving and desiring, developing tolerance and respect for differences, concern and love for others, and moving from competition to cooperation. Peace can be installed through education in cooperation and mutual support, deep-seated concern for others over concern for self. Peace can be explained in positive terms as well. The presence of happiness, health, good economy, social justice, freedom of expression, and creative support for personal growth at all levels are some elements of peace. Such a peace can be termed as positive peace.

According to UNESCO, in *Learning the Way of Peace*, these meanings of peace come easily under three basic sources. These are: inner peace, social peace, and peace with nature.[8]

---

8. UNESCO, *Seeds for Peace*, 8–18.

Inner Peace: Inner peace is peace with self—self-contentedness. One "whose mind remains unperturbed amid sorrows, whose thirst for pleasure has altogether disappeared, and who is free from passion, fear and anger" is said to have achieved inner peace.[9] For example, harmony and peace with oneself, good health, the absence of inner conflicts, joy, a sense of freedom, insight, spiritual peace, feelings of kindness, compassion, content, and an appreciation of art.

Social Peace: Social peace is "learning to live together," indeed, one of the important four pillars of learning as enunciated in the UNESCO report, "Learning: The Treasure Within."[10] Human beings are social beings; they cannot live in isolation. The tapestry of the living community is fast changing from living in homogeneous cultural, linguistic, and religious groups to a cosmopolitan community that is multi-cultural, multi-lingual, and multi-religious. For an enriched and meaningful life, it is necessary to learn to live together within diversity. Again, for social peace, tolerance for diversity is not enough; respect and love for diversity is the precondition. Social peace implies harmony in human relationships, conflict reconciliation and resolution, love, friendship, unity, mutual understanding, co-operation, brotherhood, tolerance of differences, democracy, community building, human rights, morality, etc.

Peace with Nature: Planet earth is the cradle of human civilization. Symbolically, she is the mother earth. Peace with nature implies stopping the violation of her dignity through environmental and ecological degradation, exploitation, etc. Peace with nature is harmony with our natural environment and mother earth. These sources of peace are important for they provide the necessary basis on which peace can be built. Each source could be further analyzed in detail so that many more sub-components can be identified. Often, some projects confine themselves into a single source and neglect the others or even work.

2. Peace in Yoruba Religion

In the Yoruba Religion, "Peace is good relationship well lived, health, absence of pressure and conflict, being strong and prosperous. Peace is the totality of well-being: fullness of life here and hereafter."[11] What the Yoruba call *alafia* is "the sum total of all that man may desire: an undis-

---

9. Samiran and Tagore, *Complete Poems of Rabindranath Tagore's Gitanjali*, 367.
10. See Samwaad, "Role of Teacher."
11. Rweyemamu, "Religion and Peace," 380.

turbed harmonious life."[12] If one is therefore lacking in any of the basic things (such as good health, a wife or a husband, children, or means of sustenance of one's family) or if one, though possessing these things, does not enjoy a good relationship with the other members of the community (living or dead), one cannot be said to have peace. Mere material wealth or progress that is not accompanied by an integral moral life is neither regarded as fullness of life nor is it envied in traditional African societies. Any action that is capable of hindering another from attaining the fullness of life is considered a breach of peace. A selfish or unjust person, even when he or she is not violent, is anti-social and therefore regarded by the Africans as an enemy of peace.

The centrality of harmony is the prayer for peace: elders speaking with one voice, tranquillity, agreement between the gourd cup and the vessel, and the banishment of every ill word. These are all fundamental requirements for the realization of the peace prayed for. The harmony that is to be maintained for humans to experience peace is not only social but also spiritual and cosmic. In *The Primal Vision*, John V. Taylor asserts that:

> A man's well-being consists in keeping in harmony with the cosmic totality. When things go well with him, he knows he is at peace and of a piece with the scheme of things and there can be no greater good than that. If things go wrong then somewhere he has fallen out of step. The whole system of divination exists to help him discover the point at which the harmony has been broken and how it may be restored.[13]

In many African societies, there are specific periods of the year marked out for the promotion of peace. During this period—which may last for a week or a month—litigations are suspended while quarrels and all forms of violent and unjust acts are avoided for fear of incurring the wrath of God, the deities, and the ancestors. This sacred period sometimes proceeds the planting season, and it is believed that any breach which is not adequately atoned for would lead to a poor harvest. If a person breaks either the spiritual or cosmic harmony, the lack of peace that ensues reverts on the entire community. Sometimes individual reparations in terms of sacrifices are not enough to restore the harmony, and all

---

12. Rweyemamu, "Religion and Peace," 381.
13. Taylor, *Primal Vision*, 67.

the members of the community are called upon to right the wrong. There is thus a strong sense of the communal dimension of immoral conduct.

3. Peace in Islam

In Islam, peace is expressed in the Hadith: "None of you truly believes until he wishes for his brother what he wishes for himself."[14] The word "Islam" itself stems from the root meaning *silm*, or peace. There is a general agreement among the scholars of Islam that Islam as a religion has been based on values and principles that promote peace and harmony. In "Peaceful Approach to Conflict Resolution in Muslim Context," Niazi brings the following teachings of peace and non-violence initiated by Qur'an and Prophet Muhammad (pbuh), which has been long lost to the violent realities of today's Islam. It will not only enable others to understand Muslims but will also enable Muslims to understand themselves and actively participate in transforming their societies through democratic and peaceful means.[15]

Forgiveness is the most valued virtue in Islam. In Islamic tradition, forgiveness is held high in matters of conflict, both on a personal and a public level. Forgiveness has been given preference over anger and revenge no matter how evil the offense is. It is stated in the Qur'an: "And who shun the more heinous sins and abominations; and who, whenever they are moved to anger, readily forgive" (Q 42:37). Forgiveness is expressed in the Qur'an as *afw, ghafara,* and *maghfira*. *Afw* means to pardon, the waiver of punishment, and amnesty. The Qur'an does not limit forgiveness only to large conflicts; rather, it also mentions "forgiveness and kindness as a manner of interaction among individuals and communities for the cultivation of peace and harmonious relations within the society."[16]

The life of the Prophet (pbuh) also reflects an unwavering commitment to acts of forgiveness and mercy, in spite of all the brutalities carried out by his opponents. Oqbah Ibn Amer reported that the Messenger of Allah said: "You shall keep relationship with one who cut it off from you, you shall give one who disappointed you, and you shall pardon one who oppressed you" (Q 5:39). Forgiveness is a transformative process, simultaneously aiding in attaining other virtues associated with it. Abu

---

14. An-Nawawi, *Hadith*, 4.
15. Niazi, *Peace Education*, 71.
16. Niazi, *Peace Education*, 72.

Hurayrah reported that the Messenger of Allah said: "Moses, son of 'Imran, had asked: O my LORD! Who is the best honorable of Thy servants to Thee? He [the God] said: He who pardons when he is in a position of power."[17] Here, forgiving others while being in the position of power is a sign of magnanimity as well as humility.

4. Peace in Christianity

In Christianity, the principle of "right relationships" is represented by the Golden Rule: "Do unto others as you would have them do unto you" (Matt 7:12). The Christian concept of peace is revealed in both the Hebrew Bible and in the New Testament. In the Hebrew Bible, peace is inseparable from righteousness and justice. These concepts are embodied in one Hebrew word that connotes right relationship between two or more parties. This word is usually translated as "righteousness," referring not only to doing morally correct deeds but also to living rightly in relationship with others. Righteousness is also closely connected to justice, because the righteous person acts with justice in the civil or judicial sphere. The necessary link between righteousness and peace can be seen, for example, in Isaiah's vision of a future day when a righteous king will reign over Israel and God's Spirit will be poured out upon the people. Until a spirit from on high is poured out on us, and the wilderness becomes a fruitful field, and the fruitful field is deemed a forest, then justice will dwell in the wilderness and righteousness abides in the fruitful field. The effect of righteousness will be peace and the result of righteousness, quietness, and trust, forever (Isa 32:15–17).

In *Biblical Basis for Peacemaking*, Peggy Cowan wrote that *shalom* "is often used in reference to personal relationships, and it means 'wholeness' of relationship, i.e., a relationship with goodwill and harmony."[18] This is the reason why *shalom* was used as an identification of friend or foe when two parties encountered one another (1 Kings 2:13). *Shalom* is also used in the same sense on the level of international relations. When two countries are in the relation of *shalom*, it does not simply mean that there is no war between the two. Rather, it goes beyond that and means that a relationship of amity, alliance, and cooperation exists between them (1 Kgs 5:12).

---

17. Niazi, *Peace Education*, 72.
18. Cowan, *Biblical Basis for Peacemaking*, 1.

Shalom, of course, includes the state of peace in the sense of the absence of war. But such peace is one of many manifestations of *shalom*. *Shalom* does bring peace, and the breakdown of *shalom* often leads to war. However, the cessation of armed conflict does not automatically bring *shalom*. *Shalom* in the biblical sense is a much more comprehensive and dynamic concept than peace in a narrow sense as God's gift (Isa 26:3–12) and God's intention (Jer 29:11). It is the completion of God's purpose for creation that is described as a covenant of *shalom* (Num 25:12).

Although given by God, *shalom* is not to be passively awaited but rather actively pursued (Ps 34:14). "*Shalom* also involves positive relationships between peoples and persons. Positive relationships within the community means that the needs of all persons are met, and there is material well-being, economic security, and prosperity for all."[19] (Isa 54:13; 66:12; Jer 29:5–7; Ezra 34:27–29; Ps 37:11; 72:3; Hag 2:9). *Shalom* involves the absence of war but also goes beyond it, to include security and lack of fear. The full meaning of *shalom* can only be grasped when human well-being is balanced. After the fall, humankind became separated from the creator, from each other, and from the natural world. The wholeness of God's creation, *shalom*, was broken into chaotic fragmentation. The whole creation waited for the coming of the one who would restore the broken *shalom* to its original wholeness. In summary, "*Shalom* can be defined as the welfare and state of completion of all creatures, arising from a divine will for peace, including their peaceful coexistence in a way of life on God's commandments."[20] In Greek, Ειρήνη is the word for peace, meaning the absence of war. The New Testament includes all of the meanings of *shalom*: good relationships among peoples and nations (Mark 9:50; Rom 12:18–19; Eph 2:15; Heb 12:14), healthy relationships within the community, a quality of life in the Spirit or in relation to God, a gift of Jesus, reconciliation effected by or through Jesus, and a quality to be pursued by humans. When we have peace with God, we live in intimate fellowship with God. Similarly, peaceful (peace-full) human relationships are also characterized by *koinônia* (fellowship). Christ lived a life of peace in a world of violence, and this is what Christians are called to do. Christians are called to live a life of unconditional love, a love which casts out fear. Christians are called to "not worry about tomorrow" (Matt 6:34), to live each day like a lily of the field. So long as Christians set

---

19. Cowan, *Biblical Basis for Peacemaking*, 2.
20. Homolka, *Gate to Perfection*, 6.

conditions on peace, they do not have even a modicum of the faith which was preached by Jesus.

5. Models of Peacemakers

➤ Religious Models: Jesus and Muhammad

Jesus as the model of peacemaker: he is nonviolent. He is just, faithful, and unconditionally loving. He loves enemies; serves people; tells truth; builds community; prays to the God of peace; and risks his life in active nonviolence, even through his arrest, torture, and execution. Jesus delivered his most famous declaration about peace and nonviolence during the "Sermon on the Mount": "Blessed are the peacemakers, for they will be called the children of God" (Matt 5:9). The Sermon on the Mount was a very powerful set of blessings and guidelines for living a good spiritual life. Christians and non-Christians have been moved by its meaning.

Jesus taught his followers to eschew violence and to embrace nonviolence through his teaching and through the way he lived his life. During his life, he spoke out against violence around him. When a follower cut off the ear of the high priest's slave, he reprimanded the aggressor, but never told him anything like that again.[21] Jesus used nonviolent approaches to the point of accepting his impending execution by the Romans without fighting back.

As for Muhammad, he lived a nonviolent life and advocated nonviolent methods during his first thirteen years of preaching Islam in Mecca. One example is his response to the dominant religious group in Mecca when he was accused of blasphemy and was tortured and humiliated. He did not speak ill of his tormentors and he simply prayed for their understanding.[22] Even when an armed struggle is chosen over an unarmed one, the Qur'an and the Hadith put limitations on how much violence is permitted. The Qur'an forbids the killing of non-combatants in war—like women, children, and the elderly—and considers murder a major sin (*Satha-Anand*). Just as the Qur'an endorses violence in certain circumstances, it also calls its followers to use nonviolence and to seek peace.

---

21. Wink, *Engaging the Powers*, 2.
22. Ahmad, *Islam, Nonviolence, and Global Transformation*, 37.

6. Leaders of Nonviolence: Julius Nyerere and Martin Luther King Jr.

Two leaders of nonviolence in the twentieth century are Julius Nyerere and Martin Luther King Jr. They both dedicated their lives to humanity and stood tall for economic equity, justice, and peace; their example can inspire many in Africa and in the world.[23] The statesmanship of Mwalimu Julius K. Nyerere has allowed the formation of longitudinal efforts to bring peace and economic development to establish a new democratic identity for Africa. As for the principles of nonviolence practiced by Martin Luther King Jr. they include:

> Nonviolence as a way of life for courageous people.
> Nonviolence seeks to win friendship and understanding.
> Nonviolence seeks to defeat injustice, not people.
> Nonviolence holds that voluntary suffering can educate and transform.
> Nonviolence chooses love instead of hate.
> Nonviolence believes that the universe is on the side of justice.

To help each participant to comprehend their involvement in nonviolence, the following questions will be answered.[24]

> What is peace for me?
> In what way am I preventing peace in and around me?
> What is any special gift (spiritual or physical) I am not yet fully using to bring peace in me and around me?
> In what way am I preventing peace in my body?
> What is the gift that I am not yet using to bring peace to my body?
> In what way am I preventing peace with [name of the person/s with whom I have the greatest conflict]?
> What stops me from forgiving myself?
> How do I forgive myself?
> Can faith allow me to forgive myself?
> What is forgiveness when it comes from grace and faith?
> What is my gift for peace when I have fully forgiven myself or allowed myself to be forgiven?

---

23. Ezozo, "African Peace Education," 56.
24. Asseily, *Breaking the Cycles of Violence*, 14.

Questions for Comprehension, Analysis, and Reflection

1. Identify a set of core values that are most relevant to your community and develop a meaningful model of peace education for your school.
2. What are the features a good value education model should have? Analyze the above given model in the light of the features identified.
3. What do you mean by a core peace value? Give examples

Conclusion

Peace cannot be kept by force; it can only be achieved by educating religious leaders. In order to achieve peace and development, leaders of the society must allow people to follow and practice the religion of their choice. All religions are based on the morality that human beings act in a way that helps them and society at large.

Examples of Required Readings

Brenes-Castro, A. "An Integral Model of Peace Education." In *Educating for a Culture of Social and Ecological Peace*, edited by A. L. Wenden, 77–98. Albany: State University of New York Press, 2004.

Ezozo, A. "African Peace Education: An Initiative for a Nonviolence Curriculum." *Journal of Pan African Studies* 2.9 (2009) 27–63.

Harris, I. "Chapter 2." In *Peace Education*, 37–52. Jefferson, NC: McFarland, 2003.

Jackson, Robert, and Satoko Fujiwara. "Towards Religious Education for Peace." *British Journal of Religious Education* 29.1 (2007) 1–14.

Naht Hanh, T. *Peace Is Every Step: The Path of Mindfulness in Everyday Life*. New York: Bantam, 1992.

Navaro-Casto, L., and J. Nario-Galace. *Peace Education: A Pathway to a Culture of Peace*, 26–38. 2nd Ed. Philippines: Centre for Peace Education, 2010. http://www.peace-ed- campaign.org/resources/cpe-book-14oct2010-FINAL2.pdf.

Toh, S.H., and V. F. Cawagas. "A Holistic Understanding of A Culture of Peace." Paper presented at the APCEIU Expert Consultation on EIU. Fiji, 2002.

Chapter 2: Concept of Peace Education

Introduction

Peace education is more effective and meaningful when it takes into account the social and cultural context and the needs of a country. It should be enriched by its cultural and spiritual values and with universal human values.

Learning Objectives

At the end of this chapter, the participants will be able to:

1. Understand different definitions of peace education.
2. Understand the breadth and scope of peace education.
3. Acquire the skills of peace education and advocate for them.
4. Understand the concept of an Integrative Theory of Peace.
5. Use the various elements of the transformative model of peace education effectively.

Learning Activities

The participants will be asked come up with their own definitions of peace education considering their context and religion affiliation. In this activity, flipchart paper and markers for participants are materials that must be used. Then, a debate on different approaches of peace education will be conducted and ideas will be put on a flipchart in the classroom. In addition, students will answer the following questions: What makes peace education difficult to define? Why do we need it? Which definition applies best to your own context?

Content

1. Definitions of Peace Education

Peace education can be defined in many ways. Peace education seeks to address how to establish a global model of living in peace, where all people live in peace with one another. There is no universally accepted definition as such. Here are a few pertinent definitions from the peace literature. Peace Education is process of developing knowledge, skills, attitudes, behaviors, and values that enable learners to: identify and understand sources of local and global issues and acquire positive and appropriate sensitivities to these problems, resolve conflicts and to attain justice in a non-violent way, live by universal standards of human rights and equity by appreciating cultural diversity, respect for the earth and for each other.[25]

> Peace education is an attempt to respond to problems of conflict and violence on scales ranging from the global and national to the local and personal. It is about exploring ways of creating more just and sustainable futures.[26]

> Peace education is holistic. It embraces the physical, emotional, intellectual, and social growth of children within a framework deeply rooted in traditional human values. It is based on a philosophy that teaches love, compassion, trust, fairness, co-operation, and reverence for the human family and all life on our beautiful planet.[27]

> Peace education is skill building. It empowers children to find creative and non-destructive ways to settle conflict and to live in harmony with themselves, others, and their world. Peacebuilding is the task of every human being and the challenge of the human family.[28]

The basic concepts embedded in the above definitions are that peace education is a remedial measure to protect children from falling into the ways of violence in society. It aims at the total development of the child.

---

25. Abebe et al., *Peace Education in Africa*, 14.
26. Laing quoted in Abebe et al., *Peace Education in Africa*, 14.
27. Schmidt and Friedman, *Culture of Teaching Peace*, 31–33.
28. Schmidt and Friedman, *Culture of Teaching Peace*, 31–33.

It tries to inculcate higher human and social values in the mind of the child. In essence, it attempts to develop a set of behavioral skills necessary for peaceful living and peacebuilding from which the whole of humanity will benefit.

2. The Field of Peace Education

The field of peace education can be broadly defined as educating for a culture of peace. If we look at culture as a way of life, it implies that a culture of peace means a peaceful way of living. A culture of peace integrates concepts of both negative and positive peace and involves the transformation of society from the current culture of war and violence to a culture of peace and nonviolence. The culture of war is more than just a nation being at war; rather, it is the physical and structural violence that permeates every aspect of culture, including language, interpersonal relationships, power dynamics, and one's relationship with nature. The culture of war manifests itself in a myriad of ways and is often deeply entrenched in beliefs that can make it seem "normal" or "natural." As culture is a human construct, however, the culture of war is human-made and, as such, can be equally dismantled and replaced with a culture of peace.

3. Theories of Peace Education

In "Peace Education Theory," Harris presents five postulates of peace education that underline five different types of peace education: international, human rights, development, environmental, and conflict resolution education. These postulates are: (1) peace education explains the roots of violence; (2) it teaches alternatives to violence; (3) it adjusts to cover different forms of violence; (4) peace itself is a process that varies according to context; and (5) conflict is omnipresent.[29]

The Integrative Theory of Peace consists of four sub-theories: peace is a psychosocial and political as well as a moral and spiritual condition. Peace is the main expression of a unity-based worldview. The unity-based worldview is the prerequisite for creating both a culture of peace and a culture of healing.

A comprehensive, integrated, and lifelong education within the framework of peace is the most effective approach for a transformation

---

29. Harris, "Ideal of Peace," 6.

from the metacategories of survival-based and identity-based worldviews to the metacategory of a unity-based worldview.

4. Transformative Model of Peace Education

Turay and English proposed a new Transformative Model of Peace Education (TMPE), which includes five elements: Diversity, Participatory Learning, Globalized Perspectives, Indigenous Knowing, and Spiritual Underpinnings.[30] Transformative learning is absolutely critical to the process of peace education. If we consider peace education as a practice for transforming society from a culture of war to a culture of peace, then it is implicit that our current worldview is embedded in the culture of war. Our knowledge, behaviors, and actions are influenced by this worldview and must change in order to shift towards a culture of peace. Therefore, transformative learning is a necessary part of peace education. Transformative learning is important for all involved, including teachers, for teachers need to internalize these concepts themselves in order to be able to effectively convey them to their students.

5. Five Elements of the Transformative Model of Peace Education

> **Diversity**

According to Turay and English, an effective model of peace education celebrates diversity and difference and, at the same time, acknowledges that core values—such as respect, honor, and dialogue—are universal. By engaging participants in a critical self-reflective process, the diversity element seeks to transform their worldviews about what constitutes diversity and what constitutes peace.

> **Participatory Learning**

The guiding principle of participatory learning is that learners know what they need to learn and how they need to learn it. It is a process that includes the transformation of both the educator and the learners, and values the lived experience of all participants. Through the participatory learning process, community members name the problem, analyze its root causes, view the issue from a variety of perspectives, strategize options for addressing the root causes, and only then move to solutions.

---

30. Turay and English, "Toward a Global Culture of Peace," 286–301.

▸ Globalized Perspectives

Incorporating globalized perspectives requires the teacher and learners to negotiate the tension between the global and the local and to stress the larger sociocultural and economic sphere of which the participants are a part.[31] The teacher should promote the ability to work across cultures as well as the ability to see the linkages between immediate and so-called removed circumstances.

▸ Indigenous Knowing

The indigenous knowing aspect of the model demands that the model be contextualized to the location where it is enacted. One important aspect is acknowledging that participants may have fluency in indigenous languages and ways of life that are not considered in many international standards of literacy. The transformative model, therefore, must be contextualized in the participants' location.

▸ Spiritual Underpinnings

In this context, spirituality is the search for meaning in life. Many people have religious or spiritual beliefs and values that are central to how they deal with conflict, and we need to acknowledge and incorporate these ideas into how we educate for peace. Furthermore, peace, like spirituality, should be a thread that runs across the whole of education—classroom, recreation, and one-on-one interactions.

Questions for Comprehension, Analysis, and Reflection

1. Define peace education in your own words.
2. Name five elements of the transformative model of peace education and how to apply them in your community.

Conclusion

In this chapter, I have presented the concept of peace and peace education, the scope of peace education, and a brief outline of the curriculum. The pedagogical issues and methods of transaction of peace education will be dealt with in the second module.

31. Turay and English, "Toward a Global Culture of Peace," 295.

Examples of Required Readings

Cawagas, V., and S. Toh. "Introduction." In *Peaceful Theory and Practice in Values Education*, 2–19. Quezon City: Phoenix, 1991.
Fountain, S. *Peace Education in UNICEF.* New York: UNICEF, 1999. www.unicef.org/girlseducation/files/PeaceEducation.pdf.
Galtung, J. "Form and Content of Peace Education." In *Encyclopedia of Peace Education*, edited by Monisha Bajaj, 49–58. Charlotte, NC: Information Age, 2008.
Harris, I. "History of Peace Education." In *Encyclopedia of Peace Education,* edited by Monisha Bajaj. Charlotte, NC: Information Age, 2008. http://www.tc.edu/centers/epe/PDF%20articles/Harris_ch2_22feb08.pdf.
Kester, Kevin. "Peace Education Primer." http://journals.sfu.ca/jgcee/index.php/jgcee/article/viewFile/66/59.
Murithi, T. "An African Perspective on Peace Education: *Ubuntu* Lessons in Reconciliation." *International Review of Education* 55 (2009) 221–33.
Salomon, G. "The Nature of Peace Education: Not All Programs Are Created Equal." In *Peace Education: The Concept, Principles, and Practices Around the World*, edited by Nevo and Salomon, 3–13. Mahwah, NJ: Lawrence Earlbaum Associates, 2002.
Toh, S., et al. "Building a Peace Education Program." *Peace Education Miniprints* 38 (1992) 1–38.
United Nations. "Preamble of the UN Charter (1945)." http://www.un.org/cyberschoolbus/peace/frame2.htm.

Chapter 3: Peacebuilding

Introduction

As religious violence and terrorism increases, all efforts to learn how to build peace in our hearts and minds must be encouraged and developed. It is time to understand that we all cannot tolerate hatred, unrest, and violence.

Learning Objectives

At the end of this chapter, the participants will be able to:

1. Prevent their religious community from lapsing or relapsing into violent conflict.
2. Establish structures and incentives for peaceful mitigation of conflicts.
3. Incentivize elite commitment to peace processes.
4. Demonstrate the practical use of such concepts as negotiation, co-operative problem-solving, and decision-making under complex circumstances.
5. Develop their competences as peace ambassadors in human rights promotion and protection, conflict transformation, peacebuilding, and intercultural dialogue.
6. Enhance their capacity to take action at a local level in environments affected by previous or ongoing conflicts.
7. Advance their role in peacebuilding and conflict transformation.

Learning Activities

Allow the participants to watch the following videos on Youtube: (1) "Breaking the Cycle of Violent Conflict with Johan Galtung" and (2) "Interview with Betty Reardon." Ask each participant to write their feelings and the lessons they have learned.

Content

1. Peacebuilding: Self-identification: Having or Being?

Dale Snauwaert describes two basic dispositions to the self: having and being. The "having" disposition is expressed as "I am what I have," and through it, people identify most closely with their possessions. This is a widely shared disposition in modern society. "I have friends, I have a great job, I have a wonderful wife, I have a wonderful church community."[32] The great problem of the "having" disposition is that it leads to existential anxiety. The having self might be expressed as: "If I am what I have, and if what I have can be taken away, then my sense of self-identity is under constant threat, generating existential anxiety."[33]

Snauwaert calls for a shift from the "having" disposition to the "being" disposition. Being is experienced as "I am. I am I." The being self is experienced through a self-reflexive state of consciousness; it is consciousness of consciousness itself. The being self might be expressed as: "I am a caring friend, I am a teacher, I am a loving husband, I am a passionate contributor to my community."[34]

How do you identify yourself? What is your self-identification? Are you oriented towards a having or being sense of self? This brief exercise invites you to consider your sense of self. To begin, find a comfortable place sit and reflect. Close your eyes and take a few deep breaths. Continue to take slow, deep, and intentional breaths. When your mind begins to waver, focus on your breath. If you find your mind wandering, return to this focus on your breath. When your mind becomes generally free of external distraction, begin to contemplate the questions of self-identification below. Feel free to incorporate all of your own contemplative or meditative practices if you have them.

1. Who am I?
2. How do I see myself?
3. How do I describe who I am?
4. What are my key characteristics?
5. What is my essence?

32. National Peace Academy, "Holistic Approach," 1.
33. National Peace Academy, "Personal Peace Building," 1.
34. National Peace Academy, "Self-identification," 5.

6. What is important to my sense of self?

2. Lederach's Conception of Peacebuilding

Lederach's conception of peacebuilding emphasizes transformation as its goal. The concepts "change" and "transformation" are often used in describing the purposes, goals, and intended outcomes of peacebuilding and peace education. The term "change" describes a process of becoming different in a particular way without fully losing one's previous characteristics. Transformation(s) can be understood as deeper changes that affect ways of thinking, worldviews, values, behaviors, relationships, and social structures. We can have right relationships—relationships that acknowledge and assure the dignity of others and not necessarily agree with each other. It is also a concept that from an ethical and principled perspective we all have some familiarity with.

The preamble of the "Universal Declaration of Human Rights" begins by recognizing "the inherent dignity and the equal and inalienable rights of all members of the human family (as) the foundation of freedom, justice, and peace in the world."[35] The Golden Rule and the principle of human dignity, however, only provide us a glimpse as to what might be implied by right relationships. Right relationships can also be considered just and equitable. So to live in right relationships, we must also have a clear understanding of what is meant by justice and equity. Understanding what comprises "right relationships" requires inquiry into our own values, principles, and norms. In order to live in "right relationships" and to make this concept of peace useful, it is also useful to engage with it as an open and ongoing inquiry. In addition to understanding what a "right relationship is"—and not just what might be implied—we must also understand what is meant by "wholeness."

John Paul Lederach's definition of peacebuilding expresses peacebuilding as a holistic process that integrates both inner and outer work and development, addressing aspects of each of the five spheres. He describes peacebuilding as a "comprehensive concept that encompasses, generates and sustains the full array of processes, approaches, and stages needed to transform conflict toward more sustainable, peaceful relationships."[36]

---

35. United Nations, "Universal Declaration of Human Rights," 1.
36. Lederach, *Building Peace*, 20.

1. Peacebuilding in the Yoruba Religion

Indigenous Proverbs and Peacebuilding in Nigeria.
Proverbs are the vehicle with which socio-cultural and philosophical thoughts underlying social values and ethnic and religious issues are transmitted across generations. Thus, Owomoyela opines that language development and socialization among the Yoruba people of South-Western Nigeria is done through the use of proverbs. He asserts that the Yoruba people "approach with deliberate care, taking great pains to avoid careless or thoughtless statement, whose damage might outlast lifetimes."[37] Proverbs are central to indigenous education and various themes of traditional education were imparted through the vehicle of proverbs. Underscoring the importance of proverbs in traditional societies, Akinmade notes that in African societies, proverbs have been and will continue to be of great advantage to humankind.[38] Proverbs express the nature of African wisdom as they perform diverse functions, ranging from bringing peace where there is conflict and misunderstandings, giving hope where there is despair, and light where there is darkness in human relationships and interactions.

The following teachings promote peacebuilding:

- ✓ Avoid any action that will hinder another person from attaining the fullness of life and is considered a breach of peace.

- ✓ Avoid selfishness. A selfish or unjust person, even when he or she is not violent, is anti-social and is therefore regarded by Yoruba as an enemy of peace.

- ✓ Harmony is a fundamental category in Yoruba religion and thought.

- ✓ In the community, harmony entails smooth relationships between persons and other beings.

- ✓ No attempt is made to deny or cancel out differences; rather, all effort is devoted to find a way in which differences can continue to co-exist harmoniously.

---

37. Owomoyela, *Yoruba Proverbs*, 25.
38. Akinmade, "Decline of Proverbs," 127–48.

✓ In personal life, such harmony consists in the ability to reconcile one's desires with one's means, coordinate one's thoughts, sentiments, and their verbal expressions, as well as the ability to discharge one's religious and social duties. One who is able to do this will experience inner peace.

The centrality of harmony is the prayer for peace: elders speaking with one voice, tranquillity, agreement between the gourd cup and the vessel, and the banishment of every ill word. These are all fundamental requirements in the realization of the peace prayed for. Since human beings come in different shapes, sizes, and with all sorts of different ideas in their heads, Yorubas try to accommodate the various opinions of their members for their long, drawn-out village discussions in search of consensus. In traditional Yoruba debates, the goal is always to include everyone in any decision that will be binding on all. And in the interest of harmony, the discussion is continued until the last skeptic has been won over. It often happens that the few who do not share the opinion of the many voluntarily give up their own opinion in the interest of harmony. Any person who causes a breach in the harmonious co-existence of the members of the community is required to make up for it through just reparation or restitution, depending on the offense committed.

In Yoruba Religion, peace in the community cannot be separated from justice. Peace is honorable; it can never be achieved when you are disgraced or when you disgrace another person. People must relate to one another on equal terms. Peace is not something that happens but rather a situation that arises when justice happens. It is a pleasant state of things that happens when the state of things is just. The unwritten moral code of the Yorubas contains not only things that are forbidden but also those things that must be done as compensation and in reparation for the injury which immoral conduct inflicts on individuals and on the society at large. Such compensation and reparation are usually based on past experiences. People are usually at a loss when a person commits a sin or an immoral act hitherto unknown in the community.

The harmony that is to be maintained for humans to experience peace is not only social but also spiritual and cosmic. During a sacred period, which may last for a week or a month, litigations are suspended while quarrels and all forms of violent and unjust acts are avoided for fear of incurring the wrath of God, the deities, and the ancestors. This sacred period sometimes proceeds the planting season and it is believed that any breach which is not adequately atoned for would lead to a poor harvest. If a person breaks either the spiritual or the cosmic harmony, the lack of peace that ensues affects the entire community. Sometimes individual reparations in terms of sacrifices are not enough to restore the harmony, and all the members of the community are called upon to right the wrong. There is thus a strong sense of the communal dimension of immoral conduct.

2. Peacebuilding in Islam

Social justice is just one number of values that relate Islam to peace. Many Muslim and non-Muslim scholars have pointed to Islamic principles and values such as unity, supreme love of the creator, mercy, subjection of passion, and accountability for all actions, all of which are sported by innumerable verses in the Qur'an that command believers to be righteous and above passion in their dealings with their fellow human beings. Love, kindness, affection, forgiveness, and mercy are recommended as virtues of the true faithful.[39]

Justice is known to man through available evidence (both revelation and reason). However, knowing justice through revelation is the more dominant belief. Whether justice is the embodiment of the highest human virtues or a direct emanation from (perfection), it is an ideal notion that Muslims are obliged to pursue. Those who believe in a single, just God are the subjects of divine justice, and all others are the objects of that justice. Divine justice is conceived as divine laws—eternal, perfect, and existing irrespective of time and place—a design for universal application to all men. Even men who do not believe in one God can seek refuge in it. The standards of justice, whether determined by revelation or reason, indicate the path for right and wrong, so that all, each according to his "light," would pursue the right and reject the wrong in order to achieve the good in this life and salvation in the next.[40]

Social empowerment through *ihsan* and *khayr* (doing good) is also an important path to justice in the Islamic tradition. Islam's rapid growth was in large measure a response to its deep commitment to empower the weak, and it remains a religion of dynamic social activism in terms of individual duties and a sense of social responsibility. Struggling against

---

39. Ahmad, "Attainment of Inner Peace," 40.
40. Khadduri, *War and Peace in the Law of Islam*, 192.

oppression (*zulm*), assisting the poor, and pursuing equality among all humans are core religious values throughout the Qur'an and Hadith.

The universality of humanity is a central precept in Islam, amply affirmed throughout the Qur'an and Hadith and conveyed through the belief in the equality of origins and rights and the essential solidarity of all people. Humans are regarded as the most dignified and exalted of all creatures, with the potential for knowledge and moral action. Islamic teachings point beyond the settlement of short-term disputes; they aspire to unite humanity in a single family based on the equality of all members. This precept is based on the idea of the oneness and common origin of all people: "O mankind! We created you from a single (pair) of a male and a female, and made you into nations and tribes, that ye may know each other (not that ye may despise each other). Verify the most honored of you in the Allah is (he who is) the most righteous of you. And Allah has full knowledge and is well acquainted (with all things)" (Q 49:13). Peacebuilding approaches assume that human life is valuable and must be protected and that resources should be used to preserve life and prevent violence. The Qur'an clearly affirms the sacredness of human life: "If any one saved a life, it would be as if he saved the life of the whole people" (Q 5:32); "Nor for (idle) sport did we create the heavens and the earth and all that is between!" (Q 21:16; 44:38); "Nor take life which Allah has made sacred-except for just cause" (Q 17:33). Human actions have consequence, and life is an integral part of the great cosmic purpose. Peace in Islam is understood as a state of physical, mental, spiritual, and social harmony, living at peace with God through submission, and living at peace with one's fellow human beings by avoiding wrongdoing. In the peacebuilding field in general, open, face-to-face communication about problems and conflicts is deemed more productive than avoidance or violence, reducing the cost of conflict by addressing all the grievances of conflicting parties. Nonviolent strategies encourage creativity and innovation in dealing with conflicts and relationships by generating new options that do not compromise the sense of justice.

The forgiveness that vanquishes hatred and anger is a prized virtue in Islam, greater even than justice (Q 24:43; 42:40). In facts, believers are urged to forgive even when they are angry. The prophet said: "God fills with peace and faith the heart of one who swallows his anger, even though he is in a position to give vent to it" (Q 42:37).[41]

---

41. See also Q 42:37 on forgiveness and control of anger.

In Islam, the real test is in action. Lip service is not enough. God judges kindly those who have faith and have done good deeds: "On those who believe and work deeds of righteousness, will (Allah) Most Gracious bestow love" (Q 19:96). Involvement through individual responsibility and choice. Moral choice and rational persuasion are important, Islamic principles that emphasize responsibility for one's own actions. Even the prophet himself was not responsible for the decisions of others: "But if they turn away say: Allah sufficeth me: there is no God but He: on him is my trust—He the Lord of the Throne (of Glory) supreme!" (Q 9:129).

Muslims are encouraged to be patient and to suspend their judgment of others, whether Muslims or non-Muslims. *Sabr* (patience) is a virtue of the believers, who are expected to endure enormous difficulties and still maintain a strong belief in God.

Peacebuilding approaches assume that collaborative efforts to resolve a problem are more productive than competitive efforts by individuals. A well-known saying in Islamic tradition is: "God's hand is with the group (*jama'ah*)," which is often incited to motivate togetherness. It also contains the pragmatic idea of reducing costs and damage that might be incurred in conflicts.

The concept of the *Ummah* has been a foundation for collective action since the time of the prophet. During the early period of Islam in Mecca, the prophet propagated such values of collaboration and collection to respond to attacks of his opponents.

Peacebuilding endeavors to encourage participatory forums and inclusive procedures, deeming them more productive and effective than authoritarian, hierarchical, or exclusionary decision-making approaches. Peacebuilding strategies are based on assisting parties in negotiation based on joint interests or bringing in a third party to facilitate such a process.

Satha-Anand has developed eight theses for Muslim nonviolence that underlie the true meaning of nonviolence within Islam.[42] These are:

➤ The problem of violence is an integral part of the Islamic moral sphere.

➤ Violence, if any, used by Muslims must be governed by rules prescribed in the Qur'an and Hadith.

---

42. Satha-Anand, "Nonviolent Crescent," 7.

- If violence used cannot discriminate between combatants and non combatants, then it is unacceptable in Islam. Modern technology of destruction renders discrimination virtually impossible at present.

- In the modern world, Muslims cannot use violence.

- Islam teaches Muslims to fight for justice with the understanding that human lives are—as all parts of God's creation—purposive and sacred.

- In order to be true to Islam, Muslims must utilize nonviolent action as a new mode of struggle.

- Islam itself is fertile soil for nonviolence because of its potential for disobedience, strong discipline, sharing and social responsibility, perseverance and self-sacrifice, and the belief in the unity of the Muslim community and the oneness of mankind. Satha-Anand specifically points to many Qur'anic verses that stipulate the need for nonviolent actions. He cites the following: "Whenever they kindle the fire of war, God extinguishes it. They strive to create disorder on earth and God loves not those who create disorder" (Q 5:64); "God commands you to treat (everyone) justly, generously, and with kindness" (Q 16:90); "Repel evil with that which is best [not evil]: We are well acquainted with things they say" (Q 23:96); "But if the enemy incline toward peace, do thou (also) incline toward peace, and trust in Allah: for He is the One that heareth and knoweth all things" (Q 8:61).

Ghaffar Kahn (1890–1988), a Muslim leader and a Pashtun independence activist against the rule of the British Raj, tried to develop an army of nonviolent soldiers from a people with a strong violent reputation and culture. He reasoned that perhaps the Pashtuns might be reckless enough to make it work. His army was called the *Khudai Khidmatgans*, which means, "Servants of God." Like the regular military, recruits were drilled and disciplined. They had officers, a chain of command, uniforms, a flag, and even a bagpipe corps. All in the *Khudai Khidmatgens* were required to take a strict oath. They had to pledge:

> I am a *Khudai Khidmatgar*, and as God needs not service, but serving his creation is serving him:

I promise to serve humanity in the name of God.

I promise to refrain from violence and from taking revenge. I promise to forgive those who oppress me or treat me with cruelty.

I promise to refrain from taking part in feuds and quarrels and from creating enmity.

I promise to treat every [Pashtun] as my brother and friend.

I promise to refrain from antisocial customs and practices.

I promise to live a simple life, to practice virtue, and to refrain from evil.

I promise to practice good manners and good behavior and not to lead a life of idleness.

I promise to devote at least two hours a day to social work.[43]

3. Peacebuilding in Christianity

Study a bible passage dealing with peace and comment. Peace within the Social context. Peace is a greeting, entailing more than just "how are you?" (Rom 1:7). God wants His children to live in peace, which is one of His great blessings (Ps 29:11), and the peace He provides defies comprehension (Phil 2:6–7). There is human responsibility in pursuing peace, but we are not to seek it the way the world does. Genuine peace does not come from achieving greater success or acquiring more money; rather, it is the overflow of godly living (Ps 34:12–14). Peace can be compared to a tripod, each leg of which is necessary for stability.

First, there must be peace with God, which occurs at the point of salvation (Col 1:20); second, we must have inner peace (John 7:38); and third, we are to pursue peace with other people (Matt 5:9).

If a single component is missing, we will not experience the totality of God's intended blessing. There are many types of peace: inner peace, family peace, and community peace. The benefits of peace should be emphasized. When there is no peace, there is no physical development or prosperity in the community. Foreign investors will not be interested in investing in such a community. The creativity of the people is eroded. Name two different communities: one lives at peace and accesses their development potential and the inputs of investors, the other one lives in chaos due to violence; access their development potential and the investors' inputs. Inner peace and balance are of great importance in

---

43. Easwaran, *Nonviolent Soldier of Islam*, 111.

everyone's life. They are highly valued by most people, though few really possess them. Yet, everyone can develop them, some more, some less.

➤ What do Inner Peace and Inner Balance Mean?

They mean the presence of self-control and discipline and the ability to not let outside events influence our emotions, actions, and reactions. Their presence means the possession of common sense and good judgment and of not letting the outside world shake our inner world. What is the cause of so much unhappiness in this world? What deprives so many of inner peace? Is it not things like immorality, thefts, and murder? Is it not things like coveting, deceit, envy, and pride? Such things destroy families, friendships, and property. What, then, is the cause of these things?

Jesus declared the source of all these things to be the sinful hearts of men (Mark 7:21–23); James, the Lord's half-brother in the flesh, concurred with this diagnosis (James 4:1–2). How many times have you been overwhelmed by emotions, lost your temper, and got angry or impatient? How many times have you regretted your reactions or attitude? (Discuss these first in groups). Return from groups to share and conclude with the insights of Mark and James passages.

➤ Ways of Living in Peace

Pursue Peace with other People (Matt 5: 9). The current poverty not only denies Africans peace but also divides God's household into the rich and poor. God does not discriminate (Rom 2:11; Gal 2:6) and has no favorites (Act 10: 34). Therefore, as Children of one Father, Christians are invited to show similar universal love to all (Matt 5: 43–48; Gal 3:28). There are many other elements in our behavior that come into play when we talk about peace and how it is achieved and maintained: forgiveness, caring, sharing, positive communication, tolerance, citizenship, embracing diversity, cultural unity, caring for all living things, individuality, freedom, and so much more. Jesus' principle of love transcends all borders in Jesus' ministry. Jesus served all people, irrespective of their backgrounds (such as the Samaritan woman) to manifest his unconditional love (John 14:9). Christians are called to emulate Christ our Savior by striving for a harmonious relationship with all people rather than applying the discriminatory tendencies based on religion.

Peacemakers Commitment (Matt 5) Christians are called to build a peacemaking church that constantly prays, teaches, speaks, and acts for peace. Every liturgy must be a call to and celebration of peace.

Questions for Comprehension, Analysis, and Reflection

1. Ask each person to write a brief description of a positive image you learn in the peacebuilding of another religion.
2. What outstanding characteristics of their tradition would you like to learn now about?
3. What characteristics of other religion would you want to be committed to?

Conclusion

Peacebuilding focuses on different ways to promote peace and prevent conflict. It helps to build a peaceful society that is structured in such a way that it encourages each person to take the risk to invent new ways of living together. So for peace to exist, it has to engage in and debate with all the agendas for peace in a society.

Examples of Required Readings

Abu-Nimer, Mohammad. *Nonviolence and Peacebuilding in Islam*, 48–84. Gainsville, FL: University of Florida, 2000.

Ahmed, Razi. "Islam, Nonviolence, and Global Transformation." In *Islam and Nonviolence*, edited by Glenn D. Paige, et al., 27–52. Honolulu, HI: Centre for Global Nonviolence, 1993.

Tarimo, Aquiline. "The Role of Religion in Peacebuilding." 2012. http://binsarspeaks.net/wp-content/uploads/2012/02/The-Role-of-Religion-in-Peacebuilding.pdf.

Chapter 4: Sacred Texts or Peace Stories

Introduction

A close look at the original teachings of the oral and sacred texts of the Yoruba, Islam, and Christianity indicates that they are essentially wellsprings and resources for peace. We need to rediscover the principles and values that they uphold to remind us of the essential mission of each religion to seek peace.

Learning Objectives

At the end of this chapter, the participants will be able to:

1. Access more sacred texts and stories about peace from three religions.
2. Understand the different perspectives religions have about peace.
3. Notice differences and similarities.
4. Explore the causes of bloodshed when so many religions believe in peace.

Learning Activities

Activity 1: Conduct a debate in which the class divides either into pairs or into two groups. One side should argue that sacred texts help people to conduct their lives with morality and goodness. The other side will argue that people should work out for themselves what it means to be good, rather than relying on a text. Is it possible for the two groups to reach an agreement?

Activity 2: Ask participants to read each passage from sacred texts, think about what each one means separately, and then compare them. What beliefs do these religions hold in common based on the passages below? If peace is a shared belief, why do you think so much bloodshed has happened in the name of religion?

> From sacred text, Christianity: "Blessed are the peacemakers, for they shall be called the children of God" (Matt 5:9).

> From sacred text, Islam: "Let there be no hostility except to those who practice oppression" (Q 2:193).

> Yoruba proverb: Isokan.

Content

1. Proverbs of Peace in the Yoruba Religion

The theme of co-operation at the family and societal level is a precondition for peace in Yoruba world view. Hence the Proverb: "*Bi ede o dun, bii igbe ni iluri*," meaning, "If the home is not settled, the town is like a forest (without any allurement)." In the same vein, the theme of co-operation is reflected in: "*Owo omode ko to pepe, ti agbalagba ko wo akengbe*," meaning, "Just as a child's hand not reach the top of the mantel piece, so also does the elder's hand does not enter the gourd's neck."[44] Thus, when a child appeals to an adult for a favor, it should not be rejected, since both young and old all have responsibilities to one another and we live to complement each other. Additional proverbs are as follows: "*Okunkii ho ruru, ki a tunwa a ruru*" ("The sea does not foam violently and one rows on it violently"). Usage: care should be taken to handle any volatile/ dedicate matter. "*Ohun a ba tele mu kiibaje ohun a bafa gbara mu, li lenii le Kankan*" ("What one handles gently does not get spoilt, but if handled with force, it becomes difficult"). Usage: It is simply to advice/ to take life easy in all circumstances. "*Kafotun we osi, kafosi we out nlowo fi imo*" ("To wash the left with the right hand and wash the right hand with the left is what cleans both hands"). Usage: It is proverb that admonishes that people should co-operate with themselves. "*Okele gbigbe tountalaafia san ju*" (It signifies contentment). "*Gba fun Gbada ni leni gba fun sule loko*" ("Please give [this thing] to Gbada in town, is to help give [this thing] to Sule in the village"). Usage: We must be able to share things both amongst rich and the poor, no matter how far removed they are. "*Se fun mi, ki n se fun o niopolo fin kelodo*" ("Serve me and I serve you is what the toad is shouting in the river"). Usage: It is to express a tit for tat exchange. "*Opo eniyanni n je janmo, enikankii je awa de*" ("Very

---

44. Adeyemi, "Place of Indigenous Proverbs," 190.

many people will answer to be a crowd; no single person would say 'we have come'"). Usage: Working with others for a common end is better than singleness of purpose.

These proverbs are words of wisdom, teaching about peace. They will be interpreted and used in the context of interreligious education to enable the students to appreciate the values and contribution of Yoruba Religion.

2. Scriptures of Peace in Islam

The root of the word Islam is "*silm,*" which means peace—peace with God and with other human beings. A Muslim is one who submits to God's will. The objective of this submission is not so much the personal salvation of the individual believer but rather the successful execution of the Divine Plan and the implementation of a just and harmonious social order.[45] The following are several verses from Islam's Holy book, the Qur'an, which expresses peace-related messages: Islam and those who believe and do good are made to enter gardens (*jannah*) wherein flow rivers, abiding by their Lord's permission; "Their greeting therein is peace" (Q 14:23); "Enter paradise in peace and security" (Q 15:46); "God guideth him who seeketh his good pleasures unto paths of peace" (Q 5:16); "In paradise there is not idle chatter but only the invocation of peace, such is the greeting from the LORD all compassionate" (Q 36:58); "If two parties of believers fall to fighting, then make peace between them. And if one party of them does wrong to the other, fight that wrong-doer until it returns to the ordinance of God; then, if it returns, make peace between them justly, and act equitably. Lo! God loves the equitable" (Q 49:9); "He is who sent down peace of reassurance into the hearts of the believers, that they might add faith to their faith" (Q 48:4); "In the remembrance of God do hearts find satisfaction" (Q 13:28); "O tranquil soul, return to your Lord so pleasant and well-pleased! Enter among My servants and enter My garden!" (Q 89:27–30); "Whosoever kills a human being, except (as punishment) for murder or spreading corruption in the land, it shall be like killing all humanity; and whosoever saves a life, saves the entire human race" (Q 5:32); "Allah does not forbid you to deal justly and kindly with those who fought against you on account of religion nor drove you out of your homes. Verily, Allah loves those who deal with equity" (Q 60:8); "It is righteousness to believe in God and the Last Day and the Angels,

---

45. Mahmood-Abedin, "Islam and Global Governance," 285.

and the Book, and the Messengers; to spend of your substance, out of love for Him, for your kin, for orphans, for the needy, for the wayfarer, for those who ask; and for freeing captives; to be steadfast in prayers; and practice regular charity" (Q 2:177); "Be dutiful and good to parents, and to kindred, and to orphans and the poor, and speak good to people" (Q 2:83); "O mankind! We have created you male and female and have made you nations and tribes, that you may know one another (not despise on another)" (Q 49:13); "And fight in God's cause against those who wage war against you, but do not commit aggression—for, verily, God does not love aggressors" (Q 2:190); "God commands justice, the doing of good, and He forbids all shameful deeds, injustice and rebellion" (Q 16:90); "It is they who are the believers in truth. For them are grades of dignity with their Lord, and forgiveness and generous provision" (Q 8:4); and "Peace! A word of salutation from the Lord most merciful" (Q 36:58).

From the Hadith—the sayings of Prophet Muhammad—we find verses such as the following: God's creatures are His family, and he is most beloved by God who does real good to the members of God's family. May I tell you what is even better than prayers and fasting and giving alms to the poor? It is reconciling differences and disputes among men. And sowing discord wipes off all virtues. God fills the heart of him with faith and contentment who, having the power to avenge himself, exercises restraint and toleration. And by God he is no believer whose neighbor does not live in peace because of his mischief making. Show compassion to those on earth, so that He who is in heaven may show His mercy on you.[46]

3. Scriptures of Peace in Christianity

From the Old Testament, which is part of Christianity's Holy Scriptures, we can also derive the concept of "shalom," the Hebrew word for peace. Shalom implies wholeness and comprehensive well-being, including good health, prosperity, harmony, healing, welfare, happiness, and security.[47] It also means the absence of war: "I will break bow and sword and weapons of war and sweep them off the earth, so that all the living creatures may lie down without fear" (Hos 2:20). However, peace is not simply the absence of war. The prophets envisioned it as a reality where weapons give way to implements of peace: "They shall beat their swords

---

46. Saiyadain, "Islam," 54.
47. Lord, "Spiritual and Faith Tradition as Resources of Peace," 54.

into plowshares and their spears into pruning hooks; one nation shall not raise the sword against another nor shall they train for war again" (Isa 2:4). Peace is also envisioned as intimately connected to justice: "Justice and peace shall kiss" (Ps 85:11); "Justice will bring about peace, will produce calm and security" (Isa 32:17).

Another fundamental peace-related teaching of Christianity is that which relates to the worth of humans. In the Old Testament, Genesis says God created humans in His image and likeness (Gen 1:26–28). In the New Testament, we find Jesus saying: "Do for others what you want them to do for you." This is the meaning of the Law of Moses and of the teachings.

There are many additional scriptural passages that promote peace in Christianity.

From the Hebrew Scriptures: "God is peace, His name is peace, and all is bound together in peace" (Lev 10); "May the Lord lift up his countenance upon you, and give you peace" (Num 6:26); "Thou dost keep him in perfect peace, whose mind is stayed on thee, because he trusts in thee" (Isa 26:3); and "They shall beat their swords into plowshares, and their spears into pruning hooks; nation shall not lift up sword against nation, neither shall they learn war any more" (Isa 2:4). (See also Isa 1:16–17; 11:6–9; 32:16–17; 57:17, 19–21; Jer 6:13–14; Mic 2:1–2; 4:1–4; Lev 2:14; 26; Amos 4:1; 5:14–15a; Ps 34:14).

From the New Testament (or Second Testament): "The peace of God, which passes all understanding, will keep your hearts and your minds in Christ Jesus" (Phil 4:7); "Peace I leave with you; my peace I give to you; not as the world gives do I give to you" (John 14:27); "The peace which comes from finding union in the midst of the world's bewildering diversity is also expressed Glory to God in the highest, and on earth peace, good will toward men" (Luke 2:14); "For Christ Jesus is our peace, who has made us both one, and has broken down the dividing wall of hostility" (Eph 2:14); and "Blessed are the peacemakers, for they shall be called sons of God" (Matt 5:9). (See also Luke 12:13, 15–22; Acts 5:1–14; Gal 3:28–29). These passages can also be compared to texts in the Hebrew Bible (Jer 6:13–14; Ezek 13:10; Amos 6:1–6).

George explains that we can identify three elements in Jesus' approach to peace[48]:

> **Rejection of Violence**

---

48. George, "Radically Christian Witness for Peace," 50.

He instructed his disciples during his arrest in the Garden of Gethsemane not to take the sword: "All who take the sword die by the sword" (Matt 26:51–52); Love and Reconciliation Rather than Retaliation: "Love one another, by this love it will be known that they are His disciples" (John 13:34); and He extended this commandment of love to include enemies: "Love your enemies, do good to those who hate you, bless those who curse you, and pray for those who maltreat you" (Matt 5:43–44).

Jesus set aside the traditional lextalionis ("an eye for an eye") in favor of a loving and compassionate response. In Romans, it is said: "Never repay injury with injury.... Avenge not yourselves.... Vengeance belongs to me; I will recompense, says the Lord. But if your enemy is hungry, feed him; if he thirsts, give him to drink.... Be not overcome by evil but overcome evil with good" (Rom 12:17–21). The aim of such non-retaliatory love is reconciliation.

> **Use of transforming Initiatives**

Christians are called to actively engage in peacemaking. In Jesus' Sermon on the Mount, he said, "Blessed are the peacemakers, for they shall be called the children of God" (Matt 5:9). Jesus told his disciples to respond to violence by taking unexpected, surprising initiatives: "When a person strikes you on the right cheek, turn and offer him the other.... Should anyone make you walk a mile with him, go with him two miles" (Matt 5:39–41).

Questions for Comprehension, Analysis, and Reflection

1. Name various sacred texts on peace from your tradition and explain how it is practiced in our daily life
2. Name various sacred texts on peace that are not put in practice and why?

Conclusion

Peace is most desirable in all religion's sacred texts. In the oral and sacred texts, peace brings tranquillity to the heart and clarity to the mind. It is the absence of passions, desires, anxieties, and wandering thoughts; the heart becomes cool and content. Islam and Christianity both praise the peace and tranquillity that come to the soul that is firm in faith. Other passages describe the peace of God that brings harmony among people and nations. Outward peace is emphasized in the Abrahamic faiths, for whom the work of God has a social and historical dimension. The love of God breaks down the walls of hostility between people, and thus becomes the foundation for their lasting peace.

Examples of Required Readings

New Testament: Colossians 3
Qur'an: Chapter 5

Unit IV: Human Security

The fourth unit comprises four chapters. It looks at understanding the concept of human security, the components and teachings of human security from three religions, and understands the basic principles of human existence and peaceful development.

Chapter 1: Understanding Human Security

Introduction

To address the widespread threats facing the people of Nigeria, religious leaders must be acquainted with the concepts and skills of human security which give more tangible results that comprehensively address the roots causes behind those threats.

Learning Objectives

At the end of this chapter, the participants will be able to:

1. Define the human security concept.
2. Understand human rights standards, principles, instruments, and mechanisms of promotion and protection.
3. Analyze the causes of human rights violations.
4. Develop attitudes such as a sense of justice and equality, respect of human rights, and skills in empathy and dignity.
5. Understand the main human security threats and risks identified.

6. Understand the strategic approaches and policy tools.
7. Take action oriented toward ways of dealing with human rights violations.

Learning Activities

Post series of pictures of various situations—in conflict, human slavery, famine, etc.—and ask participants to observe the pictures. Which one has touched them and why? Ask them to reflect on what human security issues are present in the picture. Each should write down their comments and share with others. At the end, lead a discussion on participants' opinions and assist them in understanding and framing different human security issues.

Content

What is Human Security?

According to the Commission on Human Security (CHS),[1] in its final report, *Human Security Now,* human security is defined as:

> To protect the vital core of all human lives in ways that enhance human freedoms and human fulfillment. Human security means protecting fundamental freedoms—freedoms that are the essence of life. It means protecting people from critical (severe) and pervasive (widespread) threats and situations. It means using processes that build on people's strengths and aspirations. It means creating political, social, environmental, economic, military, and cultural systems that together give people the building blocks of survival, livelihood, and dignity.[2]

1. What are the Main Features of Human Security?

Human security brings together the "human elements" of security, rights, and development. As such, it is an interdisciplinary concept that displays

---

1. The Commission on Human Security (CHS) was established in January 2001 in response to the UN Secretary-General's call for a world "free from want" and "free from fear" at the 2000 Millennium Summit. The Commission consisted of twelve prominent international figures, including Mrs. Sadako Ogata (former UN High Commissioner for Refugees) and Professor Amartya Sen (1998 Nobel Economics Prize Laureate).

2. CHS, *Human Security,* 4.

the following characteristics: people-centered; multi-sectoral; comprehensive; context-specific; and prevention-oriented. As a people-centered concept, human security places the individual at the "center of analysis." Consequently, it considers a broad range of conditions which threaten survival, livelihood, and dignity, identifying the threshold below which human life is intolerably threatened. Human security is also based on a multi-sectoral understanding of insecurities. Therefore, human security entails a broadened understanding of threats and includes causes of insecurity relating for instance to economic, food, health, environmental, personal, community, and political security. Moreover, human security emphasizes the interconnectedness of both threats and responses when addressing these insecurities. That is, threats to human security are mutually reinforcing and interconnected in two ways. First, they are interlinked in a domino effect in the sense that each threat feeds on the other. For example, violent conflicts can lead to deprivation and poverty, which, in turn, could lead to resource depletion, infectious diseases, education deficits, etc. Second, threats within a given country or area can spread into a wider region and have negative externalities for regional and international security.

2. Human Security Principles and Approach

Human Security focuses primarily on protecting people while promoting peace and assuring sustainable continuous development. It emphasizes aiding individuals by using a people-centered approach for resolving inequalities that affect security. From an operational perspective, human security aims to address complex situations of insecurity through collaborative, responsive, and sustainable measures that are (i) people-centered, (ii) multisectoral, (iii) comprehensive, (iv) context-specific, and (v) prevention-oriented. In addition, human security employs a hybrid approach that brings together these elements through a protection and empowerment framework: "Human Security complements state security, strengthens human development, and enhances human rights."[3]

3. Definition of Human Rights

In the words of Toh and Cawagas: "Human rights could be generally defined as those rights which are inherent in our nature and without

---

3. CHS, *Human Security*, 2.

which we cannot live as human beings."[4] They argue that "human rights encompass those rights that make a person human and enable one to develop fully as a human being and at the same time allow people to live in community and realise the richness of their talents, culture, resources, and nonmaterial gifts."[5]

Human rights are naturally acquired and important for human beings to survive with dignity. Castro and Nario-Galace argue that: "Human dignity is the fundamental innate worth of a human being having been made in the image and likeness of God."[6] In addition, Galace sustains that: "The protection of human dignity means the protection of self-esteem. It motivates one to treat himself or herself and others with respect. Human rights and human dignity are closely interlinked."

4. Types of Human Rights

Cawagas and Toh point out five major types of human rights: "Civil rights; political rights; economic rights; social rights; and cultural rights."[7] But Galace writes: "There are two types or sets of rights. The first is the Civil and Political Rights which make certain freedom of human from fear. In this set of rights, governments are mandated to protect the life, liberty, and security of their citizens. The second set of rights is the Economic, Social, and Cultural Rights which aim to ensure freedom of human from want."[8] In spite of considering a different number of types, the content is the same. Toh and Cawagas explain: "The civil and political rights are those rights that guarantee the freedoms of individuals to be able to participate in the activities necessary to facilitate peace and harmony in society."[9] In addition, Galace argues: "Civil rights are rights belonging to a person by virtue of citizenship and political rights involve the power of citizens to participate directly or indirectly in the administration of government."[10] This author writes that: "Amnesty international describes economic, social, and cultural rights as rights that relate to the conditions

---

4. Toh and Cawagas, *Peaceful Theory and Practice*, 138.
5. Toh and Cawagas, *Peaceful Theory and Practice*, 135.
6. Nairo-Galace, "Towards a Fairer World," 60.
7. Cawagas and Toh, "Building a Peace Education Program," 233.
8. Nairo-Galace, "Towards a Fairer World," 60.
9. Toh and Cawagas, *Peaceful Theory and Practice*, 135.
10. Nairo-Galace, "Towards a Fairer World," 60.

necessary to meet basic human needs such as food, shelter, education, health care, and gainful employment."[11]

Questions for Comprehension, Analysis, and Reflection

1. Define human security in your own words.
2. From your tradition, how can you prevent various human abuses?
3. How do various religions meet basic human needs?

Conclusion

Living in a "global village," we become more conscious of the need of human beings and recognize the responsibilities to each other in applying the concept of human security. This is bound to find increasing application and wider adherence with each religion and society.

Examples of Required Readings

Cilliers, Jakkie. "Human Security in Africa: A Conceptual Framework for Review." https://www.issafrica.org/uploads/AHSIMONO1.PDF.

---

11. Nairo-Galace, "Towards a Fairer World," 60.

Chapter 2: The Yoruba Religion and Human Security

Introduction

The Yoruba traditional education for peace and security promotes human security which puts the human being in the center and focuses on an educational order that prevents peace and security menaces in Nigeria.

Learning Objectives

At the end of this chapter, the participants will be able to:

1. Understand human rights standards and principles from the Yoruba Religion.
2. Use the various proverbs on justice, equality, ecology, and good governance.
3. Analyze causes of human rights violations.
4. Develop attitudes such as a sense of justice and equality, respect of human rights, and skills in empathy and dignity.
5. Take action oriented towards an education for human rights and ways of dealing with human rights violations in a multireligious context.

Learning Activities

Post a series of pictures of various human rights situations (in conflict, human slavery, famine, etc.) and ask participants to observe the pictures. Determine which affects them the most and why. Ask them to reflect on the human rights issues present in the picture. Each should write down their comments and share with others. At the end, lead a discussion on participants' opinions and assist them in understanding and framing different human rights issues.

Ask the participants to discuss the following questions in groups:

How does your traditional religion deal with human safety from chronic threats such as hunger, disease, and repression? What are teachings on protection from sudden and hurtful disruptions in the patterns of daily life—whether in homes, jobs, or communities? Write their answers on a board.

Content

1. Human Rights

In Yoruba land, human rights are important and are taught with proverbs such as "*Agba kiiwa l'oja kori omo tuntun wo*," meaning, "An elder will not be in the market and young ones suffer guidance." Thus, the role of the elders as a repository of the wisdom, customs, and values of the society is underscored. At all times, an elder must call for caution. Discuss how elders have lost the respect accorded them in indigenous education as repository of good cultural practices. Can this be attributed to social decadence, corruption, greed, and acquisition of bad practices from foreign cultures?

2. Justice

In the Yoruba Religion, fair is not everyone getting the same thing; rather, fair is everyone getting what they need in other to be successful. In Yoruba Religion, peace in the community cannot be separated from justice. Peace is honorable; it can never be achieved when you are disgraced or when you disgrace another person. People must relate to one another on equal terms. Using the proverb *"Ika to ba se l'obaige"* ("We punish only the offender"), explain the concept of justice and how it can be applied in education.

3. Equality

The following proverbs explain the concept of equality and how it can be applied in education: (1) "*Aparo kan ko ga ju kan lo, afi eyi ti o ba gun ori ebe*" ("We are all equal unless you do otherwise"); (2) "*Ibi koju ibi, bi ase bi eru la se bi omo*" ("We are born in the same way either slave or master"); and (3) "*Ona lojineruni baba*" ("What is good for goose is also good for gander").

4. Good Governance

The following proverbs explain the concept of good governance and how it can be applied in education.

> "*Imado iba se bielede a balu je beruba joba, omo o ni ku kan*" ("Where the wild bear become the pig, it would have ruined the town; if the slave becomes the king, no decent person would have remained"). Usage: this proverb is used when someone is using his minor position to revenge himself on his enemies or for his personal advantage. Simply put, it means to rejoice over the failure of a bad person not able to be in position of authority.

> "*A Ki ijayeobakayagbesara*" ("No one relishes this kingly authority and defecates on his body"). Usage: the proverb is used in regard to a highly placed person who engages in demeaning actions.

> "*A gba kii waloja kori omo tuntun wo*" ("An elder cannot be in the market and allow the head of the newborn to bend"). Usage: it is used to challenge the elders in any gathering/community that things should not go wrong in their presence or that it is the responsibility of the elders in all situations to make sure that misunderstandings which may lead to unpleasantness are explained/removed/nipped in the bud.

> "*A kii fi ete sile ki a ma a pa lapalapa*" ("No one leaves leprosy untreated and tend ordinary ringworm"). Usage: the proverb simply means you do not throw away the substance for the shadow.

5. Ecology

> **The Concept of Environment in Yoruba Religion.**

The Yoruba are in constant consciousness and acknowledgement of God's divine Lordship over the whole earth. They also believe that man is a tenant on God's earth.[12] This fact keeps a check on their behavior and

---

12. Idowu, *African Traditional Religion*, 206.

reminds them that they ought to be careful how this earth is treated. The idea that God is the Creator of the Universe is held by most religions of the world. The idea of the creation of the Universe and all that is there is fundamental to the basis of the religious beliefs of Yoruba people. Respect for the environment has always been with them.

The Yoruba do not usually tamper with nature carelessly. Modernization has taken its toll on this aspect (just as it has affected all other aspects) of Nigerian life. All the features in nature are created and placed there for a significant purpose. The sole aim is to create a healthy and beautiful habitat for human beings. Some of these natural features are also to serve as an abode for a category of the divinities.[13]

The Osun groove in Oshogbo, whose forest and river are forbidden for hunting and fishing, is an example of the care for the environment. The Oke-Ibadan (Ibadan Hill) is a place set apart for the spirit of the hill which the people believe had offered them help in the war days and continues to pour his blessings on the people of Ibadan.[14] The same thing operates among the Egba of Abeokuta, where the Olumo Rock is dedicated to the spirit of the rock believed to have offered them assistance in war days.[15]

The environment and the people are in close relationship in Yoruba religion. The Yoruba life is at a critical junction,[16] where the natural meets the supernatural and where the ancestors and the divine intersect with the humans. Sometimes, the name of divinities tells of the natural phenomenon through which they manifest.[17] The word *okun* in Yoruba means sea, but the goddess of the sea or ocean is also called *olokun* (the owner or Lord of the sea). One important truth about Yoruba religion is that the divinities are the objective phenomena of the religion.[18] Each of them oversees a compartment of the Yoruba life, and this includes nature and the environment. This is the main reason why the creation in the environment must be treated with respect. In a typical Yoruba setting, you do not just dig the ground for any purpose without due permission from

---

13. Awolalu and Dopamu, *West African Traditional Religion*, 73.
14. Awolalu and Dopamu, *West African Traditional Religion*, 73.
15. Awolalu and Dopamu, *West African Traditional Religion*, 73.
16. Some, *Healing Wisdom of Africa*, 125.
17. Awolalu and Dopamu, *West African Traditional Religion*, 74.
18. Awolalu and Dopamu, *West African Traditional Religion*, 75.

the soil. Throughout the ages, the Yoruba people are constantly learning what their faith has to say about preserving the environment.

Furthermore, the Yoruba concept of the environment is all embracing; the humans, animals, plants, and "non-living beings" form the entire human society or community. Therefore, for a peaceful co-existence of all of these beings, the humans—who consider themselves to be in charge—must be careful not to provoke or destabilize their environment and their "co-tenants." For instance, the tiniest of insects is regarded as having rights to life. This is the reason why the ants are considered *aafa inu igbo* (the alfa of the forest). The Yoruba are known to give them food items (grains) whenever they come across them in the forest or bush path. They are known to bring good luck. In some parts of Yorubaland, motorists attempt to slow down whenever they come across ducks on the road. If by accident, a motorist runs over a duck, he or she must stop and put some money and other items on the dead duck. Failure to do this may cause an automobile accident. In addition, the Yoruba also have a saying regarding the right to life of insects that says: "*Yi ese re si apakan, ma se te kokoro nikokoro ti iwo ko naani ni Olorun lo le da a*" ("Side step your feet, do not kill that insect, that insect you do not regard, God also created").

The chameleon is also a sacred being that cannot be killed. There are multiple examples, but suffice to mention these few in support of the Yoruba attitude to the integrity of creation which by extension is the environment. Another dimension to the interconnectedness between the Yoruba and their environment is the step they take in rituals to correct a violation of nature.

Questions for Comprehension, Analysis, and Reflection

Have the participants reflect in groups of three or four on learning during this class and ask them to answer the following question: (1) What did you learn about human rights issues in Yoruba Religion? (2) Name human rights abuses and issues within their community. What human rights instruments can be used to rectify them from Yoruba Religion?

Conclusion

Yoruba Religion as a religion instructs people on how to live together in peace and harmony. It seeks peace and security in the individual as well as in the community as a whole.

Examples of Required Readings

Eze, O. "Human Rights Issues and Violations: The African Experience." In *Human Rights, Peace, and Justice in Africa: A Reader,* edited by C. Heyns and K. Stefiszyn, 40–41. Pretoria: Pretoria University Law, 2000.

Heyns, C., and M. Killander. "The African Regional Human Rights System." In *Human Rights, Peace, and Justice in Africa: A Reader,* edited by C. Heyns and K. Stefiszyn, 39. Pretoria: Pretoria University Law, 2006.

Marks, S. "Human Rights Education in UN Peace-building: From Theory to Practice." In *The People's Movement for Human Rights Learning: A Peoples' Report*, edited by PDHRE, 76–86. New York: PDHRE, 2010.

Chapter 3: Islam and Human Security

Introduction

Islam, like other religions and cultures, plays a significant role in dealing with human security. Many Qur'anic verses explain human security issues.

Learning Objectives

At the end of this chapter, the participants will be able to:

1. Understand human rights standards and principles from Islam.
2. Use various Qur'anic verses on justice, equality, ecology, and good governance.
3. Understand causes of human rights violations as a Muslim.
4. Develop attitudes such as a sense of justice and equality, respect of human rights, and skills in empathy and dignity.
5. Take action oriented towards an education for human rights and ways of dealing with human rights violations in a multireligious context.

Learning Activities

Post a series of pictures of various human rights situations (in conflict, human slavery, famine, etc.) and ask participants to observe the pictures. Determine which affects them the most and why. Ask them to reflect on the human rights issues present in the picture. Each should write down their comments and share with others. At the end, lead a discussion on participants' opinions and assist them in understanding and framing different human rights issues.

Ask the participants to discuss the following questions in groups: What are the Islamic teachings and beliefs on human safety from chronic threats such as hunger, disease, and repression? What are the teachings on protection from sudden and hurtful disruptions in the patterns of daily life—whether in homes, jobs, or communities? Write their answers on a board.

Content

1. Human Rights

The Islamic model of human rights in particular is striking in its rigor, its vision, and its relevance to modern times. The distinguishing feature of human entitlements in Islam is that they are the natural outcome of a broader practice of faith, deeds, and social behavior that Muslims believe are divinely mandated. The Qur'an says: "God commands justice, doing good, and generosity towards relatives, and He forbids what is shameful, blameworthy, and oppressive. He teaches you, so that you may take heed" (Q 16:90). Muhammad, the final prophet of Islam, established the very first Islamic society, which eliminated the spiritual and social problems rampant in the Arabian Peninsula. Freedom of religion was instituted in Medina; women were honored and respected as equals; racial discrimination was practically eliminated; tribal warfare was replaced with united ties of brotherhood; and usury and alcohol were completely forbidden.

When considering the question of human rights and Islam, it is important to distinguish the divinely prescribed rights of Islam from potential misinterpretation and misapplication by imperfect human beings. Just as Western societies still fight against racism and discrimination, many Muslim societies struggle to fully implement the rights outlined in Islam. Human rights in Islam stem from two foundational principles: dignity and equality. Dignity is a fundamental right of every human being merely by virtue of his or her humanity. As God states in the Qur'an: "We have honored the children of Adam and carried them by land and sea; we have provided good sustenance for them and favored them especially above many of those we have created" (Q 17:70).

Regarding equality, God (Allah in Arabic) clearly declares that, in His sight, the only distinguishing factors between humans are righteousness and piety: "People, We created you all from a single man and a single woman, and made you into races and tribes so that you should recognize one another. In God's eyes, the most honored of you are the ones most mindful of Him: God is all knowing, all aware" (Q 49:13).

Both men and women have responsibilities towards their families and societies as is clear from the following verse: "The Believers, men and women, are protectors one of another: they enjoin what is just and forbid what is evil: they observe regular prayers, practice regular charity, and obey Allah and His Messenger. On them will Allah pour His mercy: for Allah is exalted in power, Wise" (Q 9:71).

God promises in the Qur'an: "If any do deeds of righteousness, be they male or female, and have faith, they will enter Heaven, and not the least injustice will be done to them" (Q 4:124). In Islam, life is a sacred trust from God and the most basic right of a human being. No individual is permitted to take the life of another, unless it is for justice administered by a competent court following due process of law.

God recognizes this right in the Qur'an: "Nor take life which Allah has made sacred—except for just cause" (Q 17:33). He also says: "If anyone kills a person—unless in retribution for murder or spreading corruption in the land—it is as if he kills all mankind, while if any saves a life, it is as if he saves the lives of all mankind" (Q 5:32). Not only do human beings have the right not to be harmed, they have the right to be safeguarded from harm, physical or otherwise. For instance, under Islamic law, people are legally liable for not preventing a blind man from dying of a perilous fall if they were in a position to save him.

Even during war, Islam enjoins that one deals with the enemy nobly on the battlefield. Enemy soldiers and prisoners of war are not to be tortured or mutilated under any circumstances. Islam has also drawn a clear line of distinction between combatants and non-combatants. As far as the non-combatant population is concerned—such as women, children, and the elderly—the instructions of Prophet Muhammad are as follows: "Do not kill any old person, any child or any woman," and, "Do not kill the monks in monasteries." Hence non-combatants are guaranteed security of life even if their nation is at war with an Islamic state. It is now widely recognized that justice is intimately connected with human rights. A society cannot be a just and peaceful society if it denies human rights to its people or if it opts for the abridgement of such rights.

2. Justice

The Islamic concept of justice is another cardinal concept profoundly influencing Muslim thinking and action and carrying huge peace potentials. The term used for justice, *adl*, has an extended meaning and goes far beyond the narrower meaning of justice in the legal parlance. Along with i*hsan* (beneficence) and *rahmah* (compassion), *adl* manifests the yearning for a just social reality. "Justice rooted in divine wisdom is applicable to all times and all people,"[19] and its importance has been highlighted by both the Qur'an and tradition. According to Khadduri, and as quoted in Abu-Nimer's excellent study entitled *Nonviolence and Peacebuilding in Islam: Theory and Practice*: "In the Qur'an, there are over two hundred admonitions against injustice expressed in such words as *zulm, ithm, dalal,* and others, and no less than almost a hundred expressions embodying the notion of justice, either directly, in such words as *adl, qist, mizan,* and others noted before, or in a variety of indirect expressions."[20]

Again, and as pointed out by Abu-Nimer, justice is "an absolute and not a relative value, a duty to be pursued among the believers and with the enemies, too."[21] The Qur'an says: "Serve Allah, and join not any partner with Him; and do good—to parents, kinsfolk, orphans, those in need, neighbors who are near, neighbors who are strangers, the companion by your side, the wayfarer (ye meet), and what your right hands possess: for Allah loveth not the arrogant, the vainglorious" (Q 4:36).

Islam attaches great importance to social and economic justice achievable through sharing, poverty alleviation efforts, and concerted individual and collective initiatives, voluntary charities, and by developing the society on egalitarian lines. It obligates its followers to contribute towards the promotion of economic justice by doing well in a non discriminatory manner. It also calls upon the state for the establishment of a fair and just distributive mechanism in order to reduce poverty and powerlessness and ensure an optimum degree of equitable distribution of resources in the society. The Islamic principle of justice, one may add here, is based on Qur'anic injunctions and tradition. It encompasses all spheres and all aspects of human and societal relationships.

3. Equality

Islam regards humanity as a single family based on the equality of all members. The idea of the oneness and common origin of all the people is the foundational idea in the Qur'an and it reflects the universality and inclusiveness of Islam in dealing with mankind. The Qur'an says

---

19. Abu-Nimer, *Nonviolence and Peace Building in Islam*, 2.
20. Mehdi, "Islamic Principles and Values," 63.
21. Abu-Nimer, *Nonviolence and Peace Building in Islam*, 3.

emphatically that God has created the humans from the same pair of a male and a female and made them nations and tribes so that they may know each other, and do not despise each other (Q 49:13). Again, no privilege is granted to any one on the basis of race, ethnicity, or tribal association. What matters most is piety, righteousness, being good to others, and devotion to God. Also important to note is the fact that the requirement of mutual consultation (*shurah*) is neither a mere formality for a ruler to resort to nor a requirement to be subjected to political expediency. *Shurah* is a serious business in Islam. It is neither a mere political gimmick nor is it a sort of political sport of the Cains in the Muslim societies or elsewhere.[22] Islamic scholars, particularly those who challenge the notion that Islam and democracy are antithetical to one another, assert that *shurah* is:

> Men and women who have surrendered, believing men and believing women, obedient men and obedient women, truthful men and truthful women, enduring men and enduring women, humble men and humble women, men and women who give charity, men who fast and women who fast, men and women who guard their private parts, men and women who remember God often—for them God has prepared forgiveness and a mighty reward. (Q 73:36)

The Qur'an makes it clear that there is no gender difference where righteousness is concerned (Q 4:1, 124; 6:97; 9:71). "That God may chastise the hypocrites, men and women alike, and the idolaters, men and women alike; and that God turn again unto believers, men and women alike" (Q 33:73). Another verse notes: "I waste not the labor of any that labors among you, be you male and female—the one of you is as the other" (Q 3:194).

4. Good Governance

Islam is concerned with the politics and governance and provides clear instructions about how to run government affairs. Prophet Muhammad says in one of his Hadith: "Authority is a trust, and on the Day of judgment, it is a cause of humiliation and repentance except for one who fulfills its obligations and (properly) discharges the duties attendant thereon."[23]

---

22. Abu-Nimer, *Nonviolence and Peace Building in Islam*, 58.
23. Sahih Muslim, "Hadith 4491," 1:20.

In "Principles of Good Governance in Islam," Hassan Abbas explains that the purpose of governance in Islam is to encourage the formation of a just society based on the principles of equality, justice, rational thinking, tolerance, and equity. The two primary goals of establishing an Islamic state are promoting justice and pursuit of knowledge. The Islamic idea of governance is to nurture humane and accountable leaders who would focus on the wellbeing of ordinary people by establishing different institutions. If we go through these teachings in more detail, we shall realize that they are valuable for any person aspiring to become a future political leader, even in the modern world.[24]

He identifies the following five central principles of good governance in Islam:

- **Provision of justice for every citizen**, regardless of status in the society or financial condition.

- **Every Muslim, men and women**, has the right to obtain both religious and material education.

- **There should be centrality of consultation** in decision making; that is, the matters should be decided by consultation among people.

- **Welfare of people** is the primary goal of governance in Islam.

- **A leader should be knowledgeable**, honest, and accountable for his deeds.

5. Ecology

Islam expresses great concern for the environment. There are numerous verses in the Qur'an and the sayings of Prophet Muhammad addressing the issue of ecology. Islam's solution to environmental problems lies in man's adaptation of its guidance. Allah has stated that He made all the material objects on earth for man's use, not for his abuse. Humans are to maintain and not damage or abuse natural resources. Allah says: "But seek, through that which Allah has given you, the home of the Hereafter; and (yet), do not forget your share of the world. And do good as Allah has done good to you. And desire not corruption in the land. Indeed,

---

24. See Abbas, "Principles of Good Governance in Islam."

Allah does not like corruptors" (Q 28:77); "And eat and drink from the provision of Allah, and do not commit abuse on the earth, spreading corruption" (Q 2:60).

The Qur'an and the Sunnah of the Prophet Muhammad contain instructions for Muslims to preserve the environment, which includes not cutting down trees unnecessarily. In this respect, Prophet Muhammad pointed out that there are benefits in planting trees, which will last until the Day of Judgment. This is illustrated in the sayings: "If the Hour is imminent and anyone of you has a palm shoot (to plant) in his hand and is able to plant it before the Hour strikes, then he should do so and he will be rewarded for that action," and, "There is no creature on (or within) the earth or a bird that flies with its wings except that they are nations (communities) like you" (Q 6:38). We infer from the Prophet's statement and this Qur'anic verse that all living things are partners to man in existence and they deserve our respect. We must be merciful toward animals and strive to ensure the preservation of different species. Islam also forbids wasting water and using it without benefit. The preservation of water for the nourishment of humankind, animal life, bird life, and vegetation is a practice that gains Allah's pleasure.

Questions for Comprehension, Analysis, and Reflection

Have the participants reflect in groups of three or four on learning during this class and ask them to answer the following question: (1) What did you learn about human rights issues in Islam? (2) Name human rights abuses and issues from within their community. What human rights instruments can be used to rectify them from Islam?

Conclusion

"Islam" not only refers to a religion; rather, it is a way of life, and it instructs people on how to live together in peace and harmony. It seeks the peace and security of the individual as well as the community as a whole.

Examples of Required Readings

Ali, S. Sardar. *Gender and Human Rights in Islam and International Law: Equal Before Allah, Unequal Before Man?* The Hague: Kluwer Law International, 2000.

Altwaijri, Abdulaziz. *Human Rights in Islamic Teachings*. Malaysia: Publication of the Islamic Educational, Scientific and Cultural Organization, 2001.

Abu-Nimer. "Basic Human Needs: Bridging the Gap Between Theory and Practice." In *Conflict Resolution and Human Needs: Linking Theory and Practice*, edited by Kevin Avruch and Chris Mitchell, 165–86. New York: Routledge, 2013.

Foltz, Richard, et al., eds. *Islam and Ecology*. Cambridge, MA: Harvard University Press, 2003.

Khalid, Fazlun, and Joanne O'Brien, eds. *Islam and Ecology*. London: Cassel, 1993.

Hasan, Samiul, ed. *Human Security and Philanthropy: Islamic Perspectives and Muslim Majority Country Practices*, 31–49. New York: Springer, 2015.

Chapter 4: Christianity and Human Security

Introduction

In Christianity, human rights are part of religious commandments and are considered very important. This chapter explores how Christianity is committed to the concept of human security, to the recognition that all persons are subjects of dignity and rights, and to the protection of the defenseless and least protected members of society.

Learning Objectives

At the end of this chapter, the participants will be able to:

1. Understand human rights standards and principles from Christianity.
2. Use various Biblical verses on justice, equality, ecology, and good governance.
3. Understand causes of human rights violations as a Christian.
4. Develop attitudes such as a sense of justice and equality, respect of human rights, and skills in empathy and dignity.
5. Take action oriented towards an education for human rights and ways of dealing with human rights violations in a multireligious context.

Learning Activities

Post a series of pictures of various human rights situations (in conflict, human slavery, famine, etc.) and ask participants to observe the pictures. Determine which affects them the most and why. Ask them to reflect on the human rights issues present in the picture. Each should write down their comments and share with others. At the end, lead a discussion on participants' opinions and assist them in understanding and framing different human rights issues.

Ask the participants to discuss in group the following questions: What are the Christian teachings and beliefs on human safety from chronic threats such as hunger, disease, and repression? What are the teachings on protection from sudden and hurtful disruptions in the Patterns of daily life—whether in homes, jobs, or communities? Write their answers on a board.

Content

1. Human Rights

Christians derive human rights from traditions and doctrines. Whether the emphasis is on grace or covenant, creation or redemption, God's action calls for human response. In "Christian Support for Human Rights," Robert Traer asserts: "Christians accept as binding the commandments to love God and to love their neighbors and to keep the Golden Rule. . . . Christians affirm that human rights are derived from faith and involve duties to God and one's neighbor."[25] Human rights are not only derived from divine rights but also constitute duties toward others. Christians assert that because God loves all people, all people have rights and the corresponding duties to respect the rights of all others.

Generally, Christians agree that human rights are justified because of God's redemptive acts. As Moltmann asserts: "Human dignity is not merely known in the created order but in the Christ-event."[26] "It is in the meeting of God in the man Jesus Christ that man fully discovers his dignity and the dignity of all others whom he must love as his neighbors (Luke 10:36; Matt 5:43–48)."[27] Christians also affirm human dignity by supporting human rights because God has created and redeemed humanity. Max Stackhouse argues that logically all talk of human rights involves at least the following two presuppositions:

> Members of a society must believe that there is a universal moral law transcending their own culture, society, or period of history about which they can know something with relative clarity [and this] universal moral law must involve an affirmation of the dignity of each person as a member, a participant, in relationship with others, in a community that extends to all humankind.[28]

---

25. Traer, "Christian Support for Human Rights," 1.
26. McCormick quoted in Robert, "From Reflection to Action," 245.
27. Giblet, "Human Rights and the Dignity of Man," 2.
28. Stackhouse, "Public Theology, Human Rights, and Missions," 13.

Similarly, Methodist theologian J. Robert Nelson asserts: "Concern for the integrity, worth, and dignity of persons is the basic presupposition of human rights."[29]

2. Justice

Biblical justice involves making individuals, communities, and the cosmos whole by upholding both goodness and impartiality. It stands at the center of true religion, according to James, who says that the kind of "religion that is pure and undefiled before God, the Father, is this: to care for orphans and widows in their distress and to keep oneself unstained by the world" (Jas 1:27). Earlier Scripture says: "The righteous know the rights for the poor, the wicked have no such understanding" (Prov 29:7).

Justice flows from God's heart and character. As true and good, God seeks to make the object of his holy love whole. This is what motivates God throughout the Old and New Testaments in his judgments on sin and injustice. These judgments are both individual and corporate in scope. As Christians experience the wholeness that Jesus offers, they are to carry his justice forward in the world. Christians sense God's heart for this in James's epistle. James, like an Old Testament prophet, denounced oppression toward the poor. He saw church leaders favoring the rich and looking down on those less fortunate (Jas 2:1–13). James calls for the breaking down of these divisions, as God seeks to renew his people, making them whole.

The same problem still arises today, especially given the tendency in some Christian circles to downplay social justice while highlighting personal piety. Jesus rebuked this in the Pharisees: "Woe to you scribes and Pharisees, for your tithe mint, dill, and cummin, and have neglected the weightier matters hypocrites! You give a tenth of your spices—mint, dill and cummin. But you have neglected the more important matters of the law: justice and mercy and faith" (Matt 23:23).

> Thus says the Lord: "Maintain justice, and do what is right, for soon my salvation will come and my deliverance be revealed. Happy is the mortal, who does this, the one who holds it fast, who keeps the Sabbath, and refrains from doing any evil. Do not let the foreigner joined to the Lord say, the Lord will surely separate me from his people, and do not let the eunuch say, I am just a dry tree. For thus says the Lord: to the eunuchs who

---

29. Nelson, "Human Rights in Creation and Redemption," 1.

keep my Sabbaths, who choose the things that please me and hold fast my covenant, I will give in my house and within my walls a monument and a name better than sons and daughters; I will give them an everlasting name that shall not be cut off. (Isa 56:1–6)

3. Equality

There are multiple verses affirming equality in the New Testament: "For God shows no partiality" (Rom 2:11); "Truly, truly, I say to you, a servant is not greater than his master, nor is a messenger greater than the one who sent him" (John 13:16); "For in Christ Jesus you are all sons of God, through faith. For as many of you as were baptized into Christ have put on Christ. There is neither Jew nor Greek, there is neither slave nor free, there is no male and female, for you are all one in Christ Jesus. And if you are Christ's, then you are Abraham's offspring, heirs according to promise" (Gal 3:26–29).

4. Good Governance

In the Old Testament, good governance is expressed in terms of right relationships: between the ruler and the people and between the ruler and God. It also contains stories of when this relationship of trust was broken. In the New Testament, it means the relationship of Jesus and his followers with the religious and civil authorities of the time, describing harassment and persecution.

Psalm 72 is a prayer to God to guide the rulers of Israel. It offers an ideal governance model focused on a relationship of care for the poor and vulnerable. Good governance is shown based on the principles of justice, righteousness, and compassion, defending the rights of the poor and marginalized and protecting the people from conflict. Quoting from Isaiah 61, Jesus declares his manifesto for leadership in chapter 4 of Luke's Gospel. In Leviticus 25, the people of Israel are given guidance on how to govern the land sustainably so that all people and creation will be able to thrive. What are the signs that a people are well governed? In our time, which people today are the poor, weak, and needy in your area? What can community and local or national government leaders do to help the vulnerable in your context? What does this passage tell us about good governance in our own time? How can we help to promote good governance in our local area, in our country, and in our world? How can we work together with vulnerable people to improve their wellbeing? What practical actions are we to take to promote Jesus' example of servant leadership in our own context?

5. Ecology

Ecology can reveal more about the beauty and wonders of God's creation. The Scriptures are full of thoughtful observations that reflect the foundations of ecology. Primarily, these discussions serve to provide insight into God's character—that He has a plan for and cares about His creation. Let's consider a few biblical examples.

We should consider the sustainability of our actions: "If a bird's nest happens to be before you . . . you shall not take the mother with the young; you shall surely let the mother go, and take the young for yourself, that it may be well with you and that you may prolong your days" (Deut 22:6–7). The word sustainable describes a practice that meets present needs without jeopardizing the ability to meet future needs. It may be a recent buzzword, but the concept was emphasized long ago in the Bible. From the beginning, God commissioned man to "tend and keep" his environment (Gen 2:15). God wanted His people to be circumspect (Deut 32:29), avoid greed (Prov 1:19), plan for the future (2 Cor 12:14), and take care of the world around them (Prov 12:10).

As we read in Deuteronomy, God taught them to leave the mature generation to breed again if they found a bird with young—never to take both (Deut 22:6–7). Other passages also relate to sustainability. The Israelites were to manage their land responsibly, at regular intervals, letting it "rest" in a natural fallow (Lev 25:2–7). Even in war, the children of Israel were to take the long view: they were forbidden to destroy their enemies' fruit trees (Deut 20:20). After all, God designed ecosystems to satisfy the needs of a vast array of organisms, and He seems to delight in all of them (Job 38:26–27; 39). He does not smile on the thoughtless destruction of His creation (Rev 11:18).

It makes a difference what meats you eat: "Speak to the children of Israel, saying, 'These are the animals which you may eat among all the animals that are on the earth'" (Lev 11:2).[30] The Bible says that God provided for humans to consume animals "as the green herbs" (Gen 9:3). In short, the Bible describes and requires sustainable practices. Although modern life can pose different challenges, the ecological principles of the

---

30. See also Deut 14:3–20 and Gen 7:2.

Bible are just as relevant in today's quest for sustainability. Stocked with proteins and nutrients, meat has its advantages as a food source. Yet, in the same way that many plants are inedible or poisonous to humans, not all meats are equal. Not only do the muscular structures of fish, birds, and other animals differ broadly from each other (1 Cor 15:39), but even meat from apparently similar creatures can vary from relatively wholesome to risky based on a multitude of ecological and anatomical factors. A look at the meats God calls "clean" (okay for human consumption) and "unclean" affirms this principle. Of course, God gives laws for our good, both spiritually and physically (Deut 10:13). Studying only the science behind each commandment cannot reveal God's higher purpose, and it certainly cannot provide a replacement for obedience. Understanding the scientific wisdom packed into Leviticus 11, however, can help us appreciate that God's laws are not arbitrary but rather specifically designed to fit His purpose even if we don't fully understand it.

Although other biological concerns are just as instructive (like digestive differences, which make some meats more likely to carry disease), in this article, let's focus on the ecology surrounding God's instructions. It is noteworthy that the Bible's guidelines only require observation; you do not need to dissect an animal to discern if it is clean. Living things are composed of elements from the earth, and they decompose into earth: "In the sweat of your face you shall eat bread till you return to the ground, for out of it you were taken; for dust you are, and to dust you shall return" (Gen 3:19).

Questions for Comprehension, Analysis, and Reflection

Have the participants' reflect in groups of three or four on learning during this class and ask them to answer the following question: (1) What did you learn about human rights issues in Christianity? (2) Name human rights abuses and issues within their community. What human rights instruments can be used to rectify them from Christianity?

Conclusion

Human security addresses the *full* scope of human insecurities and is fully located within the Christian doctrine and sacred texts.

Examples of Required Readings

Engler, M. *How to Rule the World*, 110, 287–94. New York: Nation, 2008.
Klein, N. "Reclaiming the Commons." In *A Movement of Movements: Is Another World Really Possible?*, edited by T. Mertes, 219–29. London: Verso, 2004.
Madeley, J. *Big Business, Poor Peoples*, 126–43. London: ZED, 2008.
Nario-Galace, J. "Towards a Fairer World." In *Peace Education for Civil Society*, edited by V. Cawagas, et al., 51–58. San Jose, CA: University for Peace, 2009.
Shiva, V. *Earth Democracy, Justice, Sustainability, and Peace*, 145–186. Cambridge: South End, 2005.
UNESCO. *Education for Human Rights: An International Perspective*, 17–34, 47–53. Paris: UNESCO.
Wellman, James K., and Clark B. Lombardi. *Religion and Human Security: A Global Perspective*, 150–72. New York: Oxford University Press, 2012.

Unit V: Practices

The fifth unit is comprised of five chapters and focuses on various practices of reconciliation, teaches how to build a community, advances the interreligious practices from three religions, and advocates methods for the physical and spiritual healing of wounds.

Chapter 1: Reconciliation in Practice

Introduction

The reconciliation entails many activities and strategies from different religions to better understand how reconciliation is conceived, what activities promote reconciliation, and how to achieve peaceful solutions.

Learning Objectives

At the end of this chapter, the participants will be able to:

1. Be more aware of conflict styles.
2. Identify their preferred style/s in influencing others, managing conflict, and the additional strategies that they need to use to successfully resolve conflict situations.
3. Demonstrate their skills in resolving conflict and confrontation.
4. Identify a plan to apply and enhance their communication skills in the workplace to address existing conflicts.

5. Build skills for reaching effective solutions. Familiarize themselves with a wide range of tools for managing conflicts (negotiation, mediation, crisis management, coercive diplomacy, interaction conflict resolution, post-conflict stabilization, and reconstruction), to prevent conflicts from escalating, for managing crises, for ending violent conflicts, and for institutionalizing peace—building after violent conflict.

Learning Activities

The first exercise is two persons facing one another. One says, "I want it." The other responds, "You can't have it." For the second exercise, the two persons align themselves in the same way, but this time one says, "Yes," and the other says, "No." They can say yes or no in whatever way they want. It needs not be only through words; they may nod, they may turn around and say nothing, they may use non-verbal cues, etc. After each activity, ask each participant to write their feelings on the board.

Another activity is a role play. Divide the class into two groups—one group has chairs and the other does not. The have-nots have no power. They must ask the haves for what they need. The two groups can take it from there.

Content

1. Reconciliation

In his chapter on "Reconciliation in Practice: India Experience," Andreas D'Souza explains: "Reconciliation cannot take place unless our efforts toward it begin with an understanding of the root causes of violence and its endemic and spiral nature."[1] The church and the mosque can move from competition to reconciliation by engaging in interfaith dialogue, studying and understanding each other's religions in the community, and working toward the removal of misunderstanding and suspicion in order to promote justice and peace.

The religious leaders need to understand that the process of reconciliation is not: (a) an excuse for impunity; (b) only an individual process; (c) in opposition to/an alternative to truth or justice; (d) a quick answer;

---

1. D'Souza, "Reconciliation in Practice," 261.

(e) a religious concept; (f) perfect peace; (g) an excuse to forget; or (h) a matter of merely forgiving.

The process of reconciliation is: (i) finding a way to live that permits a vision of the future; (ii) the (re) building of relationships; (iii) coming to terms with past acts and enemies; (iv) a society-wide, long-term process of deep change; (v) a process of acknowledging, remembering, and learning from the past; and (vi) voluntary (it cannot be imposed).

> **Religious leaders need to study the following goals** of Islamic education by Ghulam Sarwar in "Islamic Philosophy of Education"[2]:

- ✓ Prepare and train the future generation to work as agents of Allah on Earth.

- ✓ Ensure the promotion of *ma'rif* (good) and the prevention of *munka*r (evil) in a society.

- ✓ Ensure the balanced growth of the total personality of a person.

- ✓ Promote spiritual, moral, cultural, physical, mental, and material development in children in preparation for the responsibilities, experiences, and opportunities of adult life.

- ✓ Develop all the faculties needed to realize the full potential of people.

- ✓ Develop all the skills required to enable people to face real life situations with a clear consciousness about their responsibility and accountability in the *akhirah* (life after death).

- ✓ Prepare people to work toward the economic and material growth of a society with a strong sense of the unity of the human race to ensure equitable distribution and proper use of wealth.

- ✓ Develop a sense of social responsibility for the efficient use of resources to eliminate waste, avoid ecological damage, and safeguard the well-being of all created beings.

---

2. Sarwar, "Islamic Philosophy of Education," 47.

- ✓ Encourage competition in good things to promote excellence and the highest achievements for the greater welfare of people and society.

- ✓ Ensure that children grow up with a strong belief in sharing opportunities, equity, justice, fair play, love, care, affection, selflessness, honesty, humility, integrity, and austerity.[3]

In addition, the religious leaders need to explore the "Islamic approaches to conflict resolution," described by George Irani below, and understand the Muslims' understanding and approach to reconciliation as well as how it can be used for the reconciliation process in the community at large.

- ✓ It is a communally oriented process; individuals are enmeshed in webs of relationships.

- ✓ The community legitimizes arbitration/mediation through respect for age, experience, status, and leadership in communal affairs.

- ✓ A preferred third party is used as an unbiased insider with ongoing connections to all parties

- ✓ Community and village elders (the *jaha*) legitimize and guarantee the process of acknowledgment, apology, compensation, forgiveness, and reconciliation.

- ✓ Language and ritual of reconciliation draws freely on explicit religious ideals, texts, stories, and examples.

- ✓ Emphasis is placed on the precedence of local history and customs, encompassing relationships between kinship groups and shared norms and values.

- ✓ The process manifests concern with cultivating the established "wisdom" gained through collective experience.

---

3. Merry, "Islamic Philosophy of Education," 47.

- ✓ The process is continuity-oriented: history is a source of stability and guidance that presents lessons for shaping a common future.

- ✓ Efforts are intended to empower individuals in relation to the legal system, gaining control over their problems while achieving greater efficiency.

- ✓ Efforts are intended to empower families and the community to participate directly in matters of common concern.

- ✓ Third parties promote direct, collaborative, step-by-step problem solving to isolate and confront discrete issues.

- ✓ Third parties emphasize the need to restore harmony and solidarity and secure cooperative relationships.

- ✓ Emphasis is placed on honor, face, dignity, prestige, just compensation, and respect for individuals and groups.

- ✓ Intervention is made to prevent conflict escalation and disruption of communal symbiosis in a context of scarce resources.

- ✓ The process is completed with a powerful ritual that includes *sulh* (settlement), *musalaha* (reconciliation), *musafaha* (exchange of handshakes), and *mumalaha* (breaking bread together).[4]

▶ **Religious leaders need to use all of these Islamic resources** along with the Christian reality of reconciliation defined by Dieter T. Hessel in *Reconciliation and Conflict: Church Controversy Over Social Involvement* so as to:

- ✓ Transform the world by the radical power of love;

- ✓ Expose sin and injustice, arousing repentance;

- ✓ Lead to conflict as well as to overcoming it;

---

4. Irani, "Islamic Approaches to Conflict Resolution," 17.

- ✓ Create confidence to pursue human freedom.
- ✓ Direct the church's social response.[5]

6. Reconciliation in Practice[6]

- ➤ **What is reconciliation?**
- ➤ **Reconciliation assumes different forms and different roles** at different levels of engagement and in different contexts.
  - ✓ In the case of violent conflicts, reconciliation often combines:

    The search for truth

    Justice

    Healing/forgiveness

    Reparation/accommodation

- ➤ **Types of reconciliation**
  - ✓ Top-down Reconciliation

The top down reconciliation tends to be high-profile and situated at the national level. It is also reliant on the legitimacy of statewide institutions.

  - ✓ Bottom-up reconciliation

Bottom up approaches focus on the interpersonal and community level, reducing social divisions, increasing social harmony, and preventing future violence through healing violence-induced traumas and psychosocial wounds. It also restores the humanity of the victims, takes ownership, and rebuilds respectful and cooperative relationships through multiple strategies.

- ➤ **Challenges to Reconciliation**
  - ✓ Tensions between the past and the future

---

5. Hessel, *Reconciliation and Conflict*, 32.
6. Clark-Habibi, "Reconciliation in Practice," 2.

Unit V: Practices   219

- ✓ Tension over timing

- ✓ Tensions over the role of truth: a help or a hindrance?

- ✓ Tensions over who and when to forgive

- ✓ Tensions over the role of third parties

➤ Stages of Reconciliation

Reconciliation
↑
c. Moving towards empathy
↑
b. Building Confidence and trust
↑
a. Co-existence

➤ Principles of Engagement into Reconciliation

- ✓ Listening with empathy and compassion.

- ✓ Ethical Conduct: know the limits of your competencies and do no harm.

- ✓ Universality and unity in diversity: treat all people as members of one human race with the same dignity, worth, and potential.

- ✓ Be an uplifter and unifier.

- ✓ Be vigilant to bias and partiality: insist on inclusivity.

- ✓ See the positive in your partners and even your opponents: build alliances.

- ✓ Celebrate each other's successes (big and small) to maintain enthusiasm and courage.

- ✓ Plan systematically how to amplify and multiply your impact throughout your engagement.

- ✓ Commit to learning: both as a strategy for change and as a mode of project engagement

7. Putting *Ubuntu* into Practices

According to John Kehoe in his book, *Ubuntu: African Wisdom on How to Be a Human Being Part 2*, Ubuntu is a term derived from the word "*muntu*," meaning a person, a human being. According to ancient African traditional wisdom, each individual possesses positive, loving qualities. These qualities represent our natural internal state of being, and when we express them, we are being genuine, an authentic human being. To be otherwise is to be out of harmony, and to be out of harmony brings unhappiness to ourselves, to others, and to our world. The values of Ubuntu manifest in good deeds, things like being sensitive to the needs of others, compassionate, forgiving, caring, and generous. Ubuntu is the art of being a human being. It is the living of our humanness. It is the unfolding of our natural goodness. Each living human being has this opportunity to discover their basic goodness and to practice it. "*Umuntungumuntungabantu.*" I am because you are. It is through you that I am a human being.[7]

> **Some of the pillars of Ubuntu living according to Kehoe[8] are:**

- ✓ Caring: Caring is embracing others. Their needs become your needs. Their joys and sorrows become your joys and sorrows. It is the practice of concern and oneness.

- ✓ Empathy: Empathy is the ability to successfully enter into the emotional situation of another, to listen and feel genuine sympathy because you hear and feel what others share with you.

- ✓ Sharing: In the *Ubuntu* culture, it is normal to share generously with others. "*Mahala*" is the traditional African practice that

---

7. Kehoe, "Ubuntu Part 2," 1.
8. Kehoe, "Ubuntu Part 2," 2.

teaches that it is proper to give to others without expecting anything in return.

- ✓ Respect: Respect covers many things. Respect for elders, children, and all members of your community, respect for your ancestors, traditions, and ancient teachings and practices. Respect for oneself, for if one does not respect oneself, how can one respect another? Respect for your environment and all living creatures. Respect for the Ubuntu way of life as a way to happiness and self-awareness.

> The actual process of *Ubuntu* involves five key stages:

First, after a fact-finding process, where the views of victims, perpetrators, and witnesses are heard, the perpetrators—if considered to have done wrong—are encouraged, both by the Council and other community members in the *Inkundla/Lekgotla* forum, to acknowledge responsibility or guilt. Secondly, perpetrators are encouraged to demonstrate genuine remorse or to repent. Thirdly, perpetrators are encouraged to ask for forgiveness, and victims, in their turn, are encouraged to show mercy. Fourth, where possible and at the suggestion of the council of elders, perpetrators would be required to pay an appropriate compensation or reparation for the wrong done. Fifth, seek to consolidate the whole process by encouraging the parties to commit themselves to reconciliation.[9]

The guiding principle of *Ubuntu* was based on the notion that parties need to be reconciled in order to re-build and maintain social trust and social cohesion, with a view to preventing a culture of vendetta or retribution from developing and escalating between individuals, families, and the society as a whole.

In *Ubuntu* philosophy, there are four key lessons[10] that can be incorporated into the peacemaking process for religious leaders:

- ✓ The utility of supporting victims and encouraging perpetrators as they go through the difficult process of making peace.

- ✓ The value of acknowledging guilt and remorse.

---

9. Kehoe, "Ubuntu Part 2," 3.
10. Murithi, "African Perspective on Peace Education," 154.

✓ The granting of forgiveness as a way to achieve reconciliation.

✓ The importance of referring constantly to the essential unity and interdependence of humanity, as expressed through *Ubuntu*, living out the principles which this unity suggests, namely, empathy for others, the sharing of our common resources, and working with a spirit of cooperation in our efforts to resolve our common problems.

One person practicing this *Ubuntu* philosophy was Nelson Mandela in South Africa. This is why he became a model of reconciliation. Here are a few quotes from him[11]:

- "Real leaders must be ready to sacrifice all for the freedom of their people."
- "I learned that courage was not the absence of fear, but the triumph over it. The brave man is not he who does not feel afraid, but he who conquers that fear."
- "A fundamental concern for others in our individual and community lives would go a long way in making the world the better place we so passionately dream of."
- "Everyone can rise above their circumstances and achieve success if they are dedicated to and passionate about what they do."
- "The truth is that we are not yet free; we have merely achieved the freedom to be free, the right not to be oppressed. We have not taken the final step of our journey, but the first step on a longer and even more difficult road. For to be free is not merely to cast off one's chains, but to live in a way that respects and enhances the freedom of others. The true test of our devotion to freedom is just beginning."

8. Reconciliation Practices in the Yoruba Religion

In *"Agba* (elder) as Arbitrator: A Yoruba Socio-political Model for Conflict Resolution," Bamikole cites the capacity of the *agba* (elder) to manage conflict shrewdly in traditional Yoruba society successfully is found through the combined function of the elder's personality, proverbial communicative prowess, as well as an understanding of the social principles of conflict management in Yoruba culture.

---

11. Mandela quoted in Meah, "50 Inspirational Nelson Mandela Quotes," 1–2.

There is no conflict that is not resolvable if the only parties to the conflict are willing to resolve them by showing understanding to one another.[12] Resolution of conflict sometimes requires a third-party or certain persons who enjoy the confidence of their fellow human beings in a political society that can appeal to such relationships to reconcile differences among members of the society.[13]

The concept of *agba* (elders) is a Yoruba socio-political model for conflict resolution, and it is the third-party that is responsible for effective conflict resolution in indigenous Yoruba societies. In traditional Yoruba culture, *agba* (elders) were usually relied upon as arbitrators and agents of conflict resolution in view of certain qualities possessed by this category of human beings.[14] "*Agba* (elders) are respected individuals identified by age and other qualities, which mark them out in their families, communities, nations, regions, and the world. To be identified as an *agba* (elder), s/he must be fearless person (*alakikanju*); s/he must be knowledgeable and wise but also must be someone who gives room for criticisms (*ologbon, oloye, afimotielomiran se*); s/he must be tolerant (*alamumora*); s/he must be upright in all ways (*olotito, olododo*); s/he must not be selfish (*anikanjopon*).[15]

Bamikole believes there is dearth of this model of *agba* (elders) in our contemporary world because the present generation of elders has been influenced by the prevalent consumerist nature of contemporary political system.[16]

Questions for Comprehension, Analysis, and Reflection

1. What is the importance of forgiveness in the process of healing?
2. Name the strategies learned from each tradition.
3. What are their strengths and weaknesses?

---

12. Bamikole, "Democracy in a Multicultural Society," 5.
13. Bamikole, "Democracy in a Multicultural Society," 5–6.
14. Bamikole, "Democracy in a Multicultural Society," 10.
15. Bamikole, "Democracy in a Multicultural Society," 12.
16. Bamikole, "Democracy in a Multicultural Society," 15.

Conclusion

Finding the strategies needed to overcome the enormous obstacles on the path of reconciliation and be able to mend the social fabric of religious conflict-torn societies requires us to critically assess various paradigms of reconciliation.

Examples of Required Readings

Bar-Tal, D., and G. H. Bennink. "The Nature of Reconciliation as an Outcome and as a Process." In *From Conflict Resolution to Reconciliation*, edited by Y. Bar-Siman-Tov, 11–38. Oxford: Oxford University Press, 2004.

Bloomfield, David. *Reconciliation after Violent Conflict: A Handbook*. Stockholm, Sweden: International Institute for Democracy and Electoral Assistance (IDEA), 2005.

Hessel, Dieter T. *Reconciliation and Conflict, Church Controversy Over Social Involvement*. London: Westminster, 1969.

Chapter 2: Building an Interreligious Community Together

Introduction

In building an interreligious community geared towards concrete peaceful actions, religious leaders will respond and overcome the pressing challenges of our time—such as violence and conflict—together, building mutually accountable societies based on respect and cooperation for the growth and development of their society.

Learning Objectives

At the end of this chapter, the participants will be able to:

1. Be a model of how different faiths can live together in Nigeria harmoniously.
2. Build understanding, good will, compassionate listening, and a sense of community between people of different faiths.
3. Share our knowledge and insights with others.
4. Work together to achieve common goals in Nigeria.
5. Support each other in times of difficulty.
6. Use our meetings to increase knowledge and awareness of the issues that face each of the faith communities.

Learning Activities

Ask each participant to examine their own biases. Ask them to answer the following in the classroom: Do you give more favorable attention to a person who is physically or socio-economically advantaged? Do you use inclusive and/or non-discriminating language (e.g., "human" instead of "man," "Blacks" instead of "Negroes," "elderly" instead of "old," and "heavy" instead of "fat," among others)? Do you give appropriate attention and treat each person fairly, regardless of their sex or socio-economic status? Consider if you are more inclined to give compliments to those who are physically attractive, and so on. Discover and name the misinformation that we have learned about each other. Understand the personal impact of religious stereotyping through the telling and hearing of stories. Learn new ways to become effective allies to each other across our religious diversity. They will share their responses.

Content

1. Dissolution of Boundaries

The solution to violence is the dissolution of various boundaries that keep believers of the two religions feeling separated. Believers in both religions must know how, when, and where their religions are connected and disconnected, when they are in confluence or in conflict, and how to help turn obstacles to harmony into stepping stones along the way. In order to dissolve these barriers, both religions need to communicate clearly, to be aware of their thoughts, concerns, and feelings and make them clear to others without projecting them on others. In addition, the knowledge of other religions is the first requirement if one hopes to build relationships that will be respectful and fruitful. Goodwill is necessary, but it is not enough. A planned study of the other religion is required if interreligious relationships are not to become stagnate at the superficial level of generalizations, clichés, and prejudices. Those who are in positions of responsibility or leadership in each religion have a greater obligation than their co-religionists to undertake a deeper study of the religion.

This will be put in practice by discussing the following subjects at meetings: what are the core values and how can we nurture them in each faith tradition? How does each faith tradition recognize their prejudices and how can they move beyond them? How do you discern your unique talent, gifts, contributions, and how are you called to serve the world and your community? Is forgiveness essential in each religion? How does one express gratitude in one's life? What does each tradition teach about reconciliation?

Furthermore, the acceptance of the other and the respect for differences must also be applied to break those barriers. Correct information about the other will show Muslims and Christians that their two religions do share many beliefs. Examples are belief in one God, mighty and merciful; acceptance of the role of prophets; and belief in the eschatological realities of judgment, reward and punishment. There are, nevertheless, fundamental differences as well. For Christians, belief in the Trinity and the Incarnation completely transform the relationships between God and humankind. For Muslims, the place given to the Qur'an as final revelation and the role given to Muhammad as the seal of the prophets puts a special stamp upon Islam.

2. Prejudice

Prejudice is the negative feeling or attitude towards a person or a group even if it lacks basis. Stereotype refers to the negative opinion about a person or group based on incomplete knowledge. Discrimination refers to negative actions toward members of a specific social group that may be manifested in avoidance, aversion, or even violence. Thus, stereotypes, being negative beliefs about a group, can form the basis for prejudicial feelings, which, in turn, may lead to negative action or discrimination.

➤ Theories on Prejudice

There are diverse theories as to the origin, transmission, and maintenance of prejudice. One strong theory on its cause is the Social Learning Theory.[17] Prejudice is simply passed along, sometimes for generations, and is reinforced in various institutions, including the family, school, and media. Prejudice is said to stem from ignorance or from lack of information as well.[18] It may also be due to one's tendency to think highly of oneself and of the group to which one belongs, resulting to the denigration of the attributes of others outside it.[19]

➤ Types of Prejudice

In the beginning, prejudice was simply equated with racism. Over time, however, it was realized that there were other forms of prejudice as well. Thus, the concept of prejudice has expanded and now includes the following major types:

- ✓ Racism: the belief that one's own cultural or racial heritage is innately superior to that of others, hence the lack of respect or appreciation for those who belong to a "different race."

---

17. Allport, "Nature of Prejudice," 67.
18. Betlehem, "Social Psychology of Prejudice," 67.
19. Tajfel and Turner, "Social Identity Theory," 67.

- ✓ Sexism: a system of attitudes, actions, and institutional structures that subordinates women on the basis of their sex.[20]

- ✓ Classism: distancing from and perceiving the poor as "the other."[21]

- ✓ Linguicism: negative attitudes that members of dominant language groups hold against non-dominant language groups.[22]

- ✓ Ageism: negative attitudes held against the young or the elderly.

- ✓ "Looksism": prejudice against those who do not measure up to set standards of beauty. The usual victims are the overweight, the undersized, and the dark-skinned.[23]

- ✓ Religious intolerance: prejudice against those who are followers of religions other than one's own.

➤ Education for Tolerance

Prejudice may be challenged by teaching tolerance. Tolerance is the respect, acceptance, and appreciation of the rich diversity of cultures and various forms of human expression.[24] It is the foundation of democracy and human rights. Education for tolerance aims to counter influences that lead to the fear of, aversion toward, and exclusion of others. Tolerance recognizes that others have the right to be who they are. Why teach tolerance? UNESCO asserts that education is the most effective means of preventing intolerance. There is a need for schools to educate citizens who are appreciative of other cultures, respectful of human dignity and differences, and able to prevent or resolve conflicts amicably. Discrediting hateful propaganda towards the different other through education is an imperative. Major religious traditions call on their flock to treat others with the same respect and dignity they give themselves. More so, the call to challenge prejudice is enshrined in various human rights instruments. Nations, through international agreements and treaties, have affirmed their commitment to the protection and promotion of human rights such

---

20. Mcginnis and Oehlberg, "Starting out Right," 67.
21. Lott, "Social Psychology of Interpersonal Discrimination," 67.
22. Chen-Hayes et al., "Challenging Linguicism," 68.
23. Nario-Galace, "Effects of a Peace Education Program," 68.
24. Franzoi, "Social Psychology," 67.

as the right to freedom of thought, conscience, religion, opinion, and expression. Article 1.2 of the Declaration on Race and Racial Prejudice stipulates that "all individuals and groups have the right to be different."[25] In addition, educating for tolerance is a practical alternative.

Intolerance has given rise to violence, terrorism, and discrimination within societies. A lack of respect for differences, among other factors, has given rise to conflicts between and among groups—as in the case of the Catholics and Protestants in Northern Ireland; the Israelis and Palestinians; the Bosnian Serbs and the ethnic Albanians; the Hutus and Tutsis; and some Christians and Moro's in Mindanao. The World Health Organization (2002) has placed casualties in armed conflicts at the rate of one person every one hundred seconds. Teaching for tolerance will aid in protecting human rights and saving lives.

> **Teaching-Learning Ideas**

Prejudice is based on a self-centered judgment that there is only one correct way of experiencing the world. Knowing the many ways of being right, as schooling can provide, can help students adopt more enlightened beliefs.

Here are some ways to teach and learn tolerance:

Examine your own biases. In the classroom, do you give more favorable attention to students who are physically or socio-economically advantaged?

Use inclusive and/or non-discriminating language, as language shapes consciousness (e.g., use "human" instead of "man," "Blacks" instead of "Negroes," "elderly" instead of "old," and "heavy" instead of "fat," among others).

Give appropriate attention and treat each student fairly, regardless of sex, socio-economic status, or otherwise. Examine if you are more inclined to give compliments to those who are more physically attractive, and so on.

Highlight the thought that diversity is enriching. Differences should be celebrated, not scorned, as we learn a lot of new things from one another. An analogy would be the fruit salad which is so delicious even if it is made up of different fruits that come in various flavors and colors.

---

25. Altemeyer, "Social Learning Theory," 67.

Show a variety of racial and physical features in our teaching aids as well as in our classroom decorations. Examine our textbooks, references, instructional materials, and curriculum/course outlines for biased messages about sex, race, ethnicity, and religion, for example. Know where our students are. Allow them to reflect on their views about differences. Below are some insights offered by Stern-LaRosa and Betmann[26] and by the Teaching Tolerance Project.[27] Ask your students to write their thoughts after each statement.

> ### Cultivate Compassionate Listening: 5 Core Practices[28]

Cultivating compassion in seeing and feeling the world from the other's perspective and the willingness to connect in disagreement. Developing the "fair witness" with ongoing self-exploration and developing the ability to hold complexity and ambiguity. Respecting self and others by developing boundaries that protect yet include, trusting each has the capacity to resolve and heal the conflict. Taking responsibility for our own part in what's unfolding. Listening with the heart by quieting the mind with a shift of focus from active mind to energetic core of being. Create a spaciousness that allows divergence and ways to find deeper points of connection. Speaking from the heart with a language that reflects a healing intention rather than judgments and blame. Reframing issues to get at the essence of underlying needs and feelings, truth, and meaning.

> ### Rejection of Fear by Non-Violent Coexistence in the Community

Religious leaders are responsible to initiate or sustain programs for promoting communication where there has been conflict. Or, as symbolic representatives of victims and offenders, they can initiate dialogue if those directly involved are not yet ready to talk.

The first step away from hatred, hostility, and bitterness is the achievement of non-violent coexistence between the antagonists, i.e., individuals and groups. At a minimum, this means looking for alternatives to revenge. The move toward such coexistence first of all requires that victims and perpetrators be freed from the paralyzing isolation and all-consuming self-pity in which they often live. This involves the building

---

26. Stern-LaRosa and Betmann, "Hate Hurts," 75.
27. Teaching Tolerance Project, "Teaching-Learning Ideas," 75.
28. Cohen, *Five Practices of Compassionate Listening*, 3–4.

or renewal of communication inside the communities of victims and offenders and between them.

The second step is to build confidence and trust in the community. The process requires that each party, the victim and the offender, gain renewed confidence in himself or herself and in each other. It also entails believing that humanity is present in every man and woman. An acknowledgement of the humanity of others is the basis of mutual trust and opens the door for the gradual arrival of a sustainable culture of nonviolence. This will be followed by the willingness to listen to the reasons for the hatred of those who caused their pain and with the offenders' understanding of the anger and bitterness of those who suffered.

Religious leaders should try in every process to focus on one ingredient in reconciliation and truth-seeking, but with the recognition that there may be multiple truths. Truth-telling is not only a pre-condition of reconciliation because it creates objective opportunities for people to see the past in terms of shared suffering and collective responsibility, but more importantly, it is also the recognition that victims and offenders share a common identity, as survivors and as human beings, and simply have to get on with each other.

The religious leaders should engage in direct dialogue with their counterparts. They can begin by centering on Qur'anic verses such as: "The Believers are a single Brotherhood; so make peace and reconciliation between your two brothers: and fear Allah, that ye may receive mercy" (Q 49:10). Allah fills with peace and faith the heart of one who swallows his anger, even though he is in a position to give vent to it. And the Christian scripture: "So we are ambassadors for Christ, God making his appeal through us. We beseech you on behalf of Christ, be reconciled to God" (2 Cor 5:20). These passages will explain the divine necessity of reconciliation. This dialogue can foster openness and bring understanding of differences not based on confrontation and exclusion.

Furthermore, there is a need to embrace a spirituality of reconciliation in order to practice reconciliation toward each other and live out the true spirituality. This is described by Josien Folbert as: "Concern for others and respect for life, commitment to social justice in a spirit of service, empowering people, removing social and economic inequalities and developing a new tolerance for others."[29]

---

29. Folbert, "Blueprint for the Process of Peace," 379.

Once communication is established, other steps can be taken. Religious leaders can engage in projects such as educating dropout children, teaching skills such as tailoring, empowering for the jobless, and healing ministry for the broken-hearted. This special ministry must comprise a trained nurse, a pastor, and an *Imam* for the physical healing and the spiritual healing of the community; the role of the health ministry must be for referral and spiritual care. The churches and the mosques in the community must also organize daily prayers for peace in the community, for the healing of its members, and for mending broken relationships in the community.

In addition, a space must be created for the community to come together and share their stories about their family background, struggles, achievement pains, experiences, difficulties, and blessings in order to see the commonality in every family and the need to come together for a brighter future. In order to practice dialogue, individually or collectively, church or mosque can create a space for hospitality, i.e., a place of respect, acceptance, attentive listening, and the mutual sharing of personal stories and experiences. There should be no attempt at conversion. This requires openness to the voice and experience of others, willingness to identify ourselves and make ourselves visible and available to one another, acceptance of others, and dealing with the social pressure of each faith and the problems confronting both Muslims and Christians in the community.

When Muslims and Christians come to know one another and learn to respect and accept one another, they are well poised to engage in some form of Muslim/Christian dialogue. In addition, setting up of dialogue by a local ecumenical council involving Christians and Muslims from a range of backgrounds should be introduced. Christians and Muslims should come together not only to talk to each other but also to work together for the common good. Christians and Muslims should express their desire to move beyond theological discussion into the "dialogue of engagement." The churches and their members should pursue a better understanding of Islam, encouraging both conversation and cooperation, defending the civil rights of Muslims, and rejecting religious and political demagogues. In the same way, the Muslim community should learn about Christianity and defend the rights of Christians.

Finally, interfaith celebrations can bring people of various religious faiths together in order to share parts of their respective sacred traditions (reading, story, prayer, meditation, chant, testimony, dance, and more) with one another. They can provide each participant a meaningful experience of how diverse religious people can come together to share their respective understanding and reactions to a common theme. Interfaith celebrations are made up of two elements: people and communication. Members of various religious traditions (people) come together in order to share some aspects of their religious traditions with one another and beyond (communication).

This may include the public in attendance at the celebration, the broader public reached through the media, specific individuals or groups of people on whose behalf prayers may be directed, and a divinity or all-encompassing source of power or reality. An annual interfaith celebration is best practiced in conjunction with other kinds of multireligious activities, not as an isolated case of multireligious cooperation. An interfaith celebration is not neutral. The very concept implies an openness to see religious diversity as something positive. Therefore, an interfaith celebration can be seen as a possible socio-political tool in the promotion of more tolerant and pluralistic societies. The purpose for holding an interfaith celebration will vary according to the circumstances that bring the organizers together. The only common denominator is the desire to celebrate together religiously, whatever form and content this intention may eventually reach.

An interfaith celebration will serve only a limited number of ends. For example, organizers and participants might come to express a public concern for a given theme through one's own religious sensitivity in order to: effect change in the direction promoted by the theme; share treasures from one's own religious tradition as a tool for education; gain more factual knowledge about each other's traditions; gain more insight into the sensitivities of each other's religious communities; gain appreciation for different expressions of religious and spiritual worship; and develop acquaintances and friendships with people across traditional religions.

The content of an interfaith celebration may include music and food. In terms of music, special attention needs to be paid to each tradition. As for food, it is one of the most powerful symbols to which all human beings must relate in order to survive. The choice of food during an interfaith celebration should be careful to observe the food guidelines of all traditions, allowing everyone to partake in the meal.

> **Physical and Spiritual Healing**

Another way to bring the community together is through health ministry in the community. The purpose of this ministry is to help the community care for one another and to help attain, maintain, and/or regain the best possible whole person's health, namely wellness of body, mind, and spirit. In an interreligious community, the local church/mosque must be raised to offer the spiritual, interpersonal, emotional, and physical health of its members in the community. This will be done through the help of health professionals and other interested lay members. The health ministry committee or cabinet will be composed by the pastor, the Imam, and a nurse. They will combine their knowledge and experience with their willingness to serve, and then respond to the unique needs of their congregation and the community. Their role may include health education, health counselling, a referral source, and facilitating and integrating health and healing in the community.

Questions for Comprehension, Analysis, and Reflection

1. Name the five core practices of compassionate listening and apply them to different contexts.
2. Write a plan for an interreligious celebration and state how to avoid obstacles.

Conclusion

The building of the interreligious community is to build understanding, respect, and cooperation among the various religious denominations and faith groups in a community for the wellbeing of each and every one.

Examples of Required Readings

Brown, Stuart E., ed. *Meeting in Faith: Twenty Years of Christian-Muslim Conversations Sponsored by the World Council of Churches*. Geneva: WCC, 1989.

Heckman, Bud. *Interactive Faith: The Essential Interreligious Community-Building Handbook (Walking Together, Finding the Way)*. Woodstock, VT: SkyLight Paths, 2008. Kindle Edition.

Smock, David. "Building Interreligious Trust in a Climate of Fear." *United States Institute of Peace: Special Report* 99 (2003) 1–12. http://www.usip.org/sites/default/files/sr99.pdf

World Council of Churches. *Guidelines on Dialogue with People of Living Faiths*. Fourth printing, revised ed. Geneva: WCC, 1990.

Chapter 3: Interreligious Practices

Introduction

The interreligious practices bring various practices from the Yoruba Religion, Islam, and Christianity to enlarge our scopes of practices and be better equipped as a religious leader living and practicing in an interreligious context.

Learning Objectives

At the end of this chapter the participants will be able to:

1. Understand and apply the five key practices of the three religions.
2. Understand and apply the Interreligious Practices.
3. Acquire the skills of Interreligious Practices.

Learning Activities

Break into religious groups and have them prepare presentations. First, they will discover how diverse they are in their own group. Give each participant ten minutes to present their religious practices and how they can be applied in a multireligious context. What are the strengths and weaknesses of these practices? Make templates of their responses on the board.

Content

1. Effective Interreligious Practices

For effective interreligious practices, the following points are to be considered:

> ➤ **Avoid proselytizing** through practicing the "golden rule": "listen to others as you would like them to listen to you." Encourage in particular the open articulation of the needs of each individual and religious community.

➤ **Avoid confusing the aim** of understanding and respecting the needs of each individual and religious community with agreement.

➤ **Seek the best possible sharing of responsibilities** across the participating religious communities, building on the various strengths of the respective organizing and participating individuals and communities.

➤ **Respect each organizer's voice** in building consensus, even though various degrees of commitment will soon emerge among the various organizers. More involvement should not translate into more weight in the process of decision-making.

➤ **Practice fair time-management** during both the planning sessions and the celebration itself; no individual or religious community should have more time than others to speak or make their own contribution. In case of tensions, reviewing the initially-agreed-upon guidelines—whether individually or as a group—should help find solutions that will avoid frustrations and feelings of being forced into unwanted decisions.[30]

2. Five Key Yoruba Religion Practices

➤ **The Development of Preaching (Iwaasu)**

In the Yoruba Religion, preaching is an all-encompassing involvement of God in the lives of the Yoruba people. Idowu described them as being "in all things religious." The use and importance of *ase* will be taught. *Ase* is a Yoruba concept that signifies the power to make things happen and change. It is given by *Olodumare* to everything—gods, ancestors, spirits, humans, animals, plants, rocks, rivers, and voiced words (such as songs, prayers, praises, curses, or even everyday conversation). Existence, according to Yoruba thought, is dependent upon it. In addition to its sacred characteristics, *ase* also has important social ramifications, reflected in its translation as "power, authority, command." A person who—through training, experience, and initiation—learns how to use the essential life force of things to wilfully effect change is called an *alaase*.

---

30. Folbert, "Blueprint for the Process," 379.

"*A kiigbo 'lu u' lenuagba*" ("One never hears, 'Beat him up,' in the mouth of an elder"): This means that elders resolve disputes, they do not goad the disputants on. Yoruba people respect the elders and believe in their worldview that their words are sacred and wise. They can preach love, peace, and values of self-restraint. A Yoruba proverb says: "*A kii fi ori we orii Mokusire, bi Mokusire kul'aaro, a jil'ale*" ("One does not like one's fortune to *Mokusire's*, If *Mokusire* dies in the morning, he resurrects at night").[31] This proverb means that you should never emulate people who know tricks you do not know.

▶ The Development of Interreligious Teaching (*eko*)

The teaching will focus on proverbs because the "proverb is the most powerful and potent vehicle for culture dissemination from one generation to the other. Proverbs express the nature of African wisdom as they perform diverse functions, ranging from bringing peace where there is conflict and misunderstandings, giving hope where there is despair, and light where there is darkness in human relationships and interactions."[32]

✓ Teaching about Poverty

The teaching will focuses on how poverty has always been a spark for violent conflicts. Two things are necessary for the alleviation from want: firstly, the natural resources necessary for human life must be protected; and, secondly, injustices in the distribution of material goods and access to those goods must be minimized.

✓ Teaching about Patience, Tolerance, Humility, and Perseverance

Yoruba proverbs teach of patience and perseverance. "*A kiikanjutuoluoran, igba e o to seniobe*" ("One does not gather *Olu-oran* mushrooms in haste, two hundred of them are not enough to make a stew"). Values of patience and perseverance are needed if achievement is to be attained. Through patience and tolerance, peace is ensured. On values of humility, a Yoruba proverb says: "*A kii fi ori we oriiMokusire, bi Mokusirekul'aaro, a jil'ale*" ("One does not like one's fortune to *Mokusire's*, If *Mokusire* dies in the morning, he resurrects at night").[33] Other proverbs on tolerance and humility can be added.

---

31. Owomoyela, *Yoruba Proverbs*, 30–40.
32. Smith, *Muslims, Christians*, 15.
33. Owomoyela, *Yoruba Proverbs*, 30–40.

▶ The Development of Worship Liturgy (*isin*)

In Yoruba Religion, worship is a prominent factor. It begins, controls, and ends all the affairs of life for the Yoruba people. This is also a way of celebrating and encouraging peaceful leaving. The liturgical worship of Yoruba Religion is based on ancestral spirits related to each individual extended family. The worship in Yoruba Religion takes the form of rites and ceremonies and includes prostrating, praying, invoking, hailing the spirit of the object of worship, making offerings, sounding a bell or gong, singing, drumming, and dancing as occasion demands. Worship may be private, offered by single person in a house shrine or it may be corporate. Whatever form worship takes, it is expected to be done in reverence and in the right mood and manner if the desired effect is to be achieved.

Every act of worship has distinct elements, which are liturgy, sacrifice, cultic functionaries, and sacred places. Music and dance are included as liturgy. Liturgy, is an important element, means the prescribed form of public worship among the people.

▶ The Development of a Spirit of Sacrifice and of a Community of Care: "*kase ara wa lokan*"

The interest of the community takes precedence over any individual or sub-group interests within the community. The individual is not expected to function on his/her own. He/she functions intra-psychically through the community. The community—its laws, customs, and taboos—is the only context within which individuals may pursue personal security, happiness, and success. Using proverbs in the Yoruba Religion, care, solidarity, and community assistance will be taught.

▶ The Development of a Spirit of Sacrificial Service (*iran lowo ati irepo*)

In Yoruba Religion, the purpose of our life is *community-service* and community-belongingness. The *Yoruba's* people devote themselves to *community service* by caring for elders, the young, and the children; they work together in cultivating and harvesting their lands. The conception of *community* plays an appropriate role towards achieving the good of all. The Yoruba proverb, "It takes the village to train a child," explains the role of the community to raise their children, how they support families in this service, and will determine how all the community will face the challenges of the future.

3. Five Key Islamic Practices

> ### The Development of Preaching (hkeutbajoumaa)

The Qur'an states that God sent out different prophets to different people to reveal the same truth of the oneness of God and individual moral accountability (Q 2:213). Diversity exists today as a call to know others and "view with one another to attain the subscriber's forgiveness . . . for God loves those who do God." Encourage preaching on the following:

Love of God is the testimonies of faith. The central creed of Islam consists of the two testimonies of faith or *shahadahs*. The first is: "There is no God but God, and Muhammad is the messenger of God." The second is: "Love of the neighbor." There are numerous injunctions in Islam about the necessity and paramount important of love for—and mercy towards—the neighbor. Love of the neighbor is an essential and integral part of faith in and love of God because in Islam, without love of the neighbor, there is no true faith in God and no righteousness. The prophet Muhammad said: "None of you has faith until you love for your brother what you love for yourself."[34]

"It is not righteousness that ye turn your faces to the East and the West; but righteous is he who believeth in God and last Day and the angels and the scripture and the prophets; and giveth wealth, for love of Him, to kinsfolk and to orphans and the needy and the wayfarer and to those who ask, and to set slaves free; and observeth proper worship and payeth poor-due. Those who keep their treaty when they make one, and the patient in tribulation and adversity and time of stress. Such are they who are sincere such are the pious" (Q 2:177).

> ### The Development of Interreligious Teaching (*talimiasariah*)

The teaching will be based on: (1) The conquest of self: forgiveness, humility. Beware! Whoever is cruel and hard on a non-Muslim minority, or curtails their rights, or burdens them with more than they can bear, or takes anything from them against their free will: I will complain against the person on the Day of Judgment. Islam's core message of strict moral accountability not only speaks to equality, free will, and reason but also that that there can be no mediation in the individual relationship with God. It also means that there can be no compulsion in religion on matters

---

34. Al-Bukhari, *Hadith*, 13.

of faith since the sincerity of belief can only be known to God.[35] (2) Religious tolerance: tolerance to acceptance without compromising our value system and the perceived Divine Mandate.[36]

- ✓ Explain the Seven Stages of Tolerance: in the Qur'an:

First Stage, Acknowledgement of the other: "Allah, He is the one who creates you all, some believers others Non-believers" (Q 2:256); Second Stage, "No Compulsion in religious persuasion" (Q 6:66); Third Stage, "No insult or demonization of whatever they worship" (Q 5:2); Fourth Stage, "Render protection to those who seek asylum" (Q 2:256); Fifth Stage, "Collaborate as partners in promoting good of common. Concern for the well being of all" (Q 6:108); Sixth Stage, "Humility and piety be demonstrated" (Q 9:6); and Seventh Stage, "Celebrates diversity. Christians are the closest allies of The Muslims" (Q 5:2).

- ✓ Teaching about Poverty

The teaching will focuses on how poverty has always been a spark for violent conflicts. Two things are necessary for the alleviation from want: firstly, the natural resources necessary for human life must be protected. Secondly, injustices in the distribution of material goods and access to those goods must be minimized.

> **The Development of a Prayer Ritual (*salat*)**

In Islam, worship plays a central role in people's lives. Devotion to a higher being continues to tie humanity together despite differences in customs and a variety of beliefs. The concept of worship in Islam is all-encompassing and incorporates ritual worship as well as common daily tasks. In Islam, worship is the very purpose of existence. God declares in the Qur'an, "I did not create mankind except to worship Me" (Q 49:13). Muslims worship God, the Creator and Sustainer of the universe, out of love and submission. They believe that He is the One God (Allah in Arabic) who is completely unique and only He deserves to be worshipped. Worship allows living and experiencing peace.

As part of worship, the Qur'an also seeks to cultivate internal personal fortitude and character among believers. The Conquest of the self or the struggle over the ego is an effort eliciting the highest praise in

---

35. Brodeur, "Description of the Guidelines," 571–72.
36. Akinmade, "Decline of Proverbs," 128.

Islam. As prophet Muhammad famously said, the most excellent jihad (struggle) is that for the conquest of the self.

▶ The Development of a Community of Care (*sadakat*)

"And hold fast, all of you together, to the cable of Allah, and do not separate. And remember Allah's favor unto you: how ye were enemies and He made friendship between your hearts so that ye became as brothers by His grace; and (how) ye were upon the brink of an abyss of fire, and he save you from it. Thus Allah makes clear His revelation unto you that haply ye may be guided" (Q 5:82).

"Had God willed, He would have made you into community; but (it was Hill will) to test you in what he gave you. So compete with each other in doing good works. To God you are all returning, and He will inform about how you differed" (Q 51:56).

"Those who believe (in the Qur'an), and those who follow the Jewish (scriptures), and the Christians . . . and (all) who believe in God and the last day and work righteousness shall have their reward with their Lord: on them shall be no fear, shall they grieve" (Q 3:103). Islam offers "people of the book" a broad scope of religious freedoms, protections, and minority group rights within Muslim communities as a religious moral duty.

Muslims are encouraged to engage in a dialogue about Islam with non-Muslims in a "respectful" and "gentle" manner, "wisdom and beautiful preaching" (Q 5:48). though nothing more. Where disagreement or acrimony enters into dialogue, Muslims are enjoined to part ways, saying to you your beliefs, and to me mine (Q 109:6; 1:107–9), knowing that "God will judge between you on the Day of judgment concerning the matters in which you differ" (Q 2:62).

▶ The Development of a Spirit of Sacrificial Service (*moussada*)

In Islam, social justice is rooted in a underlying egalitarian ethic based on the Qur'anic principle that the only differentiation among creation to God is in piety. The Qur'an asserts that: "The most honored of you in the sight of God" (Q 16:125; 22:67–69). The prophet informed his followers: "He who helps his fellow-creature in the hour of need, and he who helps the oppressed, him will God help in the day of Travail."[37] When asked which actions were the most excellent in the eyes of God,

---

37. Khan, *Maxims of Muhammad*, 36.

Muhammad replied: "To gladden the heart of human being, to feed the hungry, to help to afflicted, to lighten the sorrow of the sorrowful, and to remove the wrongs of the injured. Feed the hungry and visit the sick, and free the captive, if he be unjustly confined. Assist any person oppressed, whether Muslim or non-Muslim."[38]

4. Five Key Christian Practices

✓ **The Development of Preaching (*kerygma*)**

The preaching must be on Jesus' principle of love that transcends all borders. In his ministry, Jesus served all people, irrespective of their backgrounds (such as the Samaritan woman), to manifest his unconditional love (John 14:9). To emulate Jesus is to strive for harmonious relationships with all people rather than applying discriminatory tendencies based on religion. Identify what discriminatory practices exist in your community and in your country. How can these be worked on? How did Jesus strive for a different type of relationship? What do we see in his dialogue with the Samaritan woman? How can this be a part of our lives? How do we apply the love of God as the First and Greatest Commandment in the Bible? (Deut 6:4–5; Matt 22:34–40).

➤ **The Development of Interreligious Teaching (*didache*)**

✓ Teaching of Religious Tolerance

Acceptance of non-Christians into Heaven (Rom 2:14–16); avoid offending followers of other religions (1 Cor 10:31–32); and tolerance of other types of "Christianity" (Mark 9:38–40). Jesus' disciples had rejected a healer who was exorcising demons in Jesus' name, yet was not one of Jesus' direct followers. Jesus criticized his disciples and accepted the healer. Mark and Luke report the incident in parallel passages.

Jesus refused to curse non-believers: Jesus' teachings were rejected by the inhabitants of a village in Samaria. His disciples asked that he exterminate the people of the village by issuing a curse. Jesus refused to do it and simply moved on to the next village (Luke 9:52–56).

Jesus treats a Samaritan woman with respect: Jesus initiated a conversation with a Samaritan woman in Sychar, Samaria. This is unusual in at least two ways: Jewish men did not talk to women who were not their

---

38. Whitehouse, *Nature of the Sufi Path*, 216.

wives or were not from their family. Also, Jews normally treated Samaritans with contempt. Jews did not have dealings with them, because they had deviated from Judaism.

✓ Teaching Common Beliefs in Islam and Christianity. Both religions believe

- Abraham is the Father of both faiths and a role model.
- The Angel Gabriel was sent to both Sarah and Hagar.
- There is life after death.
- There is accountability before Humans and before Almighty God.
- In the messianic mission of Jesus Christ.
- In the miraculous birth of Jesus without any male intervention.
- Mary as the pure and most glorified above women of all nations.
- In the ascension of Jesus Christ to heaven.
- In destiny—that to everything there is a time.
- In the second coming of Jesus Christ.
- Almighty God Allah spoke through His Angel and Prophets.
- There will be a Day of Judgment.

✓ Teaching about Poverty

The teaching will focus on how poverty has always been a spark for violent conflicts. Two things are necessary for the alleviation from want: firstly, the natural resources necessary for human life must be protected; and, secondly, injustices in the distribution of material goods and access to those goods must be minimized.

> **The Development of a Worship Liturgy** *(leiturgia)*

It is time to clearly recognize that in the end, violence is not a solution, but more often the problem. Peacemaking is not an optional commitment. It is a requirement of the Christian faith. Christians are called to be peacemakers, not by some movement of the moment, but by the Lord Jesus. Disciples of Jesus are called to build a peacemaking church that constantly prays, teaches, speaks, and acts for peace. Therefore, Christian parishes and people need to join in regular prayers for peace. Every liturgy must be a call to and celebration of peace. Create liturgy for peace.

Discuss understanding of the call for peace that God brings to your life at this time. How will you respond? How might we live and respect each other to live into that call?

➤ The Development of a Community of Care (*paraclesis*)

Make a new friend or renew your friendship with a friend, family member, neighbor, or co-worker that you have fallen away from. Share your hopes and ideas about peace for the children of the world with everyone you meet. Learn more about peace and peacemaking. Invite your community to participate in a Peace Pole dedication ceremony, including children and senior citizens, representatives of various faith communities and/or ethnic groups, schools, clubs, scouts, and local media. Community leaders and clergy love to be asked to make speeches. Have the peace messages on the Pole read in the four different Nigerian languages by designated individuals with a connection to each language or culture.

Plant a tree of peace at your home, school, workplace, or place of worship as a symbol of peace and hope for future generations. Think deeply about how your daily activities contribute to the making of justice, the building of community, and the betterment of our culturally violent world. Explore Christian teachings about peace. Picture peace. Imagine peace. Pray for peace.

➤ The Development of a Spirit of Sacrificial Service (*diakonia*)

Christians follow Jesus Christ, who advised them to contact God the Father through him. Christians follow the advice of God as enunciated in the Bible of Solemn Friendship. God's advice is the torch of life, a guide towards Him, a source of all lives and the Father who loves human beings the most. He is the trueness, offering life forever.

Christians live under the advice of God, whom they respect as the Father of all human beings of different races. Upon their belief, therefore, everyone has the same value of dignity: the rich, poor, powerful, and weak are all the children of God. It is the basis for a community which demands social justice.

Christians believe human life is valuable as it is part of the age of God whom we respect. The rich and the poor, the powerful and the powerless—all are equal in rights and freedoms and all human beings have the right to a decent life. They have the right to sufficient food, shelter, and work from which they can make money for a decent living and education for their children.

Questions for Comprehension, Analysis, and Reflection

Have the participants' reflect in groups of three or four on learning during this class and ask them to answer the following questions: 1. What Interreligious practices will be adapted into your community? Why and how? 2. List the advantages of the various practices.

Conclusion

Interreligious practices have a major impact on reducing interreligious and communal violence. Religious leaders cannot improve our peaceful coexistence without effective interreligious practices. Interreligious practices, therefore, play a major role in creating constructive ways of harmonious and peaceful coexistence.

Examples of Required Readings

Dada, I. E. "Chapter 4." In *Defibrillation of Peace: a Christian Clergy's Approach Towards the Restoring of Peace in the Nigerian Interfaith Community.* Saarbrücken, Germany: VDM Verlag, 2009.

Yong, Amos. "Chapter 2." In *Hospitality and the Other: Pentecost, Christian Practices, and the Neighbor.* Maryknoll, NY: Orbis, 2008.

Chapter 4: Healing the Wounds of Religious Addiction and Religious Abuse

Introduction

This chapter deals with the constructive role of religious leaders to be equipped to help *heal wounds* of violence and be trained to acquire skills and knowledge on religious abuse and addiction.

Learning Objectives

At the end of this chapter, participants will be able to:

1. Understand what religious addiction is.
2. Name the stages of addiction.
3. Understand the symptoms of religious addiction.
4. Understand the consequences of religious addiction and abuse.
5. Use the twelve steps of recovery to break religious addiction.

Learning Activities

Ask each participant to express the type of emotional problems they have experienced in their lives and how they were able to solve them. Encourage them to name their feelings but also to bring out their ambitions. Invite each participant to name methods for healing from their tradition.

Content

1. Religious Addiction

When we start using God in a compulsive and bulling way, we have become addicted to a certain form, ritual, and rigidity that can do more harm than good. The words used and beliefs about God can have multiple interpretations and understandings. We may belong to a certain religion or to a sub-category of a larger religion. As individuals, we will have our own personal awareness or understanding of these concepts. They are very abstract and can often lead to confusion or misunderstanding, creating a very personal way of understanding God that is very demanding to follow and difficult explain or share with others.

Religious abuse is a hidden disease; it is often difficult to see from the outside. When you grow up in an alcoholic home, the abuse, rage, and tantrums by a drunken parent easily can be seen. The home is labelled dysfunctional. In contrast, in homes that appear to be stable, material comforts can hide emotional neglect. Children become very confused when they are punished on religious issues—especially about God! Their self-esteem and their ability to connect with God and others may be affected.

Booth explains that religious addiction can damage both the addicted person and their family's happiness. The use of a rigid religious belief system is used by some as a means of escaping or avoiding painful feelings. Like Karl Marx, Booth believes that religion can be an opiate of the people. He writes that religion can console us from deprivations of life, encourage us to accept our current status, and relieve the guilt feelings of oppressors. And yet, he says that there is nothing in the nature of religion which makes it unhealthy in itself; it is possible for a neurotic to use a healthy belief system in an unhealthy way. Booth writes that it is not necessarily the contents of the belief that make a system addictive but rather the personal rigidity of its purveyors, who discourage any kind of questioning or disbelief.[39]

> **Name and explain the various symptoms of religious addiction:**

- ✓ Inability to think, doubt, or question information or authority.

- ✓ Black and white, simplistic thinking.

- ✓ Shame-based belief that you aren't good enough, or you aren't doing it right.

- ✓ Magical thinking that God will fix you.

- ✓ Scrupulosity: rigid, obsessive adherence to rules, codes, ethics, or guidelines.

---

39. Booth, *When God Becomes a Drug*, 100–180.

- ✓ Uncompromising, judgmental attitudes.

- ✓ Compulsive praying, going to church or crusades, quoting scripture.

- ✓ Unrealistic financial contributions.

- ✓ Believing that sex is dirty—that our bodies and physical pleasures are evil.

- ✓ Compulsive overeating or excessive fasting.

- ✓ Conflict with science, medicine, and education.

- ✓ Progressive detachment from the real world, isolation, and breakdown of relationships.

- ✓ Psychosomatic illness: sleeplessness, back pains, headaches, and hypertension.

- ✓ Manipulating scriptures or texts, feeling chosen, claiming to receive special messages from God.

- ✓ Trance like state or religious high, wearing a glazed happy face.

- ✓ Cries for help: mental, emotional, physical breakdown or hospitalization.

Religious addiction, like alcohol addiction, is a disease that can be treated. Just as in Alcoholics Anonymous, using the twelve-step program, we can also use a similar twelve-steps to undo the dysfunctional behavior. With such a program, people with this addiction can be helped into having a healthy relationship with God! The author believes that there is oftentimes a pairing of an alcoholic addiction or food abuse with religious addiction. He claims that the development of religious addiction is similar to the development of alcohol addiction and makes his point with a number of case studies. The author touts the twelve-step program, made famous by Alcoholics Anonymous, as a way to recovery from religious addiction. In fact, he parallels the stages of alcoholism with similar stages of progression to chronic religious addiction.

5. Religious Addiction by Dale S. Ryan and Jeff Van Vonderen[40]

Alcoholic	Religious Addict
Mood alters up by drinking; mood alters down by not drinking or simply by thinking about the prospect of not drinking.	Mood alters up by behaving religiously; mood alters down when they don't or can't practice (attend church, read the Bible daily, pray enough, etc.)
Chooses to be with people who have a relationship with alcohol similar to their own; relationships with others become a casualty.	Chooses to be with people who have a religious belief system similar to their own, withdrawing from friends and even family members who don't.
Gravitates toward places that cater to, are sympathetic to, or even encourage using behavior (e.g., the local bar).	Attends church and activities with people who believe the same or attends activities that are sponsored by like-minded groups and organizations.

At its root, religious addiction begins when our faith stops being about a spiritual connection with God and instead becomes an attempt to control our lives—or to control God—by behaving in certain ways. These behaviors seem to help us to control our mood, but that sense of control is only an illusion. We find over time that we need to engage in the behaviors more and more frequently or with more and more intensity in order to achieve the same mood alteration; that is tolerance. And we experience depression, a sense of meaninglessness, or grief when we are not able for whatever reason to continue the behaviors; that is withdrawal. The behaviors also interfere with our ability to maintain healthy relationships or to function in daily life. The result is an exhausting, graceless, performance-oriented spiritual life that knows nothing of the "rest for your soul" that Jesus described.

6. Causes of Religion Addiction

What causes an individual to develop any kind of obsession or addiction is variable, but there are some common threads. There are genetic factors, but addictive behaviors can also be triggered by trauma, such as abuse experienced as a child. Stress, low self-esteem, and other negative feelings can contribute as well. In some cases, an addiction to religion may be transferred from another addiction. Sometimes when drug addicts or alcoholics are in recovery, they switch their compulsive behaviors from

---

40. Ryan and VanVonderen, "When Religion Goes Bad: Part 2," 3–4.

substance abuse to something more healthy, like religion. This, however, can turn into an addiction as well.

Some people turn to religion for the feeling of togetherness that they experience in a community. Becoming a part of that group may be a healthy answer to loneliness and the search for meaning, but it can also turn into an obsession. In the case of a cult, the consequences can be severe. Regardless of the motivation for seeking out comfort in religion, if worship becomes an addiction, there are ways to get help. As with any type of process addiction, a trained therapist can help the addict learn how to control his impulses and obsessions. With regular counseling and support from loved ones, there is such a thing as recovery from religious addiction.

7. Booth's Suggested Method of Recovery from Religious Addiction

The twelve steps:

i. We admitted that we were powerless over our dysfunctional religion or beliefs, that our lives had become unmanageable.

ii. Came to believe that a Spiritual Power within Ourselves could guide us to sanity.

iii. Made a decision to turn our will and our lives over to this Spiritual Power as we understood this Spiritual Power.

iv. Made a searching and fearless inventory of our dysfunctional religious beliefs and behaviors.

v. Admitted to our Spiritual Power, to ourselves, and to another human being the exact nature of those behaviors.

vi. Were entirely ready to work with our Spiritual Power in replacing all those old behaviors.

vii. Worked with our Spiritual Power to help replace our dysfunctional patterns.

viii. Made a list of all persons we had harmed, and became willing to make amends to them all.

ix. Made direct amends to such people whenever possible, except when to do so would injure them or others.

x. Continued to take personal inventory, and when we made mistakes, promptly admitted it.

xi. Sought through prayer and meditation to improve our conscious contact with our Spiritual Power, as we understood that Spiritual Power, praying only for knowledge of that Power's guidance and the willingness to carry it out.

xii. Having had a spiritual awakening as a result of these steps, we tried to carry this message to others, and to practice these principles in all our affairs.

8. Alternatives to Twelve-Step Addiction Recovery

Christina Reardon in "Alternatives to Twelve-Step Addiction Recovery," provides an analysis of the critique of the twelve step approach, by alternative groups.

> **Secularity:** The Twelve Steps as originally outlined by AA are overtly spiritual, with references to "a power greater than ourselves," God, and prayer. Other twelve-step groups have retained the same or similar language. The alternative groups, on the other hand, promote themselves as being secular in nature. The alternative groups are not anti-religion, however, and many of their members belong to a religious denomination or identify as spiritual.[41]

> **Emphasis on Internal Control:** Twelve-step programs emphasize the recovering individual's powerlessness over alcohol, other substances, or behaviors and the need to rely on a higher power for assistance in overcoming addiction. Alternative groups reject this view and instead see individuals as having adequate power within themselves to overcome addictions. This view is evident in the language of alternative organizations, which emphasize phrases such as "empowering our sober selves," "saving ourselves," and "self-management and recovery."[42]

> **Evolving Approaches:** Although the number of twelve-step groups has grown over the decades, the basic language and methods of the twelve-step approach have not changed significantly since AA's founding nearly eighty years ago. Alternative groups tend to be more open to changing their techniques in response to the development

---

41. Reardon, "Alternatives to Twelve-Step Addiction Recovery," 12.
42. Reardon, "Alternatives to Twelve-Step Addiction Recovery," 12.

of evidence-based approaches to addressing addictions, such as cognitive behavioral therapy, as they are being produced, they're evaluated and then incorporated. Nothing is frozen in time.[43]

9. Shedding of Lifelong Labels: AA and other twelve-step groups portray the battle against addiction as a lifelong one that requires constant vigilance and at least periodic attendance at meetings, even for people who have been in recovery for years. Alternative groups take a shorter-term approach, presenting themselves as tools that people in recovery can use until they no longer see the need for them. "We are not defined by our past. The idea of having to label yourself as an alcoholic or an addict for the rest of your life, that is disempowering, especially for women."[44]

10. Religion Addiction: A Self-Test

Answer seven simple questions from any of the categories below.

---

43. Reardon, "Alternatives to Twelve-Step Addiction Recovery," 12.
44. Reardon, "Alternatives to Twelve-Step Addiction Recovery," 12.

Do you use church or religion to avoid social and emotional problems the same way some people use alcohol to escape?

☐ YES

☐ NO

Are you inclined to focus on external behavior and acts of piety rather than true spirituality?

☐ YES

☐ NO

Do you find identity and value in religious disciplines or church activities?

☐ YES

☐ NO

Do you use guilt to beat yourself up or to control others?

☐ YES

☐ NO

Do you avoid people who don't believe the way you do?

☐ YES

☐ NO

Have you used religion to arrest other addictive behaviors (drugs, alcoholism, sex addiction, etc.)?

☐ YES

☐ NO

Are you preoccupied with religion to the exclusion of other important priorities or to the detriment of yourself or your loved ones?

☐ YES

☐ NO

Teach various virtues encouraged by religions in the healing of wounds (from Yoruba Religion, Islam, and Christianity) such as forgiveness, empathy, compassion, and perseverance.

Questions for Comprehension, Analysis, and Reflection

1. Wounds heal in stages; name the stages of healing from each religious tradition.
2. Propose a healing program for your community

Conclusion

As interreligious leaders, learning how to heal the wounds of religious addiction and religious abuse is important and compulsory for the growth and recovery of our members.

Required Readings

Benda, Brent B., and Thomas F. McGovern. *Spirituality and Religiousness and Alcohol/other Drug Problems: Treatment and Recovery Perspectives.* New York: Haworth, 2006.

Booth, Leo. *When God Becomes a Drug: Understanding Religious Addiction & Religious Abuse.* Long Beach, CA: SCP Limited, 1998.

Minor, Robert N. *When Religion Is an Addiction.* St. Louis, MO: Humanity Works, 2007.

Vocabulary on Feelings

This will help the students in their journal writings exercises.

Table II. Vocabulary for Feelings

Abandoned	Accepted	Affectionate	Afraid	Alarmed
Amazed	Angry	Annoyed	Anxious	Appreciative
Apprehensive	Approval	Ashamed	Balmy	Belittled
Belligerent	Bitter	Bored	Bottled up	Calm
Capable	Competent	Confident	Conflicted	Confused
Contented	Crushed	Defeated	Depressed	Desolate
Desperate	Despondent	Discouraged	Disinterested	Disparate
Dissatisfied	Dispassionate	Distressed	Ecstatic	Elated
Embarrassed	Empty	Enthusiastic	Envious	Euphoric
Excited	Exhilarated	Fearful	Friendly	Frustrated
Furious	Futile	Grateful	Guilty	Happy
Hateful	Helpless	Hopeless	Horny	Humble
Humiliated	Hurt	Identification	Inadequate	Incompetent
Inflamed	Insecure	Insignificant	Jazzed	Jealous
Joyful	Longing	Lonely	Loved	Loving
Miserable	Misunderstood	Needed	Negative	Neglected
Nervous	Passionate	Pleased	Pressured	Proud
Putdown	Puzzled	Reborn	Regretful	Rejected
Rejecting	Rejuvenated	Relaxed	Relieved	Resentful
Sad	Satisfied	Serene	Shocked	Startled

Surprised	Tearful	Tense	Terrified	Threatened
Thrilled	Transcendent	Trusting	Uncertain	Uncooperative
Understood	Uneasy	Unhappy	Unloved	Upset
Uptight	Vengeful	Vindictive	Wanted	Warm-hearted
Worthless	Worthy	Yearning		

Chapter 5: Curriculum Assessment

Introduction

This chapter provides tools for students to assess their learning experiences and measure their development of human relationships, social values, and group activities. It helps identify if the *curriculum* expectations were addressed.

Learning Objectives

At the end of this chapter, participants will be able to:

1. Understand various levels of assessing a curriculum.
2. Undertake a self-assessment.
3. Assess a curriculum.
4. Improve in their interreligious involvement.
5. Be more open the interreligious activities.
6. Discover his/her strengths and weaknesses in interreligious practices.

Learning Activities

Divide the class into groups of four and ask them to answer the following questions on a sheet of paper: What kinds of tasks were useful in the group discussions during the course? Did students achieve the learning objectives? What kinds of activities in and out of class will reinforce my learning? After the groups complete their assessment, give time for personal assessment using the questions below. See pages 261–63.

Content

1. The Four Levels in Assessment

The four levels in assessing this curriculum are:

➤ Level 1: Reaction

How do religious leaders react to the learning experience? Did they like it? In the immediate sense, did they perceive it to be of value? According to Kirkpatrick, every program should at least be evaluated at this level to provide data for its improvement. As Winfrey puts it: "Although a positive reaction does not guarantee learning, a negative reaction almost certainly reduces its possibility."[45] Levels at which we can evaluate interreligious peace education management are: student evaluation, faculty evaluation, self-evaluation, self-observation, peer evaluation, and program evaluation.

➤ Level 2: Learning

Once we know how religious leaders feel about their learning experiences, we need to measure what has actually been learned. Level 2 assesses the extent to which religious leaders have actually gained anything in the domain of interreligious peace education, including knowledge, skills, and values. Typically, this is where we might want to use pre- and post-learning tests (formal and informal, team and self) in order to find out to what extent the desired education has taken place. Outcome: change as a result of the outcome. The outcomes of church and mosques that are more effective as a result of the ministry that our graduates leaders bring to their local faith community.

➤ Level 3: Behavior

Transfer is the "golden egg" of evaluation; we are all especially happy when learners transfer their learning into practice. This level of evaluation helps us know if we are producing learners who can solidify their learning through transformed behavior. Methods are needed to measure changes that occur in students' behaviors over time—not just immediately after a course—as well as a method sound enough to make explicit the link between the transfer and the course or program itself. That is to say, we need measures that can support the claim that transfer has occurred as a direct or indirect result of the courses and overall program. Output: change as a result of the activity. These activities are designed to produce an output: graduates at the end of the program of study who show evidence of some sort of quantitative and qualitative growth as a religious leader.

---

45. Winfrey, *Kirkpatrick's Four Levels*, 1.

➤ Level 4: Results

Although this level is associated by Kirkpatrick with the return on investment and the tallying of measurable long-term impacts to a company, gathering of data from the first three levels correlates with things like graduation rates, job placement rates, and success rates in competitive scholarship or graduate school applications. In an academic setting, determining the desired results of instruction comes directly from the program mission and vision of the "ideal graduate religious leader." Impact: Longer-term societal change. God's mission of global of living at peace through the churches and mosques.

2. Evaluation of the Curriculum after Graduation

At the end of the one year course, the religious leader will point out redundancy as well as areas that have played a particularly significant role in their formation. In addition, they will be asked to undertake a self-assessment based on their profile upon entering the program of study and then again just prior to leaving. This material will become the basis for a level of quantitative analysis of the extent to which the students perceive themselves to be learning and growing through their experience of the program of study. Furthermore, alumni will be valuable voices in assessing the curriculum. Some years after graduation, they will determine what material from the program of study has been particularly meaningful for effectiveness in peace work and what material has been largely irrelevant. What significant areas of knowledge and skill were difficult in practice?

3. Engaging the Local Churches and Mosques

The voices of local lay leaders, elders, youth and women leaders, and members of churches or mosques will be engaged in the assessment. It may be a one-day event in which they will respond to the following questions: What are the contextual challenges of their community? What might be the adequate role of religious leaders for their community? The responses will be incorporated into "the improved leaders."

The community and assessment: Engaging the community for assessing the success of the program is very important. This involves many community leaders who are neither Christian nor Muslim. This process includes interviews with such questions as: (1) To what extent are the churches and mosques involved in peacemaking in the community? (2)

What is the general impression the community has about co-existence between Christians and Muslims? (3) To what extent is the church and mosque involved in violence reduction in the community? (4) The responses of the local leaders to the above questions will also be gathered to determine the implications of the leaders.

4. Student Attitude Survey

Directions: Read each statement carefully. Then, mark the letter that most closely indicates your response: (a) agree strongly, (b) agree, (c) not formed an opinion yet, (d) disagree, or (e) disagree strongly.

Question	(a) agree strongly	(b) agree	(c) not formed an opinion yet	(d) disagree	(e) disagree strongly
Religions can reduce violence.					
When violence or conflict break out, the security of the community is in danger.					
The group was opened to diversity.					
I believe my religion can be the way to solve some major differences between religions.					
All religions should be equal in status.					
If there is religious violence, it is my duty to join the peacemakers and search for peace.					
Religions have some power to influence peace-building in the society.					
Religion cannot change violence.					
Every individual has the right to choose his/her religion.					

Question	(a) agree strongly	(b) agree	(c) not formed an opinion yet	(d) disagree	(e) disagree strongly
The commandment of love and justice can reduce violence.					
The conscientization of our leaders must be encouraged.					
Religious leaders can practice and teach inter-religious peace education.					
Religious leaders can practice and teach inter-religious peace education.					
The practice of justice must begin within religious institutions.					
The ICPE program can be improved.					
I have a clear understanding of how to put my experiences in practice.					
I will encourage others to attend the course.					
I learn from others.					
I was not open to new ideas.					
The course content was adequate.					
I understand what my community says about peace.					

Self-Evaluation

The following sentences will help you learn about yourself. Score your answer by checking 3, 2, 1, or 0. Score 3: if you always do what the statement says, 2 if you do so often, 1 if you do sometimes and 0 (zero) if you never do what the statement says.

Table III. Student Attitude Survey

Questions	3: Always	2: Often	1: Sometimes	0: Never
1. What were your feelings before the course?				
2. What influenced you most during the course?				
3. Your relationship with other.				
4. The course material was useful.				
5. I was happy with the learning environment.				
6. My views were heard.				
7. I was able to contribute in the class.				
8. I took good care of my emotions.				
9. I took time to relax and revitalize myself.				
10. I am with my group.				
11. I enjoy my practical work.				
12. I have good reliable friends around me.				
13. I have people in whom I can confide.				
14. I have contributed to the happiness of others.				
15. I am satisfied with my teachers.				
16. I feel I can get what I want from life.				
17. I feel responsible for my life.				
18. I exercise control over important aspects of my life.				
19. I work towards my goals.				
20. I live up to my expectations.				
21. I am content with the acquired skills.				
22. I see how my work contributes to society.				

Questions	3: Always	2: Often	1: Sometimes	0: Never
23. I am pleased with my success and achievement.				
24. I am satisfied with my personal growth.				
25. I developed the ability to think about my experience theologically.				
26. I look forward to a peaceful world.				
27. I never feel bored.				
28. I express my creativity.				
29. I have more resources from ICPE.				
30. I am satisfied with my interreligious peace education program.				
31. I am tolerant of other people's beliefs.				
32. I compromise my moral and ethical standards.				

Score of 75+ is good; 50–75 is average; 25–50 is poor; and 0–25 means you need help.

Conclusion

The curriculum assessment provides students with grades of their learning experience that enables them to become knowledgeable, self-directed, responsible individuals, able to manage violent context and cope with a complex and rapidly changing society. It measures their development of human relationships, social values, and pride in religious and peaceful heritage.

Examples of Required Readings

Wolf, Peter, et al. "Handbook for Curriculum Assessment Winter 2006." http://docplayer.net/8970242-Handbook-for-curriculum-assessment-winter-2006.html.

CONCLUSION

In designing the interreligious curriculum of peace education, I am bringing a model of education to ensure a better formation and empowerment of religious leaders who are living and facing frequent and continuous religious violence in Nigeria. The vision of interreligious peace education as stated is to create and sustain peaceful society through programs centered on conflict resolution. This approach is based on the social-behavioral symptoms of conflict and training religious leaders to resolve inter-personal disputes through techniques of negotiation and mediation. It includes learning to manage anger and improve communication through skills such as listening, turn-taking, identifying needs, and separating facts from emotions. Its goals are: to reduce the human cost of religious violence in Nigeria; to build a more effective, interreligious community; to promote harmony and the spirit of common personhood amongst all the people of Nigeria, transcending religious, linguistic, and regional or sectional diversities; to renounce practices derogatory to the dignity of a person; and provide tools religious leaders can use to transform their faith community members.

Religious violence has not only inflicted hardship on people but also denied them the opportunity of experiencing the full benefit of an encounter with the religions of others, the enrichment of another's understanding of the Divine, the understanding that is born out of mutual respect, and a critical self-examination that deepens one's own religion conviction. From my observation and understanding of the roots of religious violence, there are various reasons contributing to religious violence in Nigeria, namely, the exclusivist discourses of both Christianity and Islam, the bad handling of the economy, the high level of poverty, and the lack of administrative or intellectual expertise to formulate and properly execute growth enhancing policies. The curriculum allows religious leaders to understand that this violence is a major problem in society and is a threat to everyone. It exposes the root causes of religious violence in Nigerian society, providing the religious leaders with the foundation for understanding the cycle of violence and how it traps people in relationships. It brings out the group dynamics and explores the sources and dynamics of violence and how it relates to religion and religious values. It proves the following: (1) that religiously inspired violence is often motivated by social injustices, unresolved frustrations, endless suffering, powerlessness, and hopelessness; (2) when injustice lingers for too long, it builds hatred and thereby becomes the source of violence among people; and (3) that religious violence is often provoked by the greed that promotes various forms of inequalities and institutionalized injustices in the economic, political, ethnic, and religious spheres of society. Consequently, all these situations lead to the feelings of hopelessness, hatred, prejudice, and a desire for vengeance. The curriculum assists leaders to familiarize themselves with primary sacred texts and stories that deal with violence. Awaken them to the various ways in which violence is viewed in these texts and stories (e.g., holy violence, apocalyptic violence, and violence against bodies). The curriculum helps them to engage in critical reflection on the study of sacred texts and stories as well as to challenge them to reflect upon the ways in which this literature has impacted modern understandings of religion, sacred texts, and violence. It contributes to the development of their own view(s) of the subject matter through reading primary and secondary sources.

In addition, in my observation, the absence and neglect of interreligious peace education as part of the peace education core program and the lack of interreligious curriculum for peace education in the training of religious leaders is identified as one of the main problems encountered when analyzing the effectiveness of Nigerian academic studies in creating a peaceful living experience. In order to solve this lack and neglect, the interreligious peace education is the spiritual soul of education, creating a shield for human survival on the planet earth. It is through an interreligious peace education that religious leaders can install peace in human minds as an antidote to religious violence. The interreligious peace education also plays an important role in the search for new methods of education that will advance broad social transformation, shifting away from a paradigm of dominance, exclusiveness, and violence and toward a new paradigm of equity, inclusiveness, and peace. The curriculum provides both theoretical and practical background information. The curriculum intends to bring interreligious education to religious leaders in order to train leaders how to affect their community at a grassroots level. It promotes how to acquire the skills of peace education from various concepts of peace such as Yoruba Religion, Islam, and Christianity. It helps to understand and comprehend how to integrate the various theories of peace and how to use various elements of a transformative model of peace education effectively.

The ICPE is a new approach in the training of religious leaders and an attempt to respond to the problems of conflict and violence on scales ranging from the global and national level to the local and personal. It explores ways of creating greater awareness of a more just and sustainable peace. It brings a better understanding of the process of breaking the cycles of violence, deconstructing the doctrine of Islamic and Christian violence, and acquiring more skills to break the cycles of violence. It also helps in acquiring skills and understanding how to deconstruct the doctrine of violence to be able to use the stages of conflict effectively: prevention before conflict, resolution during conflict, and reconstruction after conflict. Theoretically, it lays the foundation for the more practical elements of the interreligious peace education.

Furthermore, understanding the deleterious effect of violence on interreligious relations and the growing realization that multireligious efforts can be more powerful than those of a sole religious community opens the way to the type of interventions found in the ICPE. The ICPE is a practical, alternative way of enhancing the capacity of the interreligious mediation group to resolve religious conflict in Nigeria effectively. The ICPE's theoretical and practical knowledge can improve the present interreligious practices and develop the core concepts further; it conveys the peace culture-building and learning activities of peace education and training as a viable alternative to violence. The proposed interreligious peace education will not achieve the changes necessary for long-lasting peace throughout Nigeria; rather, it prepares religious leaders to achieve the changes in their respective contexts as a starting point. It aims at developing awareness of social and political responsibilities, guiding and challenging people to develop their own learning from individual and collective actions. It encourages them to explore possibilities for their own contribution to resolving the problems and achieving better conditions for living. The ICPE is a planned and guided learning experience and intended learning outcome, the primary objective of which is to help religious leaders grow into a peaceful person. It is modelled on a peace education curriculum. The model consists of eighteen chapters which can accommodate many peace values and those concepts most meaningful in the present global context. It gives the basic characteristics of a peaceful person that we wish to see developing in religious leadership. The ICPE will help leaders develop positive attitudes towards themselves as individuals and in their community, country, and humanity.

General Conclusion

This chapter, following the praxeological approach, is divided into two parts. The first part is the conclusion of the book. In the second part, I present the prospective of this interreligious curriculum for peace education in Nigeria, especially in terms of its potential benefits when it comes to enhancing a more peaceful future. In addition, it also includes envisaged obstacles in its application.

CONCLUSION OF THE BOOK

Based on my observations, the rise of religious extremism in the world in general—and in Nigeria in particular—has turned the perception about religion into the most important factor dividing the Nigerian population, itself mostly one half Muslim and the other half Christian. Despite the proliferation of mosques and churches in Nigeria, the intensification of mass religious activities, and the aggressive display of religious piety, the series of religious crises witnessed in Nigeria in the last two decades are not only injurious to Muslim-Christian relations; they are also destructive to Nigeria's socio-economic development. These crises have significantly undermined the basis of collective existence—a now fragile social fabric that took generations to build and nurture over centuries. In Nigeria, religion has failed to establish the peace which it has claimed to promote because deep historical feuds (although not necessarily religious in nature per se) have now found a religious expression. This dire situation has therefore brought religion to the forefront of Nigerian problems, making religion a core element in many of its current challenges.

The general observation, analysis, and understanding of the roots of religious violence require us to find solutions. This situation calls for the restructuring of the educational system of many if not all higher educational institutions, especially those that train future religious leaders. The curriculum needs to include peace studies courses to prevent religious leaders from engaging in violent preaching, teaching, and ultimately behavior. This compels us to put faces, events, and history behind what we are teaching and allow us to establish the problematization of religious violence and bring peace education and training as a viable alternative to violence. This peace education can only be effective if it brings together participants in an interreligious peace education experience. This is especially true where the absence and neglect of interreligious peace education as part of the peace education core program and the lack of interreligious curriculum for peace education in the training of religious leaders are identified as one of the main problems encountered when analyzing the effectiveness of Nigerian academic studies in creating a peaceful living experience. The formulation of the interreligious curriculum for peace education (ICPE) is appropriate to meet this period of crises. Peace education as the solution in Nigeria is based on concepts, principles, and pedagogies found in Yoruba religion, Islam, and Christianity. Each of these religions provides overlapping perspectives, tools which reinforce and support the foundations and principles of peace education. There is a need to construct a model of peace education that will include the various distinct values of these three religions for the teaching and reduction of violence in Nigeria. This model of peace education embraces and is developed into interreligious curriculum for peace education suitable and tailored to meet the needs of religious leaders in a multicultural context.

Increasing the interpretation of past and current events through a critical analysis will help understand the issues and causes of the problems observed. Various causes have been identified, discussed, explained, and interpreted, and the results are negative—described as dramatic situations—causing injury and pain, death, mental agony, psychic terror, feelings of helplessness, destruction of property, damage to infrastructural facilities such as electric installations, police posts, and schools, diversion of public funds from socio-economic development to security, abuse of human dignity and rights, and losses of resources and desecration of property. Frequent religious violence in Nigeria not only inflicts hardship on people; it also denies them the opportunity of experiencing the full benefit of an encounter with the religions of others, enrichment through other's understanding of the Divine, understanding born out of mutual respect, and a critical self-examination that deepens one's own religious convictions. Understanding the deleterious effects of violence on interreligious relations can further the growing realization that multireligious efforts can be more powerful than those of a sole religious community. Religion seems to be the preferred instrument to hide the real causes of various conflicts across Nigeria. It excludes potentially extraordinary sacredness by throwing a veil over the eyes of people filled with hope. But if religions can be used to heighten the fire of passion, they can also be useful in easing souls and consciences. All religions promote tolerance and forgiveness. These strong shared values must help to reinforce healing in human relationships as well as to restore order and peace. Concepts, principles, and pedagogies for peace education can be found in Yoruba religion, Islam, and Christianity. Each of these religions provides overlapping perspectives, tools which reinforce and support the foundations and principles of peace education. There is a need to construct a model of peace education that will include the various distinct values of these three religions for the teaching and reduction of violence in Nigeria. A model of how peace education can embrace these values can be developed into an interreligious curriculum for peace education suitable and tailored to meet the need of current religious leaders living in a multicultural and multireligious context.

Moreover, when a nation like Nigeria increasingly suffers death and unprecedented degrees of violence through so-called religious behaviors, it becomes obvious that each religion needs trained religious leaders with peacebuilding skills to intervene, prevent, and rebuild. For those tasks, they must be trained as peacemakers through an interreligious curriculum for peace education. Through their actions, the nature of religious conflicts can be changed and decreased. It is crucial to include interreligious peace education in the curriculum that forms future religious leaders so as to empower future generation with the necessary skills to prevent and resolve conflicts as well as practice peacebuilding in post-conflict situations. In fact, the understanding that many religious leaders have about peace is very limited. They do not know about the variety of instruments and techniques that can promote peace, and thus, in the face of some more difficult challenges, they too easily fall prey to calling for the use of violence in order to achieve a "solution" to their problems. They grew up in environments that encouraged violence, supported by often selective interpretations of specific passages in their sacred texts. The curriculum in which they have been educated—if any at all—can be qualified as dysfunctional since education should teach religious leaders to avoid resorting to violence. Interreligious peace education raises awareness of the roots and causes of interreligious conflict through channeling this energy into programs that rebuild the community and strengthen bonds between communities. Interreligious peace education can inspire religious leaders and their members to look to the future for a better tomorrow. It can stimulate and revitalize religious morale and work towards developing social justice and equality.

The ICPE will shape the growing religious activity and consciousness in Nigeria toward peace and tolerance. It will engage each religious leader to address the myriad of social issues that are often at the root of violence (injustice, poverty, illiteracy, and health care) in an interdisciplinary way. It will revive the religious virtues of compassion, love, honor, and respect for the neighbor and indeed the religious sanctity of life and property of a fellow human being. It will revamp our value system and the imperative of moral regeneration of the nation. The ICPE will help build sturdy bridges of understanding between Traditional, Muslim, and Christian communities in Nigeria. It will sustain interreligious dialogue, not regarding these dialogues as mere academic exercises. It will endeavor to carry the message of tolerance and mutual understanding, which these dialogues teach, to our mosques and churches. Since we generally fear what we do not know or understand, religious instruction must take place in all institutions of learning in the country so that adherents of all religions can know each other and avoid mutual suspicions. It will address many grievances that contribute to communal and religious conflict related to equity, fairness, and, indeed, the inability or outright refusal of local officialdom to promote them. It will also fight against poverty, enabling Muslims, Christians, and other traditional religious communities to live decent and productive lives.

If the purpose of religion is for us to know God, we must also know those created by God. If we cannot live together, how can we claim to be worshipping God? Therefore, as outlined in this book, the ICPE presents a curriculum aimed at responding to the different needs and capacities of religious leaders to be effective in knowing human beings in a multireligious context. As part of the training courses for advanced high training, the tools will ensure multiple goals to reduce the present crises arising from competition and power struggles. Furthermore, the foolish attitude of religious people who teach "truth," "benevolence," and "mercy" to be hostile to each other and repeat bloody conflicts will be replaced by religious conversations, instructions, and behaviors that address violence through dialogue.

The interreligious curriculum for peace education is not a quick fix solution or a pre-packaged tool to be imposed either locally or globally; rather, what is necessary is a paradigm shift that shapes content and pedagogy by incorporating issues of human security.[1] The ICPE will not achieve the changes necessary for short term peace; rather, it prepares religious leaders to achieve the long term changes for peace themselves. It aims at developing awareness of social and political responsibilities, guiding and challenging people to develop their own learning from individual and collective actions. It encourages them to explore possibilities for their own contribution to resolving problems and achieving better conditions for living. True peace education makes humans whole and is a life-long endeavor. It is the core aspect of all types of education. Peace education includes all the elements that constitute human life. Thus peace cannot be taught; instead, is learned by both teachers and students through dialogue, discussion, and practice.

The ICPE is a way of educating religious leaders in the creation of peace, initially among believers from different traditions, but ultimately in relation to the training of their leaders. The most valuable part of this book is the development of valuable and reliable cores from various theories of peace as well as peaceful doctrines and rites from various religious traditions. The hope for ICPE is that it will help strengthen interreligious communities throughout Nigeria by creating and deepening relationships with the sacred, the self, and a variety of others so that we can begin the creative process together. By sharing our questions, traditions, selves, cultures, worship, and work for justice, we can begin to know ourselves, the other, and the sacred better. At the same time, learning about our own religion and that of others opens up possibilities of not only understanding another tradition but also looking at our own with new eyes.

In today's world, too many people who live near each other, if not side by side, isolate themselves in communal enclaves based on their religions. This often divides them and maintains a sense of hatred and violence for other religions. The ICPE will help confront this isolation and avoidance of the other and/or conflict. Isolation and avoidance can be caused by what Augsburger describes as the difficulty of crossing over to

---

1. Ardizzone, "Towards Global Understanding," 2.

meet the other. Fear of misunderstanding, appearing insensitive, or being offensive can cause people to isolate themselves and appear uninterested. They engage in judging themselves for being wrong and inadequate, feel shamed and judged by others, and become closed, fearful, and prejudiced.[2] In finding out how adherents of other traditions are time and culture bound in the expressions of their faith, we become aware of the degree to which we ourselves are influenced by our social, cultural, and political environment as well.

In addition, due to the normalization of violence and its influence on well-being, religious leaders must learn how to teach peace, to respond to conflict, and to analyze how current problems can be avoided. Due to the deficiency of curricula in our mosques, churches, and institutions of higher learning, religious leaders who acquire their skills from the ICPE will have the responsibility of participating in a snow ball effect, creating lessons and curricula that facilitate more interreligious peace education.

The greatest collective challenge facing Nigeria today is how to find stability and peace in her process of development and growth. The world is continually facing challenges of unprecedented and continued development, acquisition of weapons of mass destruction, conflicts between states or ethnic and religious groups, the spread of tribalism, nationalism, community, violence, the huge widening gap between the rich and the poor throughout the globalized economy, violations of human rights, and the degradation of the environment. The ICPE is a tool for the transformation and emancipation of the believers, a challenge to the status quo. Its education promoting the respect of others is relevant in today's context, especially after examining the nature of religious conflicts around the world (and especially in Nigeria). There are challenges, however, to the implementation of interreligious peace education because it challenges the status quo. Only very few people are comfortable with change out of fear of a disruption of what they have always known.

Although the present challenges are enormous, it is important that we also see the signs of hope—such as the growth of social movements that work for the promotion of peace and justice in various ways and levels. This should increase our confidence and resolve to make our own contributions towards our positive vision. We need a more purposive focus on the goals of ICPE, more investment in renewable energy, and a greater commitment to peace itself. I believe that building a culture

---

2. Augsburger and Abu-Nimer, *Peace-building*, 41.

of peace is among the essential goals for today and tomorrow. Human and ecological survival and well-being, now and in the future, depend on this. Therefore, it makes good sense for religious leaders—as well as all people—to work together towards this vision.

In this book, the goals were to understand the nature and origins of religious violence and its effects on both victim and perpetrator; to create frameworks for achieving peaceful, creative societies; to sharpen awareness about the existence of relationships that are non-peaceful between people and within and between nations; to investigate the causes of conflicts and violence embedded within the perceptions, values, and attitudes of individuals as well as within social and political structures of society; to encourage the search for alternative or possible skills in nonviolence; and to equip religious leaders with personal conflict resolution skills—to think, teach, speak, and act for peace.

In conclusion, the importance of the interreligious curriculum for peace education in the training and education programs of religious leaders cannot be over emphasized, particularly at a time when the world is facing its worst crisis. This book explores a variety of theoretical and workable understandings of nonviolence and peace. It contributes to the understanding of nonviolence as a fundamental tool for the creation of a just and peaceful family, school, community, society, nation, and world. The ICPE explains the roots of violence and helps teach alternatives to violence. It covers different forms of peace education like Human Rights Education, Environmental Education, Co-existence Education, and Resolution Conflict Education, concluding that promoting these types of peace education will help to reduce violence in communities as well as society. If peace education programs become more widely used and universally accepted, ICPE could be a model peace reconciliation program and adapted to a variety of specific contexts, both in Nigeria as well as other neighboring sub-Saharan African countries in particular. If implemented, it will definitely foster the process of conflict resolution and transformation, the formation of peaceful relations, mutual trust, acceptance, tolerance, and cooperation as well as contribute to the nonviolence movement.

PROSPECTIVE

The prospective of the interreligious curriculum for peace education in Nigeria is to bring the benefits of an education that is necessary if we want to work toward a more peaceful future as well as the envisaged obstacles in its application. In designing the ICPE, I am bringing a model of education that ensures a better formation and empowerment of religious leaders who are living in and facing frequent and continuous religious violence in Nigeria. The vision of interreligious peace education as stated in this book is to create and sustain peaceful society through programs centered on conflict resolution and transformation. This approach is based on the social-behavioral symptoms of conflict and training religious leaders to resolve inter-personal disputes through techniques of negotiation and mediation. It includes learning to manage anger and improve communication through skills such as listening, turn-taking, identifying needs, and separating facts from emotions. Its goals are to: reduce the human cost of religious violence in Nigeria, build a more effective, interreligious community, and promote the harmony and spirit of common personhood amongst all the people of Nigeria—transcending religious, linguistic, and regional or sectional diversities. It seeks to renounce those practices derogatory to the dignity of a person and provide tools that religious leaders can use to transform their faith community members.

The absence and neglect of interreligious peace education as part of the peace education core program and the lack of an interreligious curriculum for peace education in particular has been identified as one of the main problems encountered when analyzing the effectiveness of peaceful living in any multicultural society. According to Castro: "The ultimate goal of interreligious education (and of peace education) is to learn new ways of thinking and acting based on mutual respect and shared responsibility so that the whole human community can live in peace and enjoy the fruits of a sustainable equitable development."[3] In developing the interreligious curriculum for peace education, my utopian dream is for our religious leaders to build the kingdom of God on earth together and to share gifts and skills for the welfare and growth of humankind. The expected achievement of this interreligious curriculum for peace education is a humanizing process whereby Nigerian religious leaders will cultivate hearts that welcome the other through religious teachings and peace education. They will enable them to manage their

---

3. Castro, "Role of Education," 4.

violent tendencies and know how to release their bitterness to prevent them from building conditions that would attract violence.

My prospective of the ICPE is to train religious leaders to play the role of religion itself effectively. Generally, religion plays various roles. According to Farideh Salili in *Religion in Multicultural Education*:

> Religion plays a double role in most communities. On the one hand, it provides meaning for life with references to higher powers, going beyond the appeal to the uniqueness of humans in creation and the freedom they enjoy in relation to the rest of creation. On the other hand, for the sake of peace and harmony, it encourages obedience to authority and adherence to rules and regulations to maintain healthy bonds within the community.[4]

The role of religion in a community is to preserve moral values and to enhance the quality of life. This is achieved through imparting beliefs and practices to their adherents and by transmitting the faith through rites, rituals, customs, institutions, and teaching. In addition, religion provides a framework for individual's lives as well as communities' lives. Religion is an important basis of identity for many people. It is an important source of legitimacy for actions they can support or oppose in their personal and social life. The role of religion is to bring people to an awareness of life. It is to transform the world, to come to see the world as God sees the world, and to bring it as close to the vision of God as we possibly can. That is why in "The Role of Religion in Today's Society," Joan Chittister asserts that:

> Real religion is not about building temples and keeping shrines. Real religion is about healing hurts, speaking for and being with the poor, the helpless, the voiceless, and the forgotten who are at the silent bottom of every pinnacle, every hierarchy, and every system in both state and church, church and state. Real religion, the scripture insists, is not about transcending life; real religion is about our transforming life. The gospel of the transfiguration calls us to Sabbath; calls us to become enlightened; calls us to change our attitudes about the role of religion; calls us to understand the nature of religion itself; because the so-called rational has failed. Religion calls us to the Beatitudes, to the works of mercy, to the casting out of demons, to the doing of miracles for those in need, to the being and act of irrational love and burning justice of God.[5]

4. Salili and Hoosain, *Religion in Multicultural Education*, 14.
5. Chittister, *Role of Religion in Today's Society*, 1.

In Nigeria, religion is a very important factor in the current condition of the society. It contains vital ingredients that can contribute to the development of a healthy and stable order in the nation or it may be the reinforcer of ethnic conflict. Religion has contributed to the Westernization that Christianity brought to the South of Nigeria in particular, which included education, literacy, and access to jobs in colonial service. Islam brought a new system of ideas, a new way of life, and literacy in the North of Nigeria in particular. Religion can correct the division it has caused Nigeria. It has not only divided the country, but this imperfect division has also affected the relationship between people of various religious traditions. Religion has a strong influence on the social and moral lives of Nigerians. Instead of religion acknowledging and promoting the right of others to believe and to act differently in a multicultural society, instead, religion has too often contributed to many atrocities and acts of destruction.

Peace is essential to humanity. Peace defeats disharmony and celebrates serenity. It believes in giving, sharing, caring, and respecting life. Peace is necessary for individuals within the same religious community, between two or more religions, and between peoples and states, regionally and globally. All religions preach peace and believe that the abode of God is where peace is fully experienced. Peace is a divine attribute in every religion because in each religion it is God's commandment to live in peace with each other. Christians and Muslims have a duty to promote this tranquility of order. For Christians, although it is also the expectation of a perfect stage at the end of history, the Kingdom of God does not just come in one dramatic event sometime in the future; the kingdom is present in every act of love, in every manifestation of truth, in every moment of joy, and in every experience of the holy.

If nurturing peaceful characteristics within all humans could eventually lead to the development of a culture of peace, religious leaders will contribute to this process by teaching about peace: what it is, why it doesn't exist, and how to achieve it and build the beloved community. They will use their interreligious peace education skills to teach about how to create peaceful communities. They will teach about how conflicts get started, the effects of violent solutions to conflict, alternatives to violent behavior, and how to resolve disputes non-violently. They will establish practices of religion and education to prevent violence or even abolish it, all of which would be of significant importance to avoid recurring crimes against human dignity.

Additionally, an expected achievement of the ICPE is that religious leaders will hope to create a commitment to the way of peace in human consciousness, to solve problems caused by violence, and inculcate resistance to the evil effects of violence to their members by teaching skills to manage conflicts non-violently and by creating a desire to seek peaceful resolutions of conflicts. Humans have the potential to build peace, and this potential can be educated and nourished.

Through ICPE, religious leaders should become more alarmed about the dangers of violence, learn how to promote peace, and change our behavior and political systems by teaching conflict resolution skills. They can reduce levels of violence since education implies at best a change in consciousness, learning facts and theories that may result in a change in attitude and behavior. In the face of the deadly threats that confront both humanity and the earth itself today, religious leaders in Nigeria should identify and develop the best ways to teach about the religious causes, perceptions, and behaviors that contribute to the continuous violence in Nigeria. They should contribute to the building capacity of the two main faith communities to face the enormous possibilities for collaboration between these communities: to work together for social and ethnic justice, for the defense of human rights and people's rights, for safeguarding and promoting religious freedom, for resolving conflicts peacefully, and for addressing the plight of refugees and displaced people. Religious leaders will educate their communities where they live, encouraging Christians and Muslims to share spiritual insights, to stand hand-in-hand in the face of common threats or in struggling together towards shared social and political goals, to bring exchanges and mutual transformation, and to discover resources that will help the community become more humane, more sensitive to the needs of others, and more obedient to God's will for all creation—thus fulfilling the purpose for which God has created humankind.

Leaders will be able to teach how to overcome misconceptions, combat prejudice and bias, and dispel religious ignorance. They will become educated on how to eliminate inherited ideas and negative stereotypes, which marked their mutual perceptions and false images of the other developed in both communities, resulting in fear and misunderstanding. They will re-examine and reject prejudices against other religions. The leaders will help Christians who have often (but not always) perceived Islam as too political, an economic and a theological threat, and have painted Islam in negative colors, in contrast to their own positive self-image. They will assist Muslims who, in turn but not always, have been inclined to regard Christianity and Christendom—often identified with each other and with the West—as engaged in an ongoing crusade against the Muslim world, to see Christians in a new light.

They will provide models for building healthier interreligious relations, soothing discords, righting wrongs, and nurturing respect. The leaders will be enabled to educate their members that dialogue is neither conversion nor is it only conversation (a dialogue of ideas); rather, it is an encounter between people (dialogue of life). Dialogue depends on mutual trust, demands respect for the identity and integrity of the other, and requires a willingness to question one's own self-understanding as well as an openness to understand others on their own terms. Dialogue includes the understanding that involvement does not water down their own tradition. They will expand the understanding that in dialogue, we are invited to listen in openness to the possibility that the God we know in each tradition may be encountered in individuals and community in the lives of our neighbors of other faiths.

Religious leaders will learn to help the Christian-Muslim community to reduce conflict, rivalry, or violence by continuing to deepen our mutual understanding and trust. They will establish one of the main objectives of dialogue in the common search for a viable model of society and cooperation in building a really human community which—in law and practice—guarantees equality for all, safeguards religious liberties, and respects differences and particularities.

They will not only point out that there are many points of convergence between Christian and Muslim beliefs but also acknowledge that there are real and substantial differences between them—many of which stem directly or indirectly from our respective scriptures. Given these and other differences, it is essential for the continuing improvement of relations that both Christians and Muslims make greater efforts to learn more about each other's faith.

They will focus interreligious practices around the notion of human security. Christians and Muslims seriously need to explore models of governance that further a balance between individual and community rights. Such situations also challenge the community to develop new forms of political involvement. This involvement necessitates an ability to liberate religion from narrow, sectional interests with the aim of engaging critically in issues of human rights, social and political justice, and striving towards the peaceful resolution of conflicts.

In addition, the new policy of dialogue will encourage and engage their communities in a one-on-one conversation that will allow them to think and talk about the future and the development of the community. The two religions will be able to come up with a joint strategy on addressing the issues facing the poor and what the government could do to alleviate their situation. The mission will be to promote mutual understanding, respect, appreciation and cooperation among people of faith in the community through extending hospitality, offering educational opportunities, providing moral leadership, sharing in service, and working for justice. Its vision will be to promote mutual understanding, appreciation, and respect among the region's diverse religions and cultures; to honor each other's religious festivals and, where appropriate, share together in common prayer; to seek opportunities for conversation, partnership, education, hospitality, and celebration among its members; to address concerns and pursue common goals that impact religious communities; to provide moral leadership on mutually agreed-upon issues; to serve poor, hungry, homeless, and marginalized people; to foster peace, compassion, kindness, openness, and trust; and to encourage one another in embracing these commitments. In short, this ICPE will engage new spiritual strategies to bring our spiritual powers together to fight the darkness that we all face and those spiritual issues destroying the peace and progress of the community to achieve better living conditions, both individually and collectively.

The eventual transformations this curriculum will bring will directly contribute towards better harmony in Nigeria. This harmony will need to be maintained for humans to experience peace, for it is not only social but also spiritual and cosmic. In addition, new practices for effective interreligious peace education will be practiced. These practices will emphasize ways to treat others with filial piety, fraternal love, loyalty, trustworthiness, and humanity in order to coexist with others courteously, justly, honorably, and peacefully.

The success of the ICPE will promote the image of religious leaders and allow the public sector and the government to use this approach in changing our national security policy and the educational curriculum. This new policy will bring change about how to equip the military so that violence can be prevented and teach that violence cannot be resolved by violence. This may change the mindset of our leaders and our society from the current culture of war to a *culture of peace*.

While I believe in these expected achievements, there are other challenges that I need to enumerate for future generations of trained religious leaders. In the application of the ICPE, so far, three praxeological challenges have been identified that might affect its application. That is to say, how can the newly trained leader deal with: (1) conducting praxeological observations in a pastoral milieu; (2) addressing extremism and the legitimation of violence; and 3) adopting the five interreligious practices?

The first challenge—praxeological observation in a pastoral milieu—requires setting the parameters of praxeological observation by seeking clarification of an encountered problem, starting with the "who, what, when, where, why, and how" questions. The milieu of applying the ICPE is pastoral and interreligious. While African native religious communities will be included, the principle objective is to address Christian and Muslim religious communities. How does one go about observing both communities in their respective places as well as their interaction in common, public spaces? Moreover, how does one gain access to communities whose discourses are exclusivist, sectarian, and politically radical? The situation is even more challenging in the current precariousness of socio-political conditions in Nigeria.

The second challenge is how to address extremism and the legitimation of violence: how will the trained religious leaders address extremism and the religious legitimation of violence? With the continued rise of political extremism in Nigeria, how will they deal with the threat and fear of reversion to an earlier state of subordination, the perceptions of injustice leading to anger and blame (including the stereotyping of innocents), and humiliation and shame? How will they identify other causes leading to extremist behavior and apply the ICPE, especially when actors within the Nigerian extremist Islamist group *Boko Haram* seek the complete Islamization of the country, intending to fight all heretics, apostates, hypocrites, sinners, and unbelievers (including any Muslim who does not ascribe to and participate in their understanding of *jihad*)? Likewise, the exclusivist Christian discourse—which claims that an allegiance to Christianity presents itself as a choice and entails renouncing all other religious options—is also problematic in many families and areas where the co-existence of both traditions is a matter of daily life. Christians who hold strongly to this view are concerned that engaging with other religions might be disloyal or even lead to conversion to the other faiths, without understanding that this also often leads to exclusivist behaviors in inter-community relations.

The third challenge is that of adapting five interreligious practices. There are several challenges in using the five key practices that need to be included when designing the ICPE: (1) *kerygma* (proclamation), (2) *didache* (instruction/teaching), (3) *leiturgia* (worship/prayer), (4) *koinonia* (community), and (5) *diakonia* (service). The first challenge concerns the development of *kerygma* or preaching (*hkeutbajoumaa*), which focuses on human security by addressing "economic, food, health, environmental, political, community, and personal security needs."[6] A second challenge concerns the development of an interreligious catechetic or didactic practice (*didache/talimiasariah*) that is based on knowledge about the revelation and salvation of God in history, in the sacred scriptures, and in the confessional traditions of both Christianity and Islam. The third challenge concerns the development of a community of care and comfort (*paraclesis/sadakat*). Similarly, the fourth challenge arises in developing a community of fellowship, sharing, and interaction among believers (*koinonia/jamaa*), which includes mutual care between Christians and Muslims. The fifth challenge occurs in developing witness and missionary outreach (*marturia/houhoud*) in order to empower people to transform the world. A sixth challenge arises in developing a worship liturgy compatible for both religions (*leiturgia/salat*). Finally, the seventh challenge concerns the development of a spirit of sacrificial service in the churches and mosques (*diakonia/moussada*) as agents of change and community development. Even though these practices are fundamentally from a Christian paradigm, they are similar to what a peacemaker must do in Islam. According to the Qur'an, "The worshippers of the All-Merciful are they who tread gently upon the earth, and when the ignorant address them, they reply peace!" (Q 25:63), and a Hadith on peace stipulates that, "What actions are most excellent? To gladden the heart of a human being, to feed the hungry, to help the afflicted, to lighten the sorrow of the sorrowful, and to remove the wrongs of the injured."[7]

Some other challenges are: (1) The willingness of the university to accept and implement this new curriculum. (2) The financial implications and sources of funding this interreligious curriculum for peace education cannot be implemented free of cost. Funding will be required for developing ICPE material, training, and capacity building of teachers. It may not be very easy to find sources, however, because of the tremendous

---

6. Sommaruga, "Global Challenge of Human Security," 208.
7. Sita, *True Meaning and Implications of Jihad*, 84.

pressure of limited finances on education—particularly university education. (3) Undertaking the creation of centers and the training of religious leaders: sourcing and gaining funding for interreligious curriculum peace education has proven to be difficult because many donors will be hesitant to support religious activities. In facing those many challenges and hopes, the future of the ICPE is uncertain. Nevertheless, its potential application on the ground in Nigeria is a necessity that is self-evident for the Nigerian community to be transformed towards a more sustainable peaceful and multicultural society.

Bibliography

Abbas, Haider. "Principles of Good Governance in Islam." http://blog.mile.org/principles-of-good-governance-in-islam.
Abdalla, Amr. *Peace Education: Islamic Perspectives*. Colón, Costa Rica: University for Peace, 2009.
Abdulkarim, Siraj B. "Religion, Peace, and National Development: a Look at Interreligious Conflicts in Nigeria." http://www.iua.edu.sd/publications/iua_magazine/african_studies.
Aboud, Frances. *Children and Prejudice*. New York: Basil Blackwell, 1998.
Abu-Nimer, Mohammed. "Conflict Resolution, Culture, and Religion: Toward Training Model of Training." *Peace Research* 38.6 (2001) 685–704.
———. *Dialogue, Conflict Resolution, and Change: Arab-Jewish Encounters in Israel*. Albany, NY: State University of New York Press, 1999.
———. *Nonviolence and Peacebuilding in Islam: Theory and Practice*. Gainesville, FL: University Press of Florida, 2003.
Abu-Nimer, Mohammed, and D. W. Augsburger. *Peace-building by, Between, and Beyond Muslims and Evangelical Christians*. Lanham, MD: Lexington, 2009.
Abu-Nimer, Mohammed, A. Khoury, and E. Welty. "Muslim Peacebuilding Actors in Africa and the Balkan Context: Challenges and Needs." *Peace and Change* 33.6 (2008) 549–81.
———.*Unity in Diversity: Interfaith Dialogue in the Middle East*. Washington, DC: United States Institute of Peace, 2007.
Ackerman, Peter, and J. A. Duvall. *Force More Powerful: a Century of Nonviolent Conflict*. New York: Palgrave, 2000.
Adams, Maurianne. *Readings for Diversity and Social Justice: An Anthology on Racism, Antisemitism, Sexism, Heterosexism, Ableism, and Classism*. New York: Routledge, 2000.
Adeboye, M. *Awon Owe Yoruba*. Ile-Ife, Nigeria: Craft, 2010.
Adetunji, Labiran. "Health Workforce Profile: Nigeria." www.afro.who.int/index.php.
Adeyemi, Adeniyi Babatunde. "Indigenous Proverbs and Peacebuilding in Nigeria." *International Journal of Humanities and Social Science* 4.2 (2014) 186–92.
Adolf, Antony. *Peace: A World History*. Cambridge: Polity, 2009.
Agi, S. P. I. *The Political History of Religious Violence in Nigeria*. Calabar, Nigeria: Pigasiann & Grace International, 1998.
Ahmad, Hadhrat M. T. "Attainment of Inner Peace." www.alislam.org/library/links/00000193.html.

Ahmed, Zahib S. "Human Rights in Islam." In *Peace Education: Islamic Perspectives*, edited by S. S. Niazi & N. Kakar, 115–36. Colón, Costa Rica: University for Peace, 2009.

Ahmed, Razi. "Islam, Nonviolence, and Global Transformation." In *Islam and Nonviolence*, edited by Glenn D Paige, et al., 27–52. Honolulu, Hawaii: Centre for Global Nonviolence, 1993.

Akinade, Akintunde. E. *Christian Responses to Islam in Nigeria: A Contextual Study of Ambivalent Encounters*. New York: Palgrave, 2014.

———. *Fractured Spectrum: Perspectives on Christian-Muslim Encounters in Nigeria*. New York: Peter Lang, 2013.

Akinmade, Arinola C. "The Decline of Proverbs as a Creature Oral Expression: A Case Study of Proverb Usage among the Ondo in the South Western Part of Nigeria." *AFRREV LALIGENS: An International Journal of Language, Literature, and Gender Studies* 1.2 (2012) 186–92.

Alan, Race. *Christians and Religious Pluralism: Patterns in the Christian Theology of Religions*. Maryknoll, NY: Orbis, 1983.

Ali, Muhammad, ed. *The Holy Quran: Arabic Text, with English Translation and Commentary*. Translated by Muhammad Ali. Lashore, India: Ahmadiyyah Anjuman Isha'at Islam, 1963.

Ali, Shaheen S. *Gender and Human Rights in Islam and International Law: Equal Before Allah, Unequal Before Man?* New York: Springe, 2000.

Ali-Akpajak, Sofo C. A., and T. Pyke. *Measuring Poverty in Nigeria*. Oxford: Oxfam, 2003.

Allport, Gordon W. *The Nature of Prejudice*. Abridged. Albany, NY: Doubleday Anchor, 1958.

Altwaijri, Abdulaziz. *Human Rights in Islamic Teachings*. Rabat: ISESCO, 2001.

Amartya, Sen. "The Violence of Illusion." In *Identity and Violence: The Illusion of Destiny*, 1–17. New York: Penguin, 2006.

Anderson, Paul N. "Religion and Violence: From Pawn to Scapegoat." In *Sacred Scriptures, Ideology, and Violence*, edited by J. Halord Ellens, 265–83. Vol. 1 of *The Destructive Power of Religion: Violence in Judaism, Christianity, and Islam*. Westport, CT: Praeger, 2004.

Ankerberg, John, and E. F. Caner. *The Truth about Islam and Jesus*. Eugene, OR: Harvest House, 2009.

Appleby, Scott, and Carnegie Commission on Preventing Deadly Conflict. *The Ambivalence of the Sacred: Religion, Violence, and Reconciliation*. Lanham, MD: Rowman & Littlefield, 2000.

Appleby, Scott. *The Oxford Handbook of Religion, Conflict, and Peacebuilding*. New York: Oxford University Press, 2015.

Arbuckle, Gerald A. *Violence, Society, and the Church: a Cultural Approach*. Collegeville, MN: Liturgical, 2004.

Ardizzone, Leonissa. "Towards Global Understanding: The Transformative Role of Peace Education." *Current Issues in Comparative Education* 2 (2001) 16–25.

Ashton, Carolyne. "Using Theory of Change to Enhance Peace Education Evaluation." *Conflict Resolution Quarterly* 25.1 (2007) 39–53.

Assefa, Hizkias. *Peace and Reconciliation as a Paradigm: a Philosophy of Peace and its Implications on Conflict, Governance, and Economic Growth in Africa*. Nairobi, Kenya: Nairobi Peace Initiative, 1993.

Asseily, Alexandra. *Breaking the Cycles of Violence in Lebanon and Beyond.* Brighton, East Sussex: Guerrand-Hermès Foundation for Peace, 2007.
Assman, Jan. "No God but God: Exclusive Monotheism and the Language of Violence." In *Of God and Gods: Egypt, Israel, and the Rise of Monotheism,* 106–26. Madison: University of Wisconsin Press, 2008.
Astley, Jeff, et al. *Peace or Violence: the Ends of Religion and Education?* Cardiff: University of Wales, 2007.
Augsburger, David W. *Hate Work: Working through the Pain and Pleasures of Hate.* Louisville: Westminster John Knox, 2004.
Avalos, Hector. *Fighting Words: The Origins of Religious Violence.* Amherst, NY: Prometheus, 2005.
Avruch, Kevin, and M. Chris, eds. "Basic Human Needs: Bridging the Gap between Theory and Practice." In *Conflict Resolution and Human Needs: Linking Theory and Practice,* 40–58. New York: Routledge, 2013.
Awolalu, Omosade, and P. A. Dopamu. *West African Traditional Religion.* Ibadan, Nigeria: Onibonoje, 1979.
Ayeni, Toyin. *I am a Nigerian, not a Terrorist.* Indianapolis, IN: Dog Ear, 2010.
Bajaj, Monisha. *Encyclopedia of Peace Education.* Charlotte, NC: IAP, 2008.
Bamikole, Lawrence. "An Indigenous Yoruba Socio-political Model of Conflict Resolution." http://www.davidpublishing.com/davidpublishing/Upfile/2/28/2013/2013022881869185.pdf.
———. "Democracy in a Multicultural Society." *Philosophy and Praxis* 4 (2008) 8.
Bar-Tal, Daniel. "The Elusive Nature of Peace Education." In *Peace Education: The Concept, Principles, and Practices Around the World,* edited by Gabriel Salomon, 27–36. Mahwah, NJ: Lawrence Erlbaum Associates, 2002.
Bar-Tal, Daniel, and G. H. Bennink. "The Nature of Reconciliation as an Outcome and as a Process." In *Conflict Resolution to Reconciliation,* edited by Y. Bar-Siman, 11–38. Oxford: Oxford University Press, 2004.
Barash, David P., and C. Webel. *Peace and Conflict Studies.* London: Sage, 2002.
Bartoli, Andrea. "Christianity and Peacebuilding." In *Religion and Peacebuilding,* edited by Harold Coward and Gordon S. Smith, 147-166. Albany, NY: Sunny, 2004.
Barrett, Loletta M. "Community Building of Peacemaking Through Interfaith Dialogue, Religious Education, and Social Justice Action." DMin thesis, Claremont School of Theology, 2009.
Bateson, Gregory. *Mind and Nature: A Necessary Unity.* New York: E. P. Dutton, 1979.
Beck, Sanderson. *Nonviolent Action Handbook.* Ojai, CA: World Communications, 2003.
Becker, James M. "Toward a Coherent Curriculum for Global Education." *Louisiana Social Studies Journal* 15.1 (1988) 13–16.
Beer, Francis A. *Peace Against War: the Ecology of International Violence.* San Francisco: W. H. Freeman, 1981.
Bennett, Georgette. "Interfaith Peace in the Face of Escalating Christian-Muslim Conflict." *Huffington Post,* January 3, 2012. http://www.huffingtonpost.com/georgette-bennett-phd/an-example-of-interfaith-_b_1175107.html.
Berquist, Jon L., ed. *Strike Terror No More: Theology, Ethics, and the New War.* St. Louis: Chalice, 2002.
Berling, Judith A. *Understanding Other Religious Worlds: A Guide for Interreligious Education.* Maryknoll, NY: Orbis, 2004.

Best, Shedrack G., ed. *Introduction to Peace and Conflict Studies in West Africa: a Reader*. Ibadan, Nigeria: Spectrum, 2006.
Bethlehem, Douglas W. *A Social Psychology of Prejudice*. London: Croom Helm, 1985.
Bistolfi, Robert. *Politique et Religion en Pays d'Islam: Diversités Méditerranéennes*. Paris: L'Harmattan, 2000.
Blackmore, Paul, and C. Kandiko. *Strategic Curriculum Change: Global Trends in Universities*. New York: Routledge, 2012.
Bloomfield, David. *Reconciliation After Violent Conflict: A Handbook*. Stockholm: IDEA, 2005. http://www.un.org/en/peacebuilding/pbso/pdf/Reconciliation-After-Violent-Conflict-A-Handbook-Full-English-PDF.pdf.
Blumenthal, Monica D., et al. *Justifying Violence: Attitudes of American Men*. Ann Arbor, MI: Institute for Social Research, University of Michigan, 1972.
Bonner, Monica D. *Le Jihad: Origines, Interprétations, Combats*. Paris: Téraèdre, 2004.
Booth, Leo. *When God Becomes a Drug: Breaking the Chains of Religious Addiction & Abuse*. Long Beach, CA: SCP, 1998.
Boyer, Pascal. "Why Doctrines, Exclusion, and Violence?" In *Religion Explained: The Evolutionary Origins of Religious Thought*, 265–97. New York: Basic, 2001.
Brantmeier, Edward J., et al. *Spirituality, Religion, and Peace Education*. Charlotte, NC: IAP, 2010.
———, et al. *Transforming Education for Peace*. Charlotte, NC: IAP, 2008.
Brenes-Castro, Abelardo. "An Integral Model of Peace Education." In *Educating for a Culture of Social and Ecological Peace*, 77–99. Albany: State University of New York Press, 2004.
Brent, Benda B., and T. F. McGovern. *Spirituality and Religiousness and Alcohol/Other Drug Problems: Treatment and Recovery Perspectives*. New York: Haworth, 2006.
Brockopp, Jonathan E. *Islamic Ethics of Life: Abortion, War, and Euthanasia*. Columbia, SC: University of South Carolina Press, 2003.
Brock-Utne, Birgit. *Feminist Perspectives on Peace and Peace Education*. New York: Pergamon, 1989.
Brodeur, Patrice. "Description of the Guidelines for Interfaith Celebration." *Ecumenical Studies* 34.4 (1997) 57–72.
———. "Identity and Power Dynamics: Interworldview Dialogue for Peacebuilding." Paper presented at the Institute of Peace and Dialogue Program. Vienna, Austria, 2013.
Brown, C. "The Family and the Subculture of Violence." In *Violence in the Family*. 262–68. New York: Harper and Row, 1974.
Brueggemann, Walter. *Living Toward a Vision: Biblical Reflections on Shalom*. Philadelphia: United Church, 1976.
Bryant, M. Darrol, and F. K. Flinn, eds. *Interreligious Dialogue: Voices from a New Frontier*. New York: Paragon House, 1989.
Buchan, John. *Greenmantle, etc.* London: Pan, 1947.
Bukhari, Muhammad, et al. *English Translation of Sahih al-Bukhari*. Lahore: Ahmadiyya Anjuman Isha`at-i-Islam, 1956.
Burgat, François. *Face to Face with Political Islam*. New York: Palgrave Macmillan, 2003.
Burrowes, Robert J. "Cross-Border Nonviolent Intervention: A Typology." In *Nonviolent Intervention Across Borders: A Recurrent Vision*, edited by Yeshua Moser-Puangsuwan and Thomas Weber, 45–72. Hawaii: University of Hawaii Press, 2000.

———. *The Strategy of Nonviolent Defense: A Gandhian Approach.* Albany: State University of New York Press, 1996.
Burns, Robin J., and R. Aspeslagh. "Three Decades of Peace Education Around the World." *British Journal of Educational Studies* 46.2 (1998) 413.
Câmara, Helder, and Pax Christi. *Peace Spirituality for Peacemakers.* London: Pax Christi, 1983.
Campbell, John. *Nigeria: Dancing on the Brink.* Lanham, MD: Rowman & Littlefield, 2011.
Caner, Ergun M. *Unveiling Islam: An Insider's Look at Muslim life and Beliefs.* Grand Rapids, MI: Kregel, 2002.
Castro, Loreta, et al. *Peace Education Initiatives in Metro Manila.* Quezon City: UNDP and UP-CIDS, 2005.
———. "The Role of Education in Promoting Interfaith Cooperation." http://niu.edu/iserve/PDFs/The_Role_of_Education_in_Promoting_Interfaith_Cooperation.pdf.
Cavanaugh, William. "Does Religion Cause Violence?" *Harvard Divinity Bulletin* 25.2/3 (2007) 22–35.
Cawagas, Virgina, and S. Toh. *Peaceful Theory and Practice in Values Education.* Quezon City: Phoenix, 1991.
Central Intelligence Agency. "The World Factbook: Nigeria." https://www.cia.gov/library/publications/the-world-factbook/geos/ni.html.
Central Intelligence Agency. "The World Factbook." https://www.cia.gov/library/publications/the-world-factbook/fields/2116.html.
Charron, André. "La Spécificité Pastorale du Projet d'Intervention. " In *La Praxéologie Pastorale, Orientation et Parcours 2*, edited by Nadeau J. G., 153–84. Montréal: Fides, 1987.
Charron, Jean-Marc, and Jean-Marc Gauthier. *Entre l'Arbre et l'Écorce.* Saint-Laurent, Québec: Fides, 1993.
Chen-Hayes, Stuart, et al. "Challenging Linguicism: Action Strategies for Counselors and Client-colleagues." http://eric.ed.gov/?id=ED435907.
Cheng, Shu-ju, and L. Kurtz. "Third World Voices Redefining Peace." *Peace Review* 10 (1998) 5–11.
Chittister, Joan. "The Role of Religion in Today's Society." http://www.csec.org/csec/sermon/chittister.
Chrétien, Jean-Pierre. *L'Invention Religieuse en Afrique: Histoire et Religion en Afrique Noire.* Paris: Karthala, 1993.
Christian Peace Witness. "Christian Peace Witness for Iraq." http://christianpeacewitness.org/march08.
Clark-Habibi, Sara. "Reconciliation in Practice." Paper presented at the Institute of Peace and Dialogue, Vienna, Austria, 2013.
Clift, Wallace B. *Jung and Christianity: The Challenge of Reconciliation.* New York: Crossroad, 1982.
Cobb, John B., Jr. *Transforming Christianity and the World: A Way Beyond Absolutism and Relativism.* Edited by Paul F. Knitter. Maryknoll, NY: Orbis, 1999.
Cohen, Jaqueline, and J. A. Canela-Cacho. "Incarceration and Violent Crime: 1965–1988." In *Consequences and Control*, edited by A. J. Reiss Jr. and J. A. Roth, 296–397. Vol. 4 of *Understanding and Preventing Violence*. Washington, DC: National Academy, 1994.

Cook, David. *Understanding Jihad*. Berkeley: University of California Press, 2005.
Collins, John J. *Does the Bible Justify Violence?* Facets Series. Minneapolis: Fortress, 2005.
Compass Direct News. "Violence in Yobe State, Nigeria Aimed Mainly at Christians." *Christian Post*, November 14, 2011. http://www.christianpost.com/news/violence-in-yobe-state-nigeria-aimed-mainly-at-christians-61691.
Conde-Frazier, Elizabeth, et al. *A Many Colored Kingdom: Multicultural Dynamics for Spiritual Formation*. Grand Rapids, MI: Baker Academic, 2004.
Country Studies. "Nigeria Labor." http://www.country-studies.com/nigeria/labor.html.
Couture, Pamela D. *Complex Identities in a Shifting world: Practical Theological Perspectives*. Zürich: Lit, 2015.
Cruickshank, Paul, and Tim Lister. "Al Qaeda-linked Group Finds Fertile Territory in Nigeria as Killings Escalate." *CNN*, December 26, 2011. http://www.cnn.com/2011/11/18/world/africa/nigeria-militants/index.html.
Cully, Iris. *Planning and Selecting Curriculum for Christian Education*. Valley Forge, PA: Judson, 1983.
D'Souza, Andreas. "Reconciliation in Practice: India Experience." In *Religion, Conflict, and Reconciliation: Multifaith Ideals and Realities*, edited by Jerald D. Gort and H. M. V. Henry Jansen. Amsterdam: Rodopi, 2002.
Dada, Isaiah E. "Defibrillation of Peace: a Christian Clergy's Approach Towards the Restoring of Peace in the Nigerian Interfaith Community." DMin thesis, Claremont School of Theology, 2008.
———."Praxeological Challenges in Formulating an Interreligious Curriculum for
Peace Education (ICPE) in Nigeria." In *Complex Identities in a Shifting World: Practical Theological Perspectives*, edited by P. D. Couture, 197–207. Zürich: Lit, 2015.
Dale, S. R., and J. VanVonderen. "When Religion Goes Bad." *Spiritual Abuse Recovery Resources*. http://www.spiritualabuse.com/?page_id=45.
Danesh, Hossain B. "The Education for Peace Integrative Curriculum: Concepts, Contents, and Efficacy." *Peace Education* 5.2 (2008) 157–73.
Danesh, Hossain B., and S. Clarke-Habibi. *Education for Peace Curriculum Manual: A Conceptual and Practical Guide*. Vancouver, Canada: International Education for Peace Institute, 2007.
Danfulani, Umar H. D. "Briefing: the September 2001 Events in Jos, Nigeria." *African Affairs* 101403 (2002) 243–55.
Dear, John. *The God of Peace: Toward a Theology of Nonviolence*. Eugene, OR: Wipf and Stock, 2005.
DeKeseredy, W. S., and B. Perry, eds. "A Critical Perspective on Violence." In *Advancing Critical Criminology: Theory and Application*, 150–53. Latham, MD: Lexington, 2006.
de Rivera, Joseph H. "Assessing the Basis for a Culture of Peace in Contemporary Societies." *Journal of Peace Research* 41 (2004) 531–41.
———."Introduction: Assessing Cultures of Peace." *Peace and Conflict* 10 (2004) 89–103.
De Souza, Marian. *International Handbook of the Religious, Moral, and Spiritual Dimensions in Education*. London: Springer, 2009.
Desai, Zubeida, et al. *Educational Challenges in Multilingual Societies: LOITASA Phase Two Research*. South Africa: African Minds, 2010.

Demmers, Jolle. *Theories of Violent Conflict: An Introduction*. New York: Routledge, 2012.
Dieter, Hessel T., and L. L. Rasmussen. *Earth Habitat: Eco-injustice and the Church's Response*. Minneapolis, MN: Fortress, 2001.
———. *Reconciliation and Conflict, Church Controversy Over Social Involvement*. London: Westminster, 1969.
Drake, Susan M. *Creating Standards-based Integrated Curriculum: the Common Core State Standards Edition*. Thousand Oaks, CA: Corwin, 2012.
Dubensky, Joyce. *A Look at Religion, Diversity, and Conflict Through a Practical Lens*. Münster: Westf LIT, 2011.
Easwaran, Eknath. *Nonviolent Soldier of Islam: Badshah Khan, a Man to Match his Mountains*. Tomales, CA: Nilgiri, 1999.
Eisner, Elliot W. *The Educational Imagination: On the Design and Evaluation of School Programs*. 3rd ed. New York: Macmillan, 1994.
El-Ansary, W. A., and D. K. Linnan. *Muslim and Christian Understanding: Theory and Application of "A Common Word."* 1st ed. New York: Palgrave Macmillan, 2010.
Ellens, J. Harold. "Introduction: The Destructive Power of Religion." In *Violence in Judaism, Christianity, and Islam*, edited by J. Harold Ellens, 2. Vol. 1 of *The Destructive Power of Religion*. Westport, CT: Praeger, 2004.
Encyclopedia of the Nations. "World Leaders: Nigeria 2003." http://www.nationsencyclopedia.com/World-Leaders-2003/Nigeria.html.
Engebretson, Kath. *International Handbook of Inter-religious Education*. New York: Springer, 2010.
Engler, Mark. *How to Rule the World*. New York: Nation, 2008.
Esposito, John L. *The Islamic Threat: Myth or Reality?* Oxford: Oxford University Press, 1992.
———. *Unholy War: Terror in the Name of Islam*. Oxford: Oxford University Press, 2002.
Evans, Robert A. "From Reflection to Action." In *Human Rights: A Dialogue Between the First and Third Worlds*. Maryknoll, NY: Orbis, 1983.
Eze, O. "Human Rights Issues and Violations: The African Experience." In *Human Rights, Peace and Justice in Africa: A Reader*, 35–40. Pretoria: Pretoria University Law, 2006.
Ezegbobelu, Edmund E. *Challenges of Interreligious Dialogue Between the Christian and the Muslim Communities in Nigeria*. Berlin: Peter Lang, 2009.
Ezozo, O. Agrippa. "African Peace Education: Initiative for a Nonviolence Curriculum." *Pan African Studies* 9.9 (2009) 1–27.
Faber, Claude. *Ensemble pour la Paix: Comprendre, Agir, Espérer*. Toulouse: Milan Jeunesse, 2006.
Falola, Toyin. *History of Nigeria*. Ikeja: Longman Nigeria, 1989.
———. *Violence in Nigeria: The Crisis of Religious Politics and Secular Ideologies*. Rochester: University of Rochester Press, 1998.
Fanslow, Janet. "Beyond Zero Tolerance: Key Issues and Future Directions for Family Violence Work in New Zealand." Wellington: Families Commission, 2005. http://www.familiescommission.org.nz/publications/research-reports/beyond-zero-tolerance.
Farrington, David P. "Early predictors of adolescent aggression and adult violence." *Violence and Victims* 4.2 (1989) 79–100.

Fayemi, Ademola K. "Agba (elder) as Arbitrator: A Yoruba Socio Political Model for Conflict Resolution." *Journal of Law and Conflict Resolution* 13 (2009) 60–67.
"Federal Republic of Nigeria." http://www.axl.cefan.ulaval.ca/afrique/nigeria.htm.
Finley, Laura L. *Building a Peaceful Society: Creative Integration of Peace Education.* Charlotte, NC: IAP, 2011.
Fisher, Simon. *Working with Conflict: Skills and Strategies for Action.* London: Zed, 2000.
Firestone, Reuven. *Jihad: The Origin of Holy War in Islam.* Oxford: Oxford University Press, 1999.
Folbert, Josien."A Blueprint for the Process of Peace and Reconciliation." In *Religion, Conflict and Reconciliation: Multifaith Ideals and Realities,* edited by Jerald D. Gort, et al., 261. Amsterdam: Rodopi, 2002.
Foley, Edward, et al. *Religion, Diversity, and Conflict.* Wien: Lit, 2011.
Foltz, Richard, et al., eds. *Islam and Ecology.* Cambridge, MA: Harvard University Press, 2003.
Fountain, Susan. *Peace Education in UNICEF.* New York: UNICEF, 1999. http://www.unicef.org/girlseducation/files/PeaceEducation.pdf.
Francis, David J. "Peace and Conflict Studies: An African Overview of Basic Concepts." In *Introduction to Peace and Conflict Studies in West Africa,* edited by S. D. Best, 26–36. Ibadan: Spectrum, 2004.
———. *Peace and Conflict in Africa.* New York, NY: Zed, 2008.
McCandless, Erin, and T. Karbo. "Peace, Conflict, and Development in Africa a Reader 2011." http://www.upeace.org/pdf%5CREADER_webpages.pdf.
Franzoi, Stephen L. *Social Psychology.* Madison: Brown & Benchmark, 1996.
Freire, Paulo. *The Politics of Education: Culture, Power, and Liberation.* South Hadley, MA: Bergin & Garvey, 1985.
Forsyth, Donelson R. *Human Aggression.* Pacific Grove, CA: Brooks & Cole, 1990.
Fourchard, Laurent. "Violence et Ordre Politique au Nigeria." http://hal.archives-ouvertes.fr/hal-00629064.
Galtung, Johan. "Form and Content of Peace Education." In *Encyclopedia of Peace Education,* edited by M. Bajaj, 49–59. Charlotte, NC: IAP, 2008.
———. *Peace by Peaceful Means: Peace and Conflict, Development and Civilization.* Thousand Oaks, CA: Sage, 1996.
———. "Peace Theory: An Introduction." In *World Encyclopedia of Peace,* edited by E. Laszlo & J. Y. Yoo, 251–61. New York: Pergamon, 1986.
———. *Transcend and Transform: An Introduction to Conflict Work.* Boulder, CO: Paradigm, 2004.
Galtung, Johan, et al. *Searching for Peace: The Road to Transcend.* 2nd ed. Sterling, VA: Pluto, 2002.
Garver, Newton. "What Violence Is." *The Nation* 209 (1968) 817–22.
Gelles, Richard J., and M. A. Straus. "Violence in the American Family." *Journal of Social Issues* 35.2 (1979) 15–39.
Giblet, Jean. "Human Rights and the Dignity of Man." *Convergence* 2.2 (1979).
Gier, Nicholas F. *The Origins of Religious Violence: An Asian Perspective.* New York: Lexington, 2014.
Girard, Rene. *De la Violence à la Divinité.* Paris: B. Grasset, 2007.
Gopin, Marc. *Between Eden and Armageddon: the Future of World Religions, Violence, and Peacemaking.* New York: Oxford University Press, 2000.

———. *Holy War, Holy Peace: How Religion can Bring Peace to the Middle East*. New York: Oxford University Press, 2002.
Government of Newfoundland and Labrador. "Violence Prevention Initiatives 2014." http://www.gov.nl.ca/VPI/types.
Graham, Hugh David. "The Paradox of American Violence." In *Violence in America: Historical and Comparative Perspectives*, edited by H. D. Graham and T. R. Gurr, 475–490. Rev. ed. Beverly Hills, CA: Sage, 1979.
Griff, W. "Violence: Its Source Is Not Always What It Seems." *Nieman Reports* (2007) 5.
Guidelines on Dialogue with People of Living Faiths. Rev. ed. Geneva: WCC, 1990.
Gülen, Fethullah. *Advocate of Dialogue*. Compiled by Ali Unal. Fairfax: Fountain, 2000.
Gurr, T. R. *Why Men Rebel*. Princeton: Princeton University Press, 1970.
Haar, G. T., and J. J. Busuttil. *Bridge or Barrier: Religion, Violence, and Visions for Peace*. Boston: Brill, 2005.
Haar, G. T., and J. D. Wolfensohn. *Religion and Development: Ways of Transforming the World*. London: Hurst & Co, 2011.
Hambly, W. D. "Culture Areas of Nigeria: 1935." https://archive.org/stream/cultureareasofni213hamb/cultureareasofni213hamb_djvu.txt.
Hamilton, M. Gregory. *Self and Others: Object Relations Theory in Practice*. Northvale, NJ: Jason Aronson, 1987.
Harris, Ian. "Conceptual Underpinnings of Peace Education." In *Peace Education: The Concept, Principles, and Practice Around the World*, edited by G. Salomon and B. Nevo. London: Lawrence Erlbaum, 2002.
———."History of Peace Education." In *Encyclopedia of Peace Education*, edited by Monisha Bajaj. Charlotte, NC: IAP, 2008. http://www.tc.edu/centers/epe/PDF%20articles/Harris_ch2_22feb08.pdf.
———. *Peace Education*. Jefferson, NC: McFarland, 1988.
———. *Peace Education*. 3rd ed. Jefferson, NC: McFarland, 2013.
———. "Peace Education Theory." *Journal of Peace Education* 1.1 (2004) 5–20.
———. "The Ideal of Peace." *CURI Curriculum Inquiry* 34.1(2004) 109–22.
———. "The Promises and Pitfalls of Peace Education Evaluation." In *Transforming Education for Peace*, edited by J. Lin, et al., 245–65. Charlotte, NC: IAP, 2008.
———. "Types of Peace Education." In *How Children Understand War and Peace*, edited by A. Raviv, et al., 299–317. Somerset, NJ: John Wiley, 1999.
Harris, Ian M., and M. L. Morrison. *Peace Education*. 2nd ed. Jefferson, NC: McFarland, 2003.
Harris, Ian M., et al. *Peace Studies in the West*. Malmö, Sweden: Lund University, 1997.
Harris, Ian, and O. Caviglioli. *Think it-map it!: How Schools use Mapping to Transform Teaching & Learning*. Stafford: Network Educational, 2003.
Harris, Maria. *Fashion Me a People: Curriculum in the Church*. Louisville, KY: Westminster John Knox, 1989.
Hashmi, S. H. "Jihad." In *Encyclopedia of Politics and Religion*, edited by R. Wuthnow, 425–26. Washington DC: Congressional Quarterly, 1998.
Heckman, Bud. *Interactive Faith: The Essential Interreligious Community-Building Handbook*. Kindle. Woodstock, VT: Sky Light Paths, 2008.
Hertog, Katrien. *The Complex Reality of Religious Peacebuilding*. Lanham, MD: Lexington, 2010.

Heyns, C., and M. Killander. "The African Regional Human Rights System." In *Human Rights, Peace, and Justice in Africa: A Reader*, edited by C. Heyns & K. Stefiszyn, 195. Pretoria: Pretoria University Law, 2006.

Hicks, David. *Education for Peace: Issues, Dilemmas, and Alternatives.* Lancaster: St. Martin's College, 1985.

———. *Education for Peace: Issues, Principles, and Practice in the Classroom.* New York: Routledge, 1988.

———. "Teaching for Tomorrow: How can Futures Studies Contribute to Peace Education?" *Journal of Peace Education* 1.2 (2004).

Higazi, Adam. *Jos Crisis: A Recurrent Nigerian Tragedy.* Abuja: Nigeria Friedrich-Ebert-Stiftung (FES), 2011.

Hoffman, Bob. "The Encyclopedia of Educational Technology." http://edweb.sdsu.edu/people/rhoffman.

Homolka, Walter. *The Gate to Perfection: The Idea of Peace in Jewish Thought.* Providence: Berghahn, 1994.

Huitt, W. "An Important Factor of Mind." http://chiron.valdosta.edu/whuitt/col/regsys/conation.html.

Huston, D. L. *New Tools for International Understanding: A Peace Education Curriculum For Elementary School Students.* Manoa: Spark M. Matsunaga Institute for Peace, 1992.

Ibrahim, Jibrin. "Religion and Political Turbulence in Nigeria." *Journal of Modern African Studies* 29 (1991) 115–36.

Ijeoma, E. Okey. *Africa's New Public Policy: Imperatives for Globalization & Nation-building in Nigeria.* Pretoria, South Africa: Africa Institute of South Africa, 2010.

Ikenga Metuh, Emefie. *Comparative Studies of African Traditional Religions.* Onitsha, Nigeria: IMICO, 1987.

———. "Religion as an Instrument of Peace in Nigeria." In *Religion and Peace in Multi-faith Nigeria*, edited by J. K. Olupona. Ile-Ife, Nigeria: Obafemi Awolowo University, 1992.

Information Nigeria Business. "Investment Opportunities." http://www.nigeriabusinessinfo.com/energy.htm.

Isasi-Diaz, Ada Maria. "Reconciliation: An Intrinsic Element of Justice." In *Explorations in Reconciliation: New Directions in Theology*, edited by David Tombs and Joseph Liechty, 69–81. Burlington: Ashgate, 2006.

Irani, George. "Islamic Approaches to Conflict Resolution." http://www.ciaonet.org.

Jackson, Cari. *The Gift to Listen, the Courage to Hear.* Minneapolis, MN: Augsburg, 2003.

Jackson, Robert, and S. Fujiwara. "Towards Religious Education for Peace." *British Journal of Religious Education* 29.1 (2007) 1–14.

Jackson, Robert, and S. Fujiwara, eds. *Peace Education and Religious Plurality: International Perspectives.* New York: Routledge, 2008.

Jafari, Sheherazade, and Abdul Aziz Said. "Islam and Peacemaking." In *Peacemaking: From Practice to Theory*, edited by N. S. Allen, 228–43. Vol. 1. Santa Barbara, CA: Praeger, 2012.

Jakkie, Cilliers. "Human Security in Africa: A Conceptual Framework for Review." https://www.issafrica.org/uploads/AHSIMONO1.pdf.

Jega, Attahiru. "The State and Identity Transformation under Structural Adjustment in Nigeria." In *Identity Transformation and Identity Politics under Structural*

Adjustment in Nigeria, edited by Attahiru Jega, 24–40. Uppsala, Sweden: The Nordic Africa Institute, 2000.
Johnson, David W., and R. T. Johnson. "Peace Education in the Classroom: Creating Effective Peace Education Programs." In *International Handbook of Interreligious Education*, edited by K. Engebretson, 223–41. New York: Springer, 2010.
Johnson, James T. "Jihad and Just War." *First Things: A Monthly Journal of Religion and Public Life* 124 (2002).
Johnson, Roger A. *Peacemaking and Religious Violence: From Thomas Aquinas to Thomas Jefferson*. Eugene, OR: Pickwick, 2009.
Johnson, Roger A., and E. Wallwork. *Critical Issues in Modern Religion*. Englewood Cliffs, NJ: Prentice-Hall, 1973.
Johnston, Douglas. "Reconciliation Possible in Nigeria." http://www.humantrustees.org/blogs/muslim-christian-dialog/item/64-reconciliation-possible-in-nigeria.
Joseph, Pamela B. *Cultures of Curriculum*. Mahwah, NJ: L. Erlbaum Associates, 2000.
Juergensmeyer, Mark. "Is Religion the Problem?" *Hedgehog Review* 6.1 (2004) 21–33.
———. *Terror in the Mind of God: The Global Rise of Religious Violence*. Berkeley: University of California Press, 2000.
Juergensmeyer, Mark, and M. Kitts. *Princeton Readings in Religion and Violence*. Princeton, NJ: Princeton University Press, 2011.
Juergensmeyer, Mark, et al. *The Oxford Handbook of Religion and Violence*. New York: Oxford University Press, 2013.
Kadayifici-Orellana, S. Ayse. "Religion, Violence and the Islamic Tradition of Nonviolence." *Turkish Yearbook of International Relations* 34 (2003).
Kaltner, John. *Islam: What non-Muslims Should Know*. Minneapolis: Fortress. 2003.
Kalu, Hyacinth. *Together As One: Interfaith Relationships Between African Traditional Religion, Islam, and Christianity in Nigeria*. Bloomington: iUniverse, 2011.
Karade, Ifa. "The Handbook of Yoruba Religious Concepts." http://search.ebscohost.com/login.aspx?direct=true&scope=site&db=nlebk&db=nlabk&AN=522329.
Kayaoglu, Turan. "Explaining Interfaith Dialogue in the Muslim World." *Politics and Religion* 8.2 (2015) 236.
Kehoe, Joe. "Ubuntu: African Wisdom on How to Be a Human Being Part 2." http://www.learnmindpower.com/articles/ubuntu-african-wisdom-how-be-human-being-part2.
Kellie, D. A., and W. G. Rollins. *Psychological Insight into the Bible: Texts and Readings*. Grand Rapids, MI: Eerdmans, 2007.
Kepel, Gilles. *Jihad: Expansion et Déclin de l'Islamisme*. Paris: Gallimard, 2003.
Kepel, Gilles, and P. Clark. "The Origins and Development of the Jihadist Movement: From Anti-communism to Terrorism." *Asian Affairs* 34.2 (2003).
Kenny, Joseph. "Shari'a and Christianity in Nigeria: Islam and a Secular State." *Journal of Religion in Africa* 26.4 (1996).
Kevin, Kester. "Peace Education Primer." http://journals.sfu.ca/jgcee/index.php/jgcee/article/viewFile/66/59.
Khadduri, Majid. *War and Peace in the Law of Islam*. Baltimore, MD: Johns Hopkins, 1995.
Khaki, J. "What Are the Basic Teachings/Tenets of Your Faith Tradition." http://www.shianews.com/hi/articles/islam/0000160.
Khalid, Fazlun, and Joanne O'Brien, eds. *Islam and Ecology*. London UK: Cassel, 1993.

Khanam, Farida. "Understanding Jihad." http://www.allaahuakbar.net/JIHAAD/understanding_jihad_islam.htm.
Kimball, Charles. *When Religion Becomes Evil*. San Francisco: Harper, 2003.
Kirkpatrick, Donald L. *Evaluating Training Programs: The Four Levels*. 2nd ed. San Francisco: Berrett-Koehler, 2002.
Klein, Naomi. "Reclaiming the Commons." In *A Movement of Movements: Is Another World Really Possible?*, edited by T. Mertes, 219–21. London: Verso, 2004.
Knauft, Bruce M. "Culture and Cooperation in Human Evolution." In *The Anthropology of Peace and Nonviolence*, edited by L. E. Sponsel and T. Gregor, 37–67. Boulder, CO: Lynne Rienner, 1994.
Komolafe, Babajide. "Nigeria's Per Capita Income Rises to $1,036." *Vanguard*, August 9, 2007. https://books.google.ca/books?isbn=1483629643.
Koss, Mary P., and S. L. Cook. "Date and Acquaintance Rape are Significant Problems for Women." In *Current Controversies on Family Violence*, edited by R. J. Gelles and D. R. Loseke, 147–56. Newbury Park, CA: Sage, 1993.
Köylü, Mustafa. "Islam and Peace Education." http://www.tc.columbia.edu/centers/epe/./KoyluIslam_22feb08.pdf.
———. *Islam and its Quest for Peace: Jihad, Justice, and Education*. Washington, DC: Council for Research in Values and Philosophy, 2003.
———. "Peace Education: An Islamic Approach." *Journal of Peace* 1.1 (2004) 1–14.
Krug, Samuel E., et al., eds. *World Report on Violence and Health*. Geneva: World Health Organization, 2002. www.who.int/violence_injury_prevention/violence/world_report/en/full_en.pdf
Kruttschnitt, Candace. "Gender and Interpersonal Violence." In *Social Influences*, edited by A. J. Reiss Jr. and J. A. Roth, 293–376. Vol. 3 of *Understanding and Preventing Violence*. Washington, DC: National Academy, 1994.
Kukah, Matthew H. *Democracy and Civil Society in Nigeria*. Ibadan: Spectrum, 1999.
———. *Religion, Politics, and Power in Northern Nigeria*. Ibadan, Nigeria: Spectrum, 1993.
———. *Religion and the Politics of Justice in Nigeria*. Lagos, Nigeria: Constitutional Rights Project, 1996.
———.*The Church and the Politics of Social Responsibility*. Ikate-Surulere, Lagos: Sovereign, 2007.
Kukah, Matthew H., and T. Falola. *Religious Militancy and Self-Assertion: Islam and Politics in Nigeria*. Brookfield, VT: Avebury, 1996.
Küng, Hans. "Global Ethics and Education in Tolerance." http://dio.sagepub.com/content/44/176/137.
———. *A Global Ethic for Global Politics and Economics*. New York: Oxford University Press, 1998.
Kurtz, L. R., and J. E. Turpin. *Encyclopedia of Violence, Peace, and Conflict*. San Diego: Academic, 1999.
Laitin, David D. *Hegemony and Culture: Politics and Religious Change Among the Yoruba*. Chicago: University of Chicago Press, 1986.
Last, Murray. "Muslims and Christians in Nigeria: An Economy of Political Panic." *The Round Table* 96 (2007) 392.
Lawrence, Bruce B. *Shattering the Myth: Islam Beyond Violence*. Princeton, NJ: Princeton University Press, 1998.

Lederach, John P. *Building Peace: Sustainable Reconciliation in Divided Societies.* Washington, DC: United States Institute of Peace, 1997.
Leirvik, Oddbjorn. "Religious Education, Communal Identity and National Politics in the Muslim World." *British Journal of Religious Education* 26.3 (2004) 223–36.
Lessard-Hébert, Michelle, et al. *La Recherche Qualitative: Fondements et Pratiques.* Paris: De Boeck Université, 1997.
Lin, Jing, E. J. Brantmeier, and C. Bruhn. *Transforming Education for Peace.* Charlotte, NC: IAP, 2008.
Linsky, Arnold Stanley, et al. *Stress, Culture, and Aggression.* New Haven: Yale, 1995.
Long, Michael G. *Christian Peace and Nonviolence: a Documentary History.* Maryknoll, NY: Orbis, 2011.
Lott, Bernice, ed. *The Social Psychology of Interpersonal Discrimination.* New York: Guilford, 1995.
Lynn, K. "Violence in American Literature and Folklore." In *Violence in America: Historical and Comparative Perspectives,* edited by H. D. Graham and T. R. Gurr, 9–23. Rev. ed. Beverly Hills, CA: Sage, 1979.
Madeley, John. *Big Business, Poor Peoples.* London: ZED, 2008.
Maier, K. *This House has Fallen: Nigeria in Crisis.* London: Penguin, 2000.
Mani, Rama. "Cure of Curse? The Role of Religion." *Global Governance* 18 (2012).
Marks, Stephen. "Human Rights Education in UN Peace-building: From Theory to Practice." In *Human Rights Learning: A Peoples' Report.* New York: PDHRE, 2010.
Marshall, Ruth. *Political Spiritualities: The Pentecostal Revolution in Nigeria.* Chicago: University of Chicago Press, 2009.
Marshall, Ellen O., et al. *Choosing Peace Through Daily Practices.* Cleveland, Ohio: Pilgrim, 2005.
Marty, Martin E., and R. S. Appleby. *Fundamentalisms and the State: Remaking Polities, Economies, and Militance.* Chicago: University of Chicago Press, 1993.
Mayton, Daniel M. "Nonviolence and Peace Psychology: Intrapersonal, Interpersonal, Societal, and World Peace." http://site.ebrary.com/id/10308868.
McCarthy, Roland, and Christopher Kruelgler. *Theory Building in the Study of Nonviolent Action.* Cambridge: The Albert Einstein Institution, 1993.
McCutcheon, Russell T. "Myth." In *Guide to the Study of Religion,* edited by Willi Braun and Russell McCutcheon, 190–208. New York: Cassell, 2000.
Mcginnis, Kathleen, and B. Oehlberg. *Starting out Right.* New York: Institute for Peace and Justice, 1991.
Mehdi, Sikander. "Islamic Principles and Values: Peace Content and Peace Potentials." In *Peace Education Islamic Perspectives,* edited by S. S. Niazi and N. Kakar, 53–62. Colón, Costa Rica: University for Peace, 2009.
Memorandum of the Council of the Evangelical Church in Germany. "Live from God's Peace—Care for Just Peace." http://archiv.ekd.de/ekd_peace_memorandum(2).pdf.
Merdjanova, Ina, and P. Brodeur. *Religion as a Conversation Starter: Interreligious Dialogue for Peacebuilding in the Balkans.* New York: Continuum, 2009.
Merry, M. S. "Islamic Philosophy of Education and Western Islamic Schools." In *Religion, Conflict, and Reconciliation: Multifaith Ideals and Realities in Practice* edited by H. J. Jerald D. Gort and Hendrik M. Vroom, 41–70. Amsterdam: Rodopi, 2002.
Metz, H. C. "Nigeria: a Country Study." http://countrystudies.us/nigeria.

Michael, J. Brown. *What They Don't Tell You: a Survivor's Guide to Biblical Studies*. Louisville: Westminster John Knox, 2000.

Midlarsky, Manus I. *Origins of Political Extremism: Mass Violence in the Twentieth Century and Beyond*. New York: Cambridge University Press, 2011.

Minuchin, Salvador. *Families and Family Therapy*. Cambridge, MA: Harvard, 1974.

Miller, Donald E. *Seeking Peace in Africa: Stories from African Peacemakers*. Scottdale, PA: Cascadisa, 2007.

Mitchell, Christopher R. *The Structure of International Conflict*. New York: St. Martin, 1981.

Moll, Rob. "Nigerian Christians Attack Muslims, Kill Dozens." *Christianity Today*, May 1, 2004. http://www.christianitytoday.com/ct/2004/mayweb-only/5-3-32.0.html.

Moltmann, Jurgen. *Creating a Just Future: The Politics of Peace and the Ethics of Creation in a Threatened World*. Philadelphia: SCM, 1989.

Montessori, Maria. *Education for a New Word*. India: Kalakshetra, 1974.

Moon, Bob, et al. *Routledge International Companion to Education*. New York: Routledge, 2000.

Morris, G. Shalom. *A Vision of a New World*. Nashville: Tidings, 1974.

Mouhleb, Naima. "Jihad in Classical and Modern Islam, 2nd ed." *Journal of Peace Research* 44.1 (2007) 129.

Murithi, Tim. "An African Perspective on Peace Education: Ubuntu Lessons in Reconciliation." *International Review of Educational Leadership* 55 (2009) 221–33.

Mwanyumba, Robert, and J. A. Mbillah. *Report on proceedings of the PROCMURA Conference on Religion, Conflict Prevention, and Peacebuilding in West Africa: M-Plaza Hotel, Accra, Ghana, July 21–24, 2009*. Nairobi: Programme for Christian-Muslim Relations in Africa, 2009.

Nadeau, Jean-Guy. *La Praxéologie Pastorale: Orientations et Parcours*. Montréal: Fides, 1987.

Naht Hanh, Thich. *Peace is Every Step: The Path of Mindfulness in Everyday Life*. Bantam: Reissue, 1992.

Nan, Susan Allen, et al. *Peacemaking: From Practice to Theory*. Vol. 1. Santa Barbara, CA: Praeger, 2012.

National Encyclopedia. "Nigeria." http://www.nationsencyclopedia.com/World-Leaders-2003/Nigeria.html.

National Peace Academy. "A Holistic Approach: Five Interrelated Spheres of Peace." https://nationalpeaceacademy.us/images/adultselfstudyguide/ADULT-2-v1.pdf.

———. "Self-identification: Having or Being." http://www.nationalpeaceacademy.us.

Nario-Galace, Jasmin. "Conflict Resolution and Peer Mediation Sourcebook." http://www.creducation.org/resources/Peace_Education_Castro_Galace.pdf.

Navaro-Casto, Loreta. "A Pathway to a Culture of Peace—Conflict Resolution Education." www.creducation.org/resources/Peace_Education_Castro_Galace.pdf.

Navaro-Casto, Loreta, and J. Nario-Galace. *Peace Education: A Pathway to a Culture of Peace*. 2nd ed. Philippines: Centre for Peace Education, 2010.

Nelson, Robert L. "Human Rights in Creation and Redemption: A Protestant View." In *Human Rights in Religious Traditions*, edited by Arlene Swidler, 10. New York: Pilgrim, 1982.

Nelson-Pallmeyer, Jack. *Is Religion Killing Us? Violence in the Bible and the Qur'an*. Harrisburg, PA: Trinity, 2003.

New Era Educational and Support Foundation. "Fifth International Conference on Youth and Interfaith Dialogue." https://events.tigweb.org/31335.
Niazi, S. S. "Peaceful Approches to Conflict Resolution in Muslim Contexts." In *Peace Education Islamic Perspectives*, edited by S. S. Niazi & N. Kakar, 68–85. Colón, Costa Rica: University for Peace, 2009.
Nicolas, Guy. "Géopolitique et Religions au Nigeria." *Hérodote* 3 (2002) 166.
Nigeria Business Information. "Investment opportunities." http://focusafrica.gov.in/Investment_Opportunities_in_Nigeria.html.
National Bureau of Statistics. "Nigerians living in poverty rise to nearly 61 percent." https://www.bbc.com/news/world-africa-17015873.
Nigeria. "Constitution 2010." www.nigeria-law.org/ConstitutionOfTheFederalRepublicOfNigeria.htm
Nipokow, Karl. "Education for Peace Dimension of Interreligious Education: Preconditions and Outlines." In *International Handbook of Interreligious Education*, edited by K. Engebretson, 641–58. New York: Springer, 2010.
Noddings, N. *The Challenge to Care in Schools: An Alternative Approach to Education*. New York: Teachers College, 1993.
Obadina, Tunde. "Africa's Crisis of Governance." http://www.afbis.com/analysis/crisis.htm.
Odejobi, C. O., and A.D.O. Adesina. "Peace Education and School Curriculum." http://nau.edu/uploadedFiles/Academic/COE/About/Projects/Peace%20Education%20and%20the%20School%20Curriculum.pdf.
Ogunade, Raymond. "Environmental Issues in Yoruba Religion: Implications for Leadership and Society in Nigeria." https://unilorin.edu.ng/publications/raymond/ENVIRONMENTAL%20ISSUES%20IN%20YORUBA%20RELIGION.htm.
———. "Yoruba Religious Worship in Modern Context." *Journal of the Institute of Cultural Studies* (2010). https://oldapena.wordpress.com/2011/11/05/yoruba-religious-worship-in-modern-context.
Okpu, Ugbana. *Ethnic Minority Problems in Nigerian Politics, 1960–1965*. Stockholm: Almqvist and Wiksell, 1977.
Oliva, Peter F. *Developing the Curriculum*. Glenview, IL: Scott, Foresman/Little, Brown College Division, 1988.
Olu-Adeyemi, Lanre. "Corruption and the deepening Crisis of Nigeria's Economic and National Development." *Journal of Economic and Financial Studies, Department of Economics, Banking, and Finance, Adekunle Ajasin University* 1.2 (2004) 160–67.
Olupona, Jacob K., ed. *Religion and Peace in Multi-faith Nigeria*. Ile-Ife, Nigeria: Obafemi Awolowo University, 1992.
Omer, Atalia. "Religious Peacebuilding: The Exotic, the Good, and the Theatrical." *Practical Matters* 5 (2012) 1–31.
Omonokhua, Cornelius A. "The Need for Inter-Religious Dialogue." https://www.academia.edu/8346715/the_need_for_inter-religious_dialogue.
Omotosho, A. O. "Religious Violence in Nigeria: The Causes and Solutions: An Islamic Perspective." *Swedish Missiological Themes* 91.1 (2003) 15–31.
Onuoha, Freedom C. *The State and Management of Religious Violence in Nigeria: A Case Study of the July 2009 Boko Haram revolt*. PhD Seminar Paper Presented to the Department of Political Science, Nsukka, Nigeria, 2010.

Otitie, O. "Nigeria's Identifiable Ethnic Groups." http://www.onlinenigeria.com/tribes/tribes.asp.

Owomoyela, Oyekan. *Yoruba Proverbs*. Lincoln: University of Nebraska, 2005.

Oxford English Dictionary. "Peace." 2nd ed. http://www.oed.com/oed2/00173403.

Oxford, Rebecca. "How Christianity Addresses Peace and What this Means for Education." In *Spirituality, Religion, and Peace Education*, edited by Edward J. Brantmeier, et al., 5. Charlotte, NC: IAP, 2010.

Ozcelik, Sezai. "Islamic Peace Paradigm and Islamic Peace Education: The Study of Islamic Nonviolence in Post-September 11 World." https://www.academia.edu/9897952/Ogretir_Ayse_Dilek_and_S._Ozcelik_Islamic_Peace_Paradigm_and_Islamic_Peace_Education_The_Study_of_Islamic_Nonviolence_in_the_Post-Sept._11_World_5-9_July_2007.

Paden, John. *Faith and Politics in Nigeria: Nigeria as a Pivotal State in the Muslim World*. Washington, DC: United States Institute of Peace, 2008.

Page, James S. *Peace Education: Exploring Ethical and Philosophical Foundations*. Charlotte, NC: IAP, 2008.

Pal, Amitabh. *"Islam" Means Peace: Understanding the Muslim Principle of Nonviolence Today*. Santa Barbara, CA: Praeger, 2011.

Paloutzian, Raymond F., and C. L. Park. *Handbook of the Psychology of Religion and Spirituality*. New York: Guilford, 2005.

Paquette, Claude. *Intervenir avec Cohérence: vers une Pratique Articulée de l'Intervention*. Montréal: Québec-Amérique,1985.

Patel, Eboo, and P. Brodeur. *Building the Interfaith Youth Movement: Beyond Dialogue to Action*. Lanham, MD: Rowman & Littlefield, 2006.

Park, J. S. "Jesus Christ the Prince of Peace." http://www.warc.ch/where/22gc/bible/06.html.

Parsons, Talcott. *Social Systems and the Evolution of Action Theory*. New York: Free Press, 1977.

Passow, A. Hermann, and H. S. Jacob. "Designing a Global Curriculum." *Gifted Education International* 6.2 (1989) 68–70.

Peel, John David Y. *Religious Encounter and the Making of the Yoruba*. Bloomington, IN: Indiana University Press. 2000.

People for Peace Project. *We Want Peace on Earth: A Guide for the Peace on Earth Movement*. Bloomington, IN: Authorhouse, 2003.

Perkins-Gough, Deborah, et al. "Curriculum for Peace: A Conversation with Sir John Daniel." *Educational Leadership* 60.2 (2002) 100.

Peters, Rudolph. *Islam and Colonialism: the Doctrine of Jihad in Modern History*. New York: Mouton, 1979.

Pipes, Daniel. "What is Jihad?"*New York Post*, December 31, 2002. http://www.meforum.org/4132/what-is-jihad.

Powers, Gerald F., and D. Philpott. *Strategies of Peace: Transforming Conflict in a Violent World*. New York: Oxford University Press, 2010.

Puett, Tiffany. "On Transforming Our World: Critical Pedagogy for Interfaith Education." *Cross Currents* 55.2 (2005) 264–73.

Race, Alan. *Christians and Religious Pluralism: Patterns in the Christian Theology of Religions*. Maryknoll, NY: Orbis, 1983.

Rahner, Karl, and H. Vorgrimler. *Concise Theological Dictionary*. London: Burns & Oates, 1965.

Rakov, Simon. "Ethnicity in Nigeria." http://www.postcolonialweb.org/nigeria/ethnicity.html.
Ramadan, Tariq. *Western Muslims and the Future of Islam*. New York: Oxford University Press, 2003.
Ramos, M. Kathy. "Lessons from WWII Comfort Women the Role of Peace Education," In *Developing Capacities for Forgiveness and Reconciliation*. Издательство: LAP LAMBERT Academic Publishing, 2012.
Razi, Ahmad. "Islam, Nonviolence, and Global Transformation." In *Islam and Nonviolence*, edited by Glenn D. Paige, et al., 27–52. Honolulu, HI: Centre for Global Nonviolence, 1993.
Reardon, Betty. *Educating for Global Responsibility: Teacher-designed Curricula for Peace Education, K–12*. New York: Teachers College, 1988.
———. *Education for a Culture of Peace in a Gender Perspective*. Paris: UNESCO, 2001.
———. "Peace Education: A Review and Projection." Reprinted from *International Companion to Education*, edited by B. Moon, et al. New York: Routledge, 2000.
Reardon, Betty, et al. "Pioneer in Education for Peace and Human Rights." http://dx.doi.org/10.1007/978-3-319-08967-6.
Reardon, Christina. "Alternatives to 12-Step Addiction Recovery." *Social Work Today* 13.6 (2013) 12. http://www.socialworktoday.com/archive/111113p12.shtml.
Reiss, Albert Jr., and J. A. Roth, eds. *Understanding and Preventing Violence: Panel on the Understanding and Control of Violent Behavior*. Washington, DC: National Academy, 1993.
Ritter, Daniel. "A Two-dimensional Theory of Nonviolence." Paper Presented at the Annual Meeting of the American Sociological Association, Philadelphia, PA, 2005.
Robert, Jackson, and S. Fujiwara. "Towards Religious Education for Peace." *British Journal of Religious Education* 29.1 (2007) 1–14.
Robert, Neil M. *When Religion is an Addiction*. St. Louis, MO: Humanity Works, 2007.
Robinson, B. A. "The Concept of Jihad ('Struggle') in Islam." http://www.religioustolerance.org/isl_jihad.htm.
Rosenberg, Marshall B. *Nonviolent Communication: A Language of Life*. 2nd ed. Encinitas, CA: Puddle Dancer, 2003.
Roy, Olivier. *The Failure of Political Islam*. Cambridge, MA: Harvard University Press, 1994.
Russell, T. McCutcheon. "Myth." In *Guide to the Study of Religion*, edited by Willi Braun and Russell McCutcheon, 190–208. New York: Cassell, 2000.
Rweyemamu, Robert. "Religion and Peace: An Experience with African traditions." *Peace* 38 (1989) 381.
Safi, Omid. *Progressive Muslims: On Justice, Gender and Pluralism*. Oxford: Oneworld, 2003.
Said, Abdul Aziz A., and N. Funk. "Peace in the Sufi Tradition: An Ecology of the Spirit." In *Peace and Conflict Resolution in Islam: A Global Philosophy*, 247–61. New York: University Press of America, 2001.
Shafiq, Muhammad, and M. Abu-Nimer. *Interfaith Dialogue: A Guide for Muslims*. Washington, DC: International Institute of Islamic Thought, 2007.
Salili, Farideh, and R. Hoosain. *Religion in Multicultural Education*. Greenwich, CT: IAP, 2006.

Salomon, Gavriel. "Does Peace Education Really Make a Difference?" *Peace and Conflict* 12.1 (2006) 112.

———. "The Nature of Peace Education: Not All Programs Are Created Equal." In *Peace Education: The Concept, Principles, and Practices Around the World*, edited by G. Nevo B. and Salomon. Mahwah, NJ: Lawrence Earlbaum Associates, 2002.

———, and B. Nevo, eds. *Peace Education: The Concept, Principles, and Practices Around the World*. Mahwah, NJ: Lawrence Erlbaum Associates, 2002.

———, and E. Cairns. *Handbook on Peace Education*. New York: Psychology, 2010.

Salomon, Sara. "Teaching Empathy: The Peace Curriculum: Reclaiming Children and Youth." *Strength-Based Interventions* 12.3 (2003).

Sampson, Cynthia, and J. P. Lederach. *From the Ground Up: Mennonite Contributions to International Peacebuilding*. New York: Oxford University Press, 2000.

Sandole, D. J. D. *Peacebuilding: Preventing Violent Conflict in a Complex World*. Malden, MA: Polity, 2010.

Sarbin, Theodore R., and J. I. Kitsuse. *Constructing the Social*. London: Sage, 1994.

Sarpong, Peter. "African Traditional Religion and Peace." *Studia Missionalia* 5.38 (1989) 351.

Satha-Anand, C. "Islam and Violence." http://nonkilling.org/pdf/b3.pdf.

Schirch, Lisa. *Ritual and Symbol in Peacebuilding*. Bloomfield, CT: Kumarian, 2005.

Schreiter, Robert J. *The Ministry of Reconciliation: Spirituality and Strategies*. Maryknoll, NY: Orbis Books, 1998.

Schreiber, Jean-Philippe. *Théologies de la Guerre*. Bruxelles: Éditions de l'Université de Bruxelles, 2006.

Schreiter, Robert J., et al. *Peacebuilding: Catholic Theology, Ethics, and Praxis*. Maryknoll, NY: Orbis, 2010.

Schwartz, Regina. "Inventing Identity," in *The Curse of Cain: The Violent Legacy of Monotheism*. Chicago: Chicago University Press, 1997.

Scott, James C. *Domination and the Arts of Resistance*. New Haven: Yale University Press, 1990.

Scott, Marvin B., and S. M. Lyman. "Accounts." *American Sociological Review* 33 (1968) 46–62.

Sedgwick, Mark. "Jihad, Modernity, and Sectarianism." http://www.academia.edu/322259/Jihad_Modernity_and_Sectarianism.

Selengut, Charles. *Sacred Fury: Understanding Religious Violence*. Walnut Creek, CA: Alta Mira, 2003.

Sen, Amartya. *The Violence of Illusion from Identity and Violence: The Illusion of Destiny*. New York: Penguin, 2006.

Shaw, Clifford R., and H. D. McKay. *Juvenile Delinquency and Urban Areas*. Chicago: University of Chicago Press, 1942.

Shiva, Vandana. *Earth Democracy, Justice, Sustainability, and Peace*. Cambridge: South End, 2005.

Sisk, Timothy D. *Between Terror and Tolerance: Religious Leaders, Conflict, and Peacemaking*. Washington, DC: Georgetown University Press, 2011.

Sita, Ahmed. *The True Meaning and Implications of Jihad*. Lincoln, NE: Writers Club, 2002.

Smith, Dan. *The Penguin Atlas of War and Peace*. New York: Penguin, 2003.

Smith, Daniel Jordan. *A Culture of Corruption: Everyday Deception and Popular Discontent in Nigeria*. Princeton: Princeton University Press, 2008.

Smith, Jane I. *Muslims, Christians, and the Challenge of Interfaith Dialogue*. New York: Oxford University Press, 2007.
Smock, David R. "Applying Islamic Principles in the Twenty-first Century: Nigeria, Iran, and Indonesia." http://books.google.com/books?id=8xzVMRojAVEC.
Smock, David R. *Religion in World Affairs: It's Role in Conflict and Peace*. Washington, DC: U.S. Institute of Peace, 2008.
Snauwaert, Dale. "Care of the Self." https://nationalpeaceacademy.us/images/adultselfstudyguide/ADULT-3-v1.pdf.
Soanes, Catherine, and Angus Stevenson. *Shorter Oxford Dictionary*. New York: Oxford University Press, 2003.
Some, M. Patrice. *The Healing Wisdom of Africa: Finding Life Purpose Through Nature, Ritual, and Community*. New York: Penguin Putnam, 1999.
Sommaruga, Cornelio. "The Global Challenge of Human Security." *Foresight* 6.4 (2004) 208–11.
Soyinka, Wole. "Religion Against Humanity." Paper presented at the Conference on the Culture of Peace and Non-Violence, United Nations Headquarters, New York, NY, 2012.
Sprey, Jetse. "On the Management of Conflict in Families." *Journal of Marriage and the Family* 33.4 (1974) 722–30.
Stackhouse, Max L. "Public Theology, Human Rights, and Missions." In *Human Rights and the Global Mission of the Church*, 13–21. Cambridge, MA: Boston Theological Institute, 1985.
Stassen, Glen H. *Just Peacemaking: The New Paradigm for The Ethics of Peace and War*. Rev. ed. Cleveland, OH: Pilgrim, 2008.
Stassen, Glen H., and L. S. Wittner. *Peace Action: Past, Present, and Future*. Boulder: Paradigm, 2007.
Staub, Ervin. "Moral Exclusion, Personal Goal Theory, and Extreme Destructiveness." http://onlinelibrary.wiley.com/doi/10.1111/j.15404560.1990.tb00271.x/abstract.
Steinmetz, Suzanne K., and M. A. Straus. "General Introduction: Social Myth and Social System in the Study of Intra-family Violence." In *Violence in the Family*, edited by Suzanne K. Steinmetz and M. A. Straus, 9–30. New York: Harper and Row, 1974.
Straus, Murray. "A General Systems Theory Approach to a Theory of Violence Between Family Members." *Social Science Information* 12.3 (1973) 105–25.
Talley-Kalokoh, Jeanine M. *Re-imagining Peace: Integrating a Spiritual Peace Practice in International Affairs*. Washington: America University Press, 2009.
Tan, Charlene. "Dialogical Education for Interreligious Engagement in a Plural Society." In *International Handbook of Interreligious Education*, 16–29. New York: Springer, 2010.
Tatah, Menta. *Africa: Facing Human Security Challenges in the Twenty-first Century*. Bamenda, Cameroon: Langaa RPCIG, 2014.
Tarimo, Aquiline. "The Role of Religion in Peacebuilding." http://binsarspeaks.net/wp-content/uploads/2012/02/The-Role-of-Religion-in-Peacebuilding.pdf.
Taylor, John V. *The Primal Vision*. London: SCM, 1963.
Teachers without Borders. "Teachers without Borders." http://www.teacherswithoutborders.org.
Tilly, Charles. *The Politics of Collective Violence*. Cambridge: Cambridge University Press, 2003.

Toh, Swee Hin, et al. *Building a Peace Education Program*. Peace Education Miniprints 38. Malmo: Preparedness for Peace, 1992.
Toh, Swee Hin, and V. F. Cawagas. "A Holistic Understanding of A Culture of Peace." http://citeseerx.ist.psu.edu/viewdoc/download?doi=10.1.1.493.1182&rep=rep1.
Traer, Robert. "Christian Support for Human Rights." http://religionhumanrights.com/Religion/Christian/christian.fhr.htm.
Turner, Heather A., and D. Finkelhor. "Corporal Punishment as a Stressor Among Youth." *Journal of Marriage and the Family* 58 (1996) 155–66.
Tutu, Desmond. *No Future Without Forgiveness*. New York: Doubleday, 1997.
UNESCO. "Global Citizenship Education: Preparing Learners for the Challenges of the Twenty-first Century." http://unesdoc.unesco.org/images/0022/002277/227729E.pdf.
UNESCO. *UNESCO Prize for Peace Education*. Paris: UNESCO, 1982.
UNESCO. *Education for Human Rights: An International Perspective*. Paris: UNESCO, 1994. https://searchworks.stanford.edu/view/3048100.
United Nations. "Preamble of the UN Charter (1945)." http://www.un.org/cyberschoolbus/peace/frame2.htm.
United Religions Initiative. "More than 30 Christian and Muslim Youth in Nigeria Participate in FACIS CC Workshop." *United Religions Initiative*, January 15, 2014. https://uri.org/uri-story/20140116-more-30-christian-and-muslim-youth-nigeria-participate-facis-cc-workshop.
Umaru, Thaddeus B. *Christian-Muslim Dialogue in Northern Nigeria: a Socio-Political and Theological Consideration*. Philadelphia: Xlibris, 2013.
Usman, Yusufu B. *Nigeria against the IMF*. Kaduna: Vanguard, 1986.
———. *The Manipulation of Religion in Nigeria 1977–1987*. Kaduna: Vanguard, 1987.
Verkuyten, Maykel. *Identity and Cultural Diversity: What Social Psychology Can Teach Us*. London: Routledge, 2013.
Volf, Miroslav, et al., eds. *Common Word: Muslims and Christians on Loving God and Neighbor*. Grand Rapids, MI: Eerdmans, 2010.
Wade, Richard. *Bridging Christianity, Islam, and Buddhism with Virtue Ethics*. Edited by K. Engebretson. New York: Springer, 2010.
Warr, Mark. "Public Perceptions and Reactions to Violent Offending and Victimization." In *Consequences and Control*, edited by A. J. Reiss Jr. and J. A. Roth, 1–66. Vol. 4 of *Understanding and Preventing Violence*. Washington, DC: National Academy, 1994.
Wellman, James K., and C. B. Lombardi. *Religion and Human Security: A Global Perspective*. Oxford: Oxford University Press, 2012.
Wien, Barbara J. *Peace and World Order Studies: A Curriculum Guide*. New York: World Policy Institute, 1984.
Winfrey, Elaine C. "Kirkpatrick's Four Levels of Evaluation." http://coe.sdsu.edu/eet/articles/k4levels/start.htm.
Wink, Walter. *Engaging the Powers: Discernment and Resistance in a World of Domination*. Minneapolis: Fortress, 1992.
Williams, Kirk R. "Social Sources of Marital Violence and Deterrence: Testing an Integrated Theory of Assaults Between Partners." *Journal of Marriage and the Family* 54 (1992) 620–29.
Wilson, William J. *The Truly Disadvantaged: The Inner City, the Underclass, and Public Policy*. Chicago: University of Chicago Press, 1987.

Witte, Griff. "Violence: Its Source Is Not Always What It Seems." *Nieman Reports* 61.2 (2007) 6–7.
Wolf, Peter, et al. *Handbook for Curriculum Assessment*. Guelph, ON: University of Guelph, 2006.
World Leadership Alliance Club de Madrid. "The Nigeria Inter-Religious Council." http://www.clubmadrid.org/en/practice/9/the_nigeria_inter_religious_council_nirec/impact.
Yllo, Kersti A. "Through a Feminist Lens: Gender, Power, and Violence." In *Current Controversies on Family Violence*, edited by R. J. Gelles and D. R. Loseke, 47–62. Newbury Park, CA: Sage, 1993.
Yoder, Perry, and W. Swartley, eds. *The Meaning of Peace: Biblical Studies*. Louisville: Westminster John Knox, 1992.
Yong, Amos. *Hospitality and the Other: Pentecost, Christian Practices, and the Neighbor*. Maryknoll, NY: Orbis, 2008.
Zeiger, Susan. "Teaching Peace: Lessons from a Peace Studies Curriculum of the Progressive Era." *Peace and Change* 25 (2000) 1–147.
Zelizer, Craig, and R. A. Rubinstein. *Building Peace: Practical Reflections from the Field*. Sterling, VA: Kumarian, 2009.
Žižek, Slavoj. *Violence: Six Sideways Reflections*. New York: Picador, 2008.
Zoppi, Irene M. "Transforming Warfare Training into Peace Education." In *Transforming Education for Peace*, edited by J. Lin, et al., 283–99. Charlotte, NC: IAP, 2008.